The BBC in Scotland

The BBC in Scotland

The First 50 Years

A Personal Memoir
by
DAVID PAT WALKER

Luath Press Limited

EDINBURGH

www.luath.co.uk

First published 2011
This edition 2016

ISBN: 978-1-910745-52-6

The paper used in this book is recyclable. It is made
from low chlorine pulps produced in a low energy,
low emissions manner from renewable forests.

Printed and bound by
Bell & Bain Ltd., Glasgow

Typeset in 11 point Sabon
by 3btype.com

All pictures © BBC unless otherwise indicated.

The views expressed in this book are those of the author,
and are not necessarily shared by the publishers or the BBC.

Contents

David Pat Walker
Assistant Controller, BBC Scotland.

Acknowledgements

THE FIRST DRAFT OF this book was written shortly after my retirement from the BBC where I had been Assistant Controller, BBC Scotland. At first an idea, it quickly became a reality thanks to the encouragement and generous support of the then Director-General of the BBC, Alasdair Milne.

The BBC's written archive at Caversham and BBC Scotland's files were valuable sources, with thanks due to Jacquie Kavanagh and Libby Stanners for their great assistance.

Equally important were the reminiscences willingly given by past and present staff and performers, particularly the few who remained from the earliest days. It was a problem deciding what to leave out.

The book was a personal journey for me. I was fortunate to be able to talk to Edinburgh's office boy, Tony Cogle, who in 1926 delivered the script of the station's startlingly effective spoof UK news bulletin to the nearest post office to be telegraphed urgently to London. I became close friends with the Very Rev Ronald Selby Wright who as the *Radio Padre* incorporated coded messages for MI9 into his weekly wartime broadcast. I also met past members of the Glasgow Orpheus Choir, banned from wartime broadcasting, who could still remember the intervention of Prime Minister Winston Churchill securing their return to the airwaves.

Finally, I must thank Mike Shaw. His unflagging commitment to the completion of the project and additional editorial and photographic research for this account of the nation's first broadcasters gained willing support from BBC Scotland, and I am grateful that what is quite simply a narrative of perseverance can now be read.

David Pat Walker

Chronology

24 January 1923	BBC secures wavelength (415m) and call sign 5SC from the General Post Office for broadcasting station in Glasgow
1923	Herbert A. Carruthers appointed Glasgow 5SC Station Director
6 March 1923	Opening of Glasgow Station 5SC at Rex House, 202 Bath Street
19 March 1923	First outside broadcast, a live relay from the Coliseum Theatre in Eglinton Street, Glasgow
15 April 1923	First studio broadcast by a minister (Rev John White)
25 April 1923	First outside broadcast with Rev White from the Barony Kirk
31 August 1923	Dramatic excerpts from Walter Scott's *Rob Roy* produced by R.E. Jeffrey at 5SC in Glasgow
6 October 1923	*Rob Roy* repeated as simultaneous broadcast for all BBC stations in the UK network
1923	R.E. Jeffrey appointed Aberdeen 2BD Station Director
10 October 1923	Opening Aberdeen Station 2BD at 17 Belmont Street
2 December 1923	First broadcast in Gaelic by 2BD in Aberdeen
21 December 1923	First Gaelic song recital from 2BD in Aberdeen
23 January 1924	John Reith presides at the inauguration of the BBC's Glasgow Educational Advisory Committee
February 1924	D. Millar Craig appointed Assistant Controller, BBC in Scotland
February 1924	First ever custom-built schools broadcast to be transmitted by the BBC produced by 5SC in

	Glasgow and heard by children at Garnetbank School
March 1924	5SC in Glasgow embarks on a series of regular broadcasts of religious services from local churches
7 March 1924	2BD in Aberdeen produces first regular sports broadcasts
March 1924	2BD in Aberdeen broadcasts community singing
April 1924	5SC in Glasgow presents three plays performed by the Scottish National Players
1924	George L. Marshall appointed Edinburgh 2EH Station Director
1 May 1924	Opening of Edinburgh Station 2EH at 79 George Street
9 May 1924	5SC in Glasgow starts regular schools broadcasts
May 1924	2BD in Aberdeen presents own Repertory Players in *Macbeth*
26 June 1924	Sir Harry Lauder makes his first broadcast from 5SC
July 1924	R.E. Jeffrey leaves 2BD in Aberdeen to become the BBC's Director of Drama in London and is succeeded by Neil McLean
7 November 1924	Opening of new 5SC premises at 21 Blythswood Square
November 1924	D. Millar Craig made Station Director 5SC in addition to Assistant Controller and Herbert A. Carruthers appointed Head of Music
1924	Eric W. Heddle appointed Dundee 2DE Station Director
12 November 1924	Opening of Dundee Station 2DE at 1 Lochee Road
November 1924	Radio acquires a first place in the crime

	statistics of Scotland with a police report that 'during the absence of a family from a house in the West End of Dundee, some person or persons entered and made a clean sweep of a complete wireless set. Nothing else in the house was touched.'
31 December 1924	Glasgow and Aberdeen stations join London at 9.30pm for a fairly muted welcome to the New Year. Dundee closes down at 10.30pm, but Edinburgh abandons London and dances away the night to midnight and *Auld Lang Syne*
27 July 1925	New long-wave transmitter opens at Daventry
16 January 1926	Father Ronald Knox's controversial spoof news bulletin *Broadcasting the Barricades* produced by 2EH in Edinburgh for the whole of the UK
1926	David Cleghorn Thomson replaces D. Millar Craig with title of Northern Area Director (to include Northern Ireland)
1926	George L. Marshall appointed Glasgow 5SC Station Director
1926	J.C.S. Macgregor appointed Edinburgh 2EH Station Director
1 Jan 1927	Staff replace stationery bearing the name British Broadcasting Company with that of the new British Broadcasting Corporation
14 July 1927	Outside Broadcast of the opening of the Scottish National War Memorial on the Castle Rock in Edinburgh by HRH, the Prince of Wales
1927	Gaelic programmes from the Aberdeen station 2BD increased to include a *Gaelic Corner* 'for those in the North of Scotland who speak the Gaelic tongue'

1928	Programmes featuring Mod winners and Mod concerts and prize-winners broadcast
24 September 1928	First Scottish News bulletin
30 September 1928	David Cleghorn Thomson's title changed to Scottish Regional Director
1928–1929	Scottish Regional Plan outlined to curtail local output and achieve full regionalisation of programmes
May 1930	Outside broadcast of the launch of the Clyde-built *Empress* with estimated world audience of over 100 million
May 1930	Edinburgh staff move into the new Scottish headquarters at 5 Queen Street and later joined by most of the Glasgow staff
29 November 1930	Formal opening of 5 Queen Street, Edinburgh
20 June 1932	Formal opening of new transmitter at Westerglen, near Falkirk, allowing a choice of two programmes on medium wave, one of which became known as the Scottish Regional Wavelength
1933	Moray McLaren replaces David Cleghorn Thomson as Scottish Regional Director on a temporary basis
1933	Melville D. Dinwiddie appointed as Scottish Regional Director
May 1933	First radio play in Gaelic produced by Gordon Gildard who neither spoke nor understood the language
10 January 1934	Series of six fortnightly lessons in Gaelic pronunciation
26 September 1934	Outside broadcast from Clydebank of the launch of *Queen Mary* by the Queen accompanied by King George V
November 1934	Number of radio licences issued in Scotland rises from 390,000 to more than 500,000

1935	Schools department claims another notable educational first with 762 schools registered as 'listening' and 83,000 pamphlets sold for the autumn courses
1 December 1935	The BBC Scottish Orchestra is formally established
28 February 1936	Broadcast of *The March of '45, A Radio Panorama in Verse and Song*, written by D.G. Bridson
1 June 1936	Gaelic producer Hugh Macphee moves from Aberdeen to Glasgow
12 October 1936	Burghead chosen as the most northerly transmitting station
3 May 1938	Opening of the Empire Exhibition, including the King's speech, the largest outside broadcast commitment of its time with over 200 broadcasts in six months
18 November 1938	Opening of new premises at Queen Margaret Drive, Glasgow
9 December 1938	Opening of new premises at Beechgrove, Aberdeen
28 March 1939	First *McFlannels* broadcast as part of *High Tea* programme
1 September 1939	Two days before the start of hostilities all regional broadcasting replaced by a single channel, The Home Service
4 December 1939	*Lift Up Your Hearts – A Thought For Today* starts in Glasgow
4 December 1939	The exercise programme *Up In The Morning Early* also starts in Glasgow
27 April 1940	BBC Scotland produces first five-minute weekly bulletin of news in Gaelic on the UK Home Service
September 1940	*Scottish Half-Hour* starts
October 1940	The BBC's Military Band is based in Glasgow

November 1940	Elizabeth Adair appointed first woman announcer in Scotland
1940	First advertisements inviting engineering applications for 'Women Operators' for duty in the Control Room
1940	A special unit for War News established in Scotland
14 March 1941	A large German land mine missed the top of Studio One by less than 50ft and exploded on the other side of the River Kelvin
June 1941	Sir Hugh S. Roberton and the Glasgow Orpheus Choir return to the airwaves at the instigation of Winston Churchill after the conductor had been banned for his pacifist views
1941	Scottish Variety Orchestra formed
1 April 1942	The *Radio Padre* talks broadcast on the Forces Programme with scripts 'amended' by MI9
29 July 1945	The broadcasters return to a peacetime system with the first discernibly Scottish item on the new Scottish Home Service, a religious service in Gaelic
1945	Major programme development to include *Scottish Life and Letters, Arts Review, The Guid Scots Tongue, Scottish News, Sports News, Topical News*
11 August 1945	*Sportsreel* takes to the airwaves
27 January 1947	First meeting of the Scottish Advisory Council in Edinburgh
1948	Melville D. Dinwiddie's title changed from Scottish Regional Director to Controller, Scotland
12 November 1949	Opening of small studio in the Coldside Library, Dundee
1951	*McFlannels* series on radio ends

1952	Introduction of FM broadcasting on VHF in Scotland
1952	Kirk o' Shotts developed as the site of the first Scottish television transmitter
15 February 1952	BBC Television service arrives in Scotland
14 March 1952	Formal opening of television service with special programme, *Television comes to Scotland*
25 November 1952	Last meeting of the Scottish Advisory Council in Glasgow
25 November 1952	Scotland contributes live to the network television programme *Other People's Jobs – The Miner* from the Tillicoultry mine
14 January 1953	First meeting of Broadcasting Council for Scotland in Edinburgh
31 December 1953	Scotland produces its first UK *Hogmanay* programme for television from Govan Town Hall with traditional New Year greetings blotted out by ships' sirens on the nearby river
19 September 1954	*Heritage* series of 40 radio programmes examining the history, tradition and culture of Scotland
1955	*Special Enquiry* television programme for UK examining problems of national concern in a local background – housing and Glasgow's slums
1955	American evangelist Billy Graham's Good Friday Service from the Kelvin Hall, Glasgow
1957	Andrew Stewart appointed Controller, Scotland
16 August 1957	Scotland-only opt-out *On View* featuring BBC's programming in action and transmitted ahead of the launch of Scottish Television's commercial service

31 December 1957	Scotland broadcasts its own *Hogmanay* studio party
12 February 1958	*The McFlannels* broadcast on television
13 March 1958	By-election in Kelvingrove first occasion on which the BBC reports an election campaign in its news bulletins and also presents radio and TV programmes featuring by-election candidates
7 May 1958	First *White Heather Club* appears as a Scottish opt-out prior to being taken up by the UK network the following year
31 December 1958	Scotland produces *Hogmanay* for the whole BBC
11 December 1959	Neil Munro's *Vital Spark* sets sail for the first time on television
June 1960	Retirement of Kathleen Garscadden from *Children's Hour*
1961	Two local radio experiments held in Dundee and Dumfries
November 1963	*Panorama* produced by London in Scotland angers Glasgow councillors
10 June 1964	Opening of new television studio at Queen Margaret Drive, the first outside London able to make programmes on 405 or 625 lines, attracting BBC 2 interest
1 July 1967	BBC launches regular colour transmissions on BBC 2 network
1965	Scotland hosts television series such as *Dr Finlay's Casebook*
1967	The BBC Scottish Symphony Orchestra is established replacing the BBC Scottish Orchestra
1 January 1968	Alasdair Milne appointed Controller, Scotland
1 April 1968	*Reporting Scotland* launched
April 1968	*Where Do We Go From Here?* 80-minute

	edition of *Checkpoint* examining the mood behind the upsurge of nationalist sentiment
October 1968	Alasdair Milne's ten-minute speech in Gaelic at Dunoon Mod. The first time a Gaelic speaker on Scottish Board of Management
1969	Scotland gets a colour mobile Control Room and videotape facilities
31 December 1969	Scotland's first colour programme *Ring in the New*
1970	*Sunset Song* starts run of six 45-minute episodes on BBC 2
1970	Scotland hosts Commonwealth Games at Meadowbank Stadium, Edinburgh
4 April 1970	'Broadcasting in the Seventies' creates four 'generic' radio channels while Scotland retains all the elements of its 'national' service as opt-out from the new Radio 4
1973	Robert Coulter appointed Controller, Scotland
6 March 1973	BBC Scotland celebrates its 50th anniversary

John C.W. Reith with BBC Senior Staff

(*back l/r*) G.L. Marshall, first Edinburgh 2EH Station Director; John C.W. Reith, General Manager, British Broadcasting Company; David Cleghorn Thomson, Northern Area Director, title later changed to Scottish Regional Director.

(*front l/r*) E.W. Heddle, first Dundee 2DE Station Director; J.C.S. Macgregor, second Edinburgh 2EH Station Director; D.H. Clark, Appointments; Neil McLean, second Aberdeen 2BD Station Director.

(*not present, pictured elsewhere*) Herbert A. Carruthers, first Glasgow 5SC Station Director; D. Millar Craig, first Assistant Controller for Scotland; R.E. Jeffrey, first Aberdeen 2BD Station Director.

Introduction

ON 6 MARCH 1973, the BBC celebrated 50 years of Scottish broadcasting with a formal lunch held in the Ca' d'Oro Restaurant in Glasgow. For many it was a meeting of old friends, eager to talk and remember the unbelievable – was it really true that *Children's Hour* once dropped the story of the blue and red fairy because an election was pending? This mood of reminiscence continued as the principal guest, Professor Sir Robert Grieve, recalled how he'd first 'listened in' with headphones and a simple 'cat's whisker' receiver. Under the gaslight of a tenement house in Glasgow, hearing the London Savoy Orchestra had been an extraordinary experience.

With a fine skill he led his audience forward through the years. Memories of pleasure, and little of violence, an occasional criticism turned to curiosity, and always excitement and enthusiasm.

'You are the best, but I say it astringently... you've had 50 years... you're so old – you have grown so big. You cannot be dismissed in a few general phrases such as I've been using.'

From a corner of the room in which he was speaking the soot-blackened carriage entrance to Glasgow Central Station was clearly visible. It was here that, early in 1923, the General Manager of the British Broadcasting Company, John Reith, had stepped from the London train to meet his Scottish staff for the first time. Had he wished, he could have counted them on the fingers of one hand. Fifty years later, the BBC's Scottish payroll listed over 1,000 people.

Sir Robert Grieve was right. BBC Scotland, a public service and enjoying considerable status within the community, did merit more than a few general phrases.

David Pat Walker

CHAPTER ONE

The First Radio Stations

THE BRITISH BROADCASTING COMPANY LTD began its first regular broadcasting service from Station 2LO in London on 14 November 1922. The Company (it wouldn't become a Corporation until the end of 1926) had been formed largely because of government fears that the 'chaos in the ether' in America, where over 1,000 stations were fighting for only 89 places on the air, might come to Britain. Determined that UK listening would not suffer a similar fate, the government decided to sidestep future conflict by delivering the whole bag of tricks into the hands of a monopoly.

A series of meetings was arranged – at the first conference no less than 24 manufacturers of wireless apparatus were represented – and after months of argument and negotiation it was finally agreed that there would be a single broadcasting company for the UK. Backed by six of the biggest communication and electrical firms in Britain, the British Broadcasting Company Ltd would have the exclusive right to operate broadcasting stations throughout the country. In return, it would guarantee an adequate service for a maximum number of people. Revenue for the new company, with profits restricted to 7.5 per cent, was to come partly from a share of the government's broadcasting receiving licence, and partly from royalties from the sale of radio sets and components, all of which had to be made in Britain.

With the ink hardly dry on the finer details (the new Company was not registered until mid-December, and was without a licence until mid-January 1923) the BBC opened its first three stations in London, Birmingham and Manchester. Progress was swift and surprisingly easy thanks to earlier amateur enthusiasts who, now off the air because of the monopoly, frequently found themselves re-employed by the BBC. By Christmas, Newcastle brought the number of new stations to four and next on the list was Cardiff. Then it would be over the border and into Scotland – to Glasgow and then to Aberdeen.

On 24 January 1923, the BBC wrote to the General Post Office in London seeking authority to 'construct a broadcasting station' in Glasgow. Broadcasting bureaucracy was still in its infancy and a reply came by

The British Broadcasting Company's request
To the General Post Office to allot a 'wave length
and call letters' for a station in Glasgow.

The General Post Office
Gives its permission for 5SC to start broadcasting.

return: commence as soon as the station is ready. The wavelength will be 415m and the allotted call sign 5SC. Demonstrating an easy nonchalance the BBC estimated five weeks to completion. Engineers from the Marconi Company moved into the Glasgow Corporation Electricity Supply Station at Port Dundas in the north of the city to install and run a 'high power' 1.5kw transmitter, and a search was started for suitable studio and office premises in the city centre.

Casting around for whatever radio expertise might already exist the BBC soon found two 'scientific amateurs' who had been broadcasting on a limited scale in Glasgow for almost a year. Early in 1922 Frank Milligan, a dealer in wireless equipment, along with his friend George Garscadden who owned a household appliance business at Rex House in Bath Street, had taken out a licence to operate station 5MG. From a small room in the city and using a transmitter designed by another enthusiast, J.M.A. Cameron, they had broadcast for a few hours every week. Frequently the main contributor was George Garscadden's daughter, Kathleen. She was an

5SC premises at Rex House, 202 Bath Street, Glasgow

(© Steve Newman Photography)

accomplished pianist and singer and the leading soprano at Park Parish Church, and when the station planned something more complex than songs at the piano the church's choirmaster and organist, Herbert A. Carruthers, was often asked to help.

As a broadcasting package station 5MG contained most of what the BBC needed and without delay the Company set about picking from it for its own station. Herbert A. Carruthers, a man interested in broadcasting and having the kind of organisational and music experience that would enable him to double as conductor of the station's house orchestra, was offered the post of Scotland's first Station Director, which he accepted. George Garscadden, the co-founder of 5MG wished to continue with his own business but was offered accommodation on the top floor and attics of his premises at Rex House, 202 Bath Street, and when this was accepted J.M.A. Cameron, now the BBC's 'Engineer', moved in with a great deal of 5MG's equipment. Kathleen Garscadden was chosen to be an 'assistant' and was joined by two others, Alex H. Swinton Paterson and Mungo M. Dewar.

Five staff and some Marconi technicians – not an overabundance of people, but in those days, enough. As the opening date for the new station approached the old hands of 5MG sensed a growing feeling of excitement in and around the city. *The Glasgow Herald* newspaper had been publishing details of programmes at other BBC stations since January and the staff of 5SC had only one thought in mind – to have their first show over and a verdict, good or bad.

Opening night for the new station was Tuesday 6 March 1923. The transmitter, with its cage-like aerial slung between two of the Port Dundas power station chimneys, was ready and connected to the Control Room in Bath Street by a rented post office telephone line. The evening's cast of civic dignitaries and performers crammed around the single microphone in the small studio sharing it with the station's house orchestra while the inevitable pipe band spilled out into the adjoining corridor. Separated from the studio by a thin partition the Control Room Engineer sat watching the minute hand move towards the hour. At 7.00pm precisely he closed a single switch and, following a short burst of music on the pipes, John Reith, the BBC's General Manager, bent to the microphone and announced 5SC, the Glasgow Station of the British Broadcasting Company, was calling.

The broadcast lasted three and a half hours. All of it was 'live' and for

The aerial slung between two of the Port Dundas Power Station chimneys
Connected to Station 5SC's Control Room in Bath Street by a rented post office telephone line.
Port Dundas generated electricity for Glasgow's trams. The Forth and Clyde Canal
can be seen in the foreground.

The British Broadcasting Company
Limited

Opening

of the

Glasgow Station

Tuesday, 6th March, 1923

Left

Front page of the official programme
For the opening of Station 5SC
in Glasgow on Tuesday 6 March 1923.

Below

Running order
For the opening broadcast of
Station 5SC.

PROGRAMME

7.0 LORD GAINFORD, Chairman of the B.B.C.
    Introduced by Mr. J. C. W. Reith, General Manager.

7.10 THE RT. HON. THE LORD PROVOST OF GLASGOW.

7.15 ORCHESTRA.
    Selection on Scotch Melodies, " The Thistle,"   *Middleton*
    Serenade,   -   -   -   -   -   -   *Drigo*
    Suite from the Ballet Russe,   -   -   -   *Luigini*
    " Allegro Marziale," " Scene," " Mazurka."

7.55 Miss EVA TURNER, Prima Donna, Royal Carl Rosa Opera Co.
    " Ritorna Vincitos " (*Aida*),   -   -   -   *Verdi*
    " Jewel Song " (*Faust*),   -   -   -   *Gounod*

    Miss MAY LYMBURN, Contralto.
    " Softly Awakes my Heart " (*Samson and*
    Delilah),   -   -   -   -   *Saint-Saens*
    " Habanera " (*Carmen*),   -   -   -   *Bizet*

    Mr. HORACE VINCENT, Principal Tenor, Royal Carl Rosa Opera Co.
    " Spirto Gentil " (*La Favorita*),   -   -   *Donizetti*
    " For You Alone,"   -   -   -   -   *Geehl*

8.25 Sir DONALD MACALISTER, Principal of the University of
    Glasgow.

8.30 Miss EVA TURNER.
    " Pipes of Pan " (*Arcadians*),   -   *Lionel Monckton*
    " By the Waters of Minnetonka,"   -   *Thurlow Lieurance*

    Miss MAY LYMBURN.
    " Ye Banks and Braes,"   -   -   -   *Traditional*
    " Braw, Braw Lads,"   -   -   -   *Macfarren*

    MR. HORACE VINCENT.
    " Flower Song " (*Carmen*),   -   -   -   *Bizet*
    " Trusting Eyes,"   -   -   -   -   *Gartner*

9.0 Sir WILLIAM NOBLE.

9.5 CLOSE DOWN.

9.30 Mr. JOHN DICKSON, 'Cellist.
    " Adagio Cantabile,"   -   -   -   *Tartini*
    " Czardas,"   -   -   -   -   -   *Fischer*

9.40 NEWS BULLETIN.

9.55 ORCHESTRA.
    MARCH,   -   -   " Colonel Bogey,"   -   *Kenneth Alford*
    BARCAROLLE,   -   -   " Tales of Hoffmann,"   -   *Offenbach*
    MORCEAU DANSANT,   " Vivienne,"   -   *Herman Finch*
    INTERMEZZO,   -   -   " Fragrance,"   -   *Ancliffe*

    " GOD SAVE THE KING."

those taking part the air seemed to thicken by the minute. The studio, which measured no more than 30ft square, was heavily draped with grey hessian, and had a thick carpeting of felt on the floor. In a corner a small fan did nothing more than suggest ventilation and, despite the invitations to 'The Opening' mentioning 'The Concert Room', many felt that they were visiting the Black Hole of Calcutta. Notwithstanding these difficulties, however, the next day it was clear that the broadcast had been a complete success. Good reception over a wide area had meant a large number of homes 'listening in' and for those without sets, *The Glasgow Herald* had installed a number of receivers in the city's Berkeley Hall where the capacity audience had applauded every item loud and long. Describing the evening's events the next day the newspaper was lyrical in its report:

> Swifter than Mercury from high Olympus the strains of the pipes bore their message to John o' Groats and Maidenkirk ushering in a new medium of social life and of expanding civilisation.

The Scotsman newspaper, published 50 miles away in Edinburgh, was less enamoured, making no mention at all of the Glasgow opening. Its silence, noted by the BBC, was not unexpected. The earliest government plans for broadcasting had proposed Glasgow or Edinburgh as one of the two Scottish stations, and though the eventual choice of Glasgow had been made on straightforward business grounds, Edinburgh had been less than pleased. Broadcasting, the city had reasoned, was a 'capital' matter, inadvertently laying down battle lines that would affect a great deal of the first 50 years of the BBC in Scotland.

5SC's successful launch, and the flood of congratulations that followed, gave particular satisfaction to John Reith. Twenty-five years later he would write: 'The General Manager of the British Broadcasting Company Ltd was more than ordinarily interested in the opening of the service in Scotland, for he was a Scot.' Reith expected much from his fellow countrymen and over the next 15 years he would frequently reach out from London to touch the Scottish operation. For the moment, however, he was content, leaving 5SC in the hands of Herbert A. Carruthers.

During the first few months the station had to generate all its own output. Simultaneous broadcasting – the ability to link stations together to share the same programme – was still some months away and the Glasgow staff found themselves feeding a voracious output. After a normal

Glasgow Station 5SC's *Children's Corner*
(*l/r*) Herbert A. Carruthers, first Station Director and later Head of Music;
Alex H. Swinton Paterson (Uncle Alex); Mungo M. Dewar (Uncle Mungo);
Kathleen Garscadden (Auntie Cyclone) with Susie the cat on the piano.

working day in the office they would gather in the studio for the start
of programmes, with *Children's Corner* at around 5.30pm. A short inter-
val and then broadcasting continued with a news bulletin at 7.00pm and
ran until 10.30pm. For anyone not involved in newsreading, producing,
rehearsing or performing, there was a commitment to be out and about
in the city talking to the many radio clubs that had sprung up.

As each new station enjoyed a state of virtual programme autonomy,
the BBC's important promise of 'under central control' was contrived in
various ways. By the selection of 'suitable' staff ensuring a unity of purpose
and by a nightly news bulletin dictated over the telephone from London
to a typist at each station (in Glasgow Mungo M. Dewar admitted to frequently reading a page of the news with an anxious eye on the door waiting
for someone to dash in with the next!) and the distribution by post of
numerous talks to be re-read at the microphone by local voices. One of
the first of these to reach 5SC was a script written by Princess Alice of
Athlone on *How to Adopt a Child*. Finding a female voice proved difficult

– people were cautious, fearing that their voices would be distorted – and Kathleen Garscadden chose to read it herself. Unfortunately, the broadcast was heard by her mother who considered it a most unsuitable subject for her young daughter. Later, however, subjects such as *The Art of Sweet-Making* and *Keeping Meals Hot* helped to right the balance, as did Kathleen's boisterous appearances as 'Auntie Cyclone' in *Children's Hour*.

As the staff of 5SC struggled to keep even two days ahead with their programme plans, music became the mainstay of the output. As well as using the station's house orchestra – in truth a quartet which could be augmented as and when there was money available – no time was lost in arranging to have music relayed from nearby locations.

Within two weeks of its opening Glasgow transmitted its first Outside Broadcast (OB), a live relay from the Coliseum Theatre in Eglinton Street at 7.30pm on 19 March 1923. Using a single Western Electric microphone buried in the footlights at the front of the stage, no amplifier and a rented telephone line from the theatre to the Control Room at 202 Bath Street, an excerpt from *Das Rheingold* sung by the British National Opera Company was broadcast to the listeners. A series of broadcasts followed and a new permanent switch was added to the Glasgow Control Room.

Swiftly, broadcasting firsts for Scotland were being notched up. Sunday 15 April marked the first studio broadcast by a minister – the Rev John White – and ten days later there was an OB with him from the Barony Kirk. The clergy were still not well-disposed to what they considered an undue obtrusion on worship and a great deal of perseverance was required. 'Yes. I will preach into a microphone but I will never pray into it!', retorted a minister when offered the chance to reach the bedridden and the housebound.

The new station also wanted to try its hand at drama. Plays were known to be popular with London listeners and the Glasgow staff were confident that they could do something similar. Gradually the favourites of the local amateur stage were tempted to the microphone and Glasgow rejoiced on hearing 'on the wireless' such people as William Chapman, Jean Taylor Smith, Elliot C. Mason, Cathie Fletcher and R.B. Wharrie. They were the forerunners of the semi-professionals who would take Scottish drama to the forefront of BBC radio over the next 15 years.

The credit for laying the foundations of 5SC's drama output must go to R.E. Jeffrey, a Glasgow elocutionist and a frequent visitor to the Bath

Street studio where he often arranged and took part in music-based programmes. Jeffrey was captivated by broadcasting. He found it exhilarating and exciting and saw tremendous possibilities ahead, particularly in 'dramatic' presentations. His ideas were simple, or so it seems now, but at the time were innovative to a degree. He wanted to explore the use of imaginative sound beyond the then staple fare of Shakespearean dialogue and occasional relays from the stage of the local theatre. So far the microphone had been used to present as faithful a reproduction as possible of what was going on around it. Jeffrey's concept was to make it a part of the production, exploiting its potential for stimulating the imagination. If the eye couldn't see what was going on, the ear could be persuaded to create a host of plausible images.

Herbert A. Carruthers, the Station Manager, liked the idea and, in any case, was anxious to proceed with some studio-based drama. Jeffery was given the go-ahead and on 31 August 1923 5SC offered the listener dramatic excerpts from Walter Scott's novel, *Rob Roy*.

R.E. Jeffrey took the part of Rob Roy and military music was supplied by the band of the 1st Royal Scots Fusiliers who also deftly changed sides and supplied the warring pipe music as well. The choir of The Lyric Club, Glasgow, provided the chorus and even the station's orchestra was involved. Effects were used frequently – the noises being made by whoever was free at the time – and there was a great deal of clamour at the door to the studio as the warring factions of Scott's novel arrived and departed on cue.

The next morning the local press hailed it with such phrases as 'striking new technique' and 'brought to life by actors'. They were right. For the first time in broadcasting an attempt had been made to create the sound of events being portrayed – creating actuality. The production had been designed from the start to be broadcast using a mixture of narration and dialogue, a liberal sprinkling of music and effects, and perspectives.

News of the production and its success reached head office in London. By a happy coincidence, two days before the *Rob Roy* broadcast, experiments using post office circuits to carry programmes over large distances had resulted in the first simultaneous broadcast of a London news bulletin over the 5SC transmitter in Glasgow. It had gone without a hitch and meant that the possibility of passing complete programmes between stations was now a reality. London, casting around for a programme to mark this advance in broadcasting, asked for a repeat performance of the Scottish play and on 6 October 1923, *Rob Roy* was repeated from the Bath Street Studio in Glasgow, this time as a simultaneous broadcast and was heard by every station in the BBC network.

It was a significant moment for 5SC – the first regional drama production to be broadcast to all stations – but that night the jubilation in the Glasgow studio was tinged with sadness. R.E. Jeffrey's talent had not gone unnoticed and already the BBC had other plans for him. Their next Scottish station, 2BD in Aberdeen, was due to open on the following Wednesday and he was expected to be there as its first Station Director.

R.E. Jeffrey
First Aberdeen 2BD Station Director
who was then appointed Dramatic Director
(Head of Drama) in London.

On Wednesday 10 October the BBC arrived in Aberdeen in some force. Accompanying the General Manager was Sir William Noble, a Director of the Company, and Captain Peter Eckersley, the BBC's Chief Engineer. John Reith was in fine form. A few months before, he had associated himself closely with Glasgow, the city where he had grown up. Now he underlined his northern birth: 'I am an Aberdonian myself', he wrote in a preview of the opening day, dismissing the 15 miles or so that separated the city from the town of Stonehaven, where he had been born.

The new station's importance to the BBC was threefold. It completed the main station 'spine' that spread northwards from London, it would be the first of the main stations to include a large element of rural listeners, and if the opening broadcast went as planned – a simultaneous broadcast between Aberdeen and London – the Company could realistically plan for a future when stations would no longer have to supply all their own programme material.

A great deal depended on the success of simultaneous broadcasting. Thankfully it was not seen as a way of enforcing a London monopoly of programmes. In the very week that Aberdeen was to open, Arthur Burrows, the BBC's first Director of Programmes, had written:

> By such a process it could easily be arranged for London alone to provide all the wireless entertainment of Great Britain but such a scheme would meet with early disaster. These islands of ours contain, as every traveller fully knows, various well-defined areas in which the majority of the people have distinct tastes in music and other forms of entertainment. It was in recognition of this fact that certain provincial stations were opened and for the maintenance of programmes catering for local tastes they will continue to be employed. In the future their supporters will have this local fare garnished with the tit-bits from other centres of art and music.

In Aberdeen the morning was going badly for the BBC. Few of the public saw the worried faces among the staff and were unaware that the trunk telephone wires in the north of the country were down because of a severe gale that had swept the country. The opening ceremony for the station, to be carried out by the Marquis of Aberdeen and Temair, was scheduled for 9.00pm that evening. All day engineers worked feverishly to ensure a trouble-free connection out of Aberdeen. The link from the studio at 17 Belmont Street to the 2BD transmitter situated at the premises of the

2BD studio at
17 Belmont Street,
Aberdeen

(l/r) A. Birch; R.E. Jeffrey,
Station Director;
W.D. Simpson, Engineering;
J.M.A. Cameron,
Superintendent Engineer
(North).

2BD premises at 17 Belmont Street, Aberdeen

(Entrance subsequently established at 15 Belmont Street as part of office development).

(© Ritchie Craib)

Aberdeen Steam Laundry at 40 Claremont Street posed no problems. In fact that transmitter, housed in the old dye-house, was to give exceedingly good service over the next 15 years. A tribute to the original installation work and the continuing devotion of the commissioning engineers, Messrs Harding, Birch and Burgess, although it has to be admitted that, like the everlasting hatchet, it had had the equivalent of six new handles and three new heads before it was finally replaced.

The worry was the complex of post office lines needed to carry the programme southwards. However, in the event, the broadcast was a success and the simultaneous broadcast arrangements worked perfectly.

The Company's Chief Engineer, Peter Eckersley, was paying his first visit to Aberdeen. He was so impressed by the occasion that he wrote an account of the day on his return:

The worst is over and from all reports we have 'simultaneous' to some effect. Relaxation comes like a ray of warming sunshine after threat of lowering storm. One might almost go and have a sandwich and, if one feels one deserves it, a soda and whisky.

Reception had indeed been good and over the next few days enthusiastic reports poured in. Ironically, one area close by did have problems – Stonehaven, John Reith's birthplace. Eckersley continued:

... owners of crystal sets were unable to get through but this experience is not necessarily a proof that this class of receiver will not be capable of hearing 2BD as the climate conditions at certain periods were none too favourable.

Returning south the London party had plenty to talk about. The relay to London had been excellent. 'Not only was the clapping of hands of the audience heard, but even the laughter at the two stories the Marquis of Aberdeen and Temair told,' reported the London correspondent of *The Press and Journal*. This was a striking example of the growing efficiency of the broadcasting system.

To begin with, distance had posed problems – anything beyond a few miles causing a considerable drop in quality and reliability. The engineers, along with post office colleagues, had worked hard and long on the problem and now programme transmission over long lines – referred to as 'land lines' – was entirely feasible. Now the Aberdeen broadcast was proof that all BBC stations could be drawn together with common programmes of music and speech. No longer was there any fear that broadcasting in Britain might develop along similar lines to that in America where it had mushroomed at great speed, with characteristic energy, and without any method of control whatsoever. In Britain it had been a government decision that the service should be under central control and in the hands of one organisation. Here now was the means of achieving that single standard and one guiding policy.

No time was lost in putting the new system into practice. An obvious first step involved the scripted texts – still being distributed by post from London to be re-read at the local microphones under the description, *A Short Talk, as told in London by...* Within a week of the Aberdeen opening John Reith wrote in the *Radio Times*:

In future the following will be broadcast simultaneously: Mr John Strachey's causerie on books every Monday; Mr Archibald Haddon's dramatic talk on Wednesdays; the discussion on music by Mr Percy Scholes on Thursdays; and on Fridays the film criticisms by Mr G.A. Atkinson.

These, along with the two general news bulletins broadcast nightly from London, were the first compulsory programmes broadcast by the provincial stations. A few weeks later music was added to the list when Station Directors were told that at least one concert per week was to be taken from London or elsewhere.

These moves to systemise the relaying of London programmes to the provinces did cause some apprehension amongst listeners who enjoyed the local friendliness that was now part of the provincial stations. Sensing this the BBC attempted to allay their fears and in the process defined the reason for, and purpose, of regional broadcasting in a way that was still broadly applicable 50 years later:

> We have not the slightest intention of cutting out local programmes. The stations will in no way suffer but will benefit. They are almost in personal touch with their 'listeners-in' because people know the artists and officials intimately and it would be as practicable for us successfully to supply and control a provincial broadcasting station from London as it would be to control and supply a local newspaper from London.
>
> By relieving a local station one or two nights during the week we should enable it to achieve a higher local standard. And by relaying the provincial programmes we hope to discover some provincial singers of exceptional talent. They perhaps cannot get to London but they will know that among the many people listening to them will at least be several experts on the lookout for singers and artists of promise.

Confidently on the way to achieving a unified standard of broadcasting, the Company next set about acquiring a larger audience. Many urban areas were still beyond crystal range of the recently established main stations, and cities such as Liverpool, Sheffield, Edinburgh and Dundee kept up a steady clamour of complaint. To satisfy their demands, and at

G.L. Marshall
First Edinburgh 2EH Station Director, later Station Director Glasgow, Newcastle
and Belfast, then Regional Director and Controller, Northern Ireland.

the same time increase the need for more sets and equipment, the BBC proposed setting up 11 new local-power transmitters. These additional stations would make full use of a simultaneous broadcasting system by being linked by land wire to a nearby main station. This would eliminate the need for anything more than a token programme commitment of local material as, for most of the time, the new transmitters would relay the output of their associated station.

On the face of it, these relay stations seemed a good idea and one that would be welcomed by the concerned areas. It was a sensible and practicable plan that took into account such engineering nightmares as signal 'jamming' and signal 'shielding'. It would also increase the BBC's crystal coverage to around three-quarters of the population of Great Britain and it paid due deference to the regional appetite of the provincial audiences. Where it failed was in not anticipating the strong inter-city jealousies that would arise when the main and relay linking was proposed.

There was little love between cities in Britain, and in Scotland, when word came that Edinburgh's proposed relay station would be fed from Glasgow, there was a distinct chill in the proceedings. Matters were not

2EH premises at 79 George Street, Edinburgh
(Moved to 87 George Street shortly afterwards to secure more accommodation).
(© RCAHMS)

helped by the Glasgow press. Mindful perhaps of this Edinburgh disdain, when Station 5SC was opened, *The Glasgow Herald* took the line of most resistance saying, in effect, that if Edinburgh's application for a wireless station was granted then Dundee would want one – where would it end?

In fact the plan to link the 12 new relay stations on a regional basis had ultimately to be abandoned. No-one was more surprised than John Reith who noted: 'the factor of inter-city civic jealousy had, however, not been reckoned on. It appears that no city counted sufficiently important to have a relay station could listen to the programme of any station other than London without loss of dignity.'

2EH Control Room
79 George Street, Edinburgh.

He and the company bowed to the inevitable: the new areas were linked with London where, they said, the best programmes came from.

The Edinburgh relay station, call sign 2EH, was opened on 1 May 1924 with a public relay meeting and concert held in the city's Usher Hall. The opening ceremony was performed by the Lord Provost of Edinburgh (Sir William Sleigh) and amongst the notables on the platform were John Reith and George L. Marshall, the newly appointed Edinburgh Station Director. Significantly, the programme opened with the sound of the chimes of Big Ben striking 9.00pm. True to their promise the BBC had linked the Edinburgh station to London.

The first local broadcast from the Scottish capital took place the following afternoon at 5.00pm. It was a talk for children and it marked the first use of the BBC studio at 79 George Street. The premises were small and had been rented from Messrs Townsend and Thomson, a city music shop. The Station Director's office was a throughway to the Control Room and the studio, measuring about 20-feet square and draped with the usual heavy curtaining, was an adaptation of one of Townsend and Thomson's front rooms.

The transmitter for 2EH was a little more than a mile away in a wooden hut in the quadrangle of the Edinburgh University buildings at Teviot Place. The aerial was suspended from a chimney and, no doubt because of the city's many hills and high tenements, reception was generally poor. The Station's Engineer-in-Chief, J.A. Beveridge, took every possible care but the equipment was not up to the task. A replacement was sought and a few months later, after the first Wembley Exhibition, the Wembley transmitter, which had been erected for special broadcasts, was taken to Edinburgh to replace the original installation. The new equipment had more than twice the power of the original and in order to accommodate it the wooden hut had to be extended by building an additional storey. The replacement did help to alleviate some of the

Edinburgh staff (1924)

(*l/r*) Alec Cameron; Nancy Forres; H.K. Brown; Mamie Irvine; G.L. Marshall, 2EH Station Director; Betty B.C.; Jacky Beveridge; (*at front*) Tony Coghill, Office Boy.

reception troubles and none too soon. To the concern of the civic fathers a few of the city's listeners had already gone to considerable lengths to achieve good reception and in some cases aerials had been stretched from one side of the street to another – just over the live tramway wires!

Within six months of the opening of Edinburgh the final piece of the Scottish jigsaw was set in place. As prophesied by *The Glasgow Herald*, albeit tongue-in-cheek, the BBC acquired premises in Dundee to house 2DE, the last but one of its relay chain. For a time negotiations had been touch and go. After promising a station as part of the relay development the BBC later withdrew on the grounds that stations were being allotted according to population and that Dundee would not qualify. It took some weighty negotiations by the two MPs for Dundee and pressure from a committee appointed by the Lord Provost before Dundee went back on the list, this time to stay.

THE STAFF OF THE DUNDEE WIRELESS STATION

Back row—Mr L. W. Benson, Assistant Maintenance Engineer; Miss B. L. Braid, Secretary; Mr Alex. Cameron, B.Sc., Engineer in Charge; Mrs G. E. Cuthbert, Lady Organiser, "Auntie Gwen,"; Mr H. W. Dewar, Assistant Maintenance Engineer. In front—Mr Eric Heddle, M.C., M.A.(Hons.), B.Sc. (Director).

The Station Director, who is the Director as well as Announcer, is Mr Eric W. M. Heddle, M.C., M.A., B.Sc., who was educated at Hamilton Academy and Glasgow University. During the war Mr Heddle served with the Gordons and Highland Infantry, holding a special reserve commission. He was in France with the 32nd and 9th Divisions, and was wounded, gassed, and mentioned in despatches, and awarded the M.C. After the Armistice Mr Heddle held various posts as education officer, &c., in Germany, and during the last two years has been a Lecturer on the staff of the Royal Technical College.

Mr Alexander Cameron, B.Sc., A.R.T.C., is the engineer-in-chief. He is a native of Fort-William. He has been an assistant in the Royal Technical College, and for the last six months has acted as assistant maintenance engineer at the Edinburgh Relay Station. At the College he was the Montgomerie-Neilson medallist.

Mr F. R. Benson, assistant maintenance engineer, served in the Royal Navy during the war, and was decorated with the Russian Order of St George for services in the Baltic.

Mr Harold W. Dewar, who belongs to Glasgow, is another assistant maintenance engineer. He formerly belonged to the Mercantile Marine.

Mrs Cuthbert, Bingham Terrace, Dundee, is Lady Organiser, has already achieved much popularity in Glasgow as "Auntie Gwen." For the last six months Mrs Cuthbert had travelled to Glasgow every week to take her place at the children's hour. Mrs Cuthbert has also broadcast in London. She is a very versatile lady, and has exhibited both in painting and sculpture at the Royal Scottish Academy, the Society of Scottish Artists, and the Glasgow Institute. Recently Mrs Cuthbert published a book of children's poems, and she is also the joint author of an educational book of the world travel series. With such versatile gifts, Auntie Gwen is certain to be an instant favourite with her juvenile audiences.

Auntie Joe, Assistant Lady Organiser, is Miss E. M. Barrow, who is mistress of the Preparatory School at Broughty Ferry. The Secretary is Miss Barbara Braid, Leuchars.

First Dundee staff

(l/r) L.W. Benson, Asst Maintenance Engineer; Miss B.L. Braid, Secretary; Alex Cameron, Engineer-in-Charge; Miss G.E. Cuthbert, Ladies Organiser ('Auntie Gwen'); H.W. Dewar, Asst Mt Engineer (*front*) Eric W. Heddle, 2DE Station Director.
Miss GE Cuthbert left the station after barely a year, but would later make her mark as Wendy Wood, one of the early members of the National Party of Scotland (a forerunner party to the SNP). Cuthbert was her name from her first marriage. Her maiden name was Meacham, but she adopted her mother's maiden name, Wood, ca 1927.
(Extract from *Dundee Courier* © DC Thomson & Co Ltd)

The opening ceremony and programme took place in the Caird Hall on 12 November 1924. Eric W. Heddle was present as the new Station Director while the BBC's London representative was Vice-Admiral C.D. Carpendale, Assistant General Manager. The formal part of the evening was conducted by the Lord Provost of Dundee, Sir William High. In the various speeches reference was made to the fact that, 'it was an illustrious citizen of Dundee, the great Dr Bell, who was the real father of the telephone.' It was a pertinent theme for the occasion as the Dundee station would depend on the telephone system's network of lines for over 80 per cent of its programmes leaving the small studio at 1 Lochee Road to produce little more than some light music and the ubiquitous children's broadcasting.

2DE premises at 1 Lochee Road, Dundee
(Indicated by arrow as the building was demolished though one to its rear can still be seen).
(© University of Dundee Archive Services)

Scotland could now boast four BBC stations, quite a feat of expansion

2DE studio premises at 1 Lochee Road, Dundee
Artist's impression shows the BBC's offices (ex-Gilroy's) in the centre of the image with a tram approaching from the right. The ornate garden at the back was probably the result of the licence allowed the artist at the period.
(© RCAHMS)

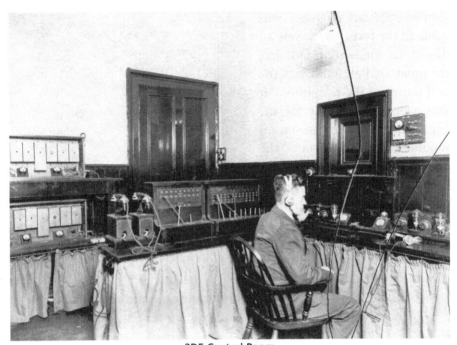

2DE Control Room
Alex Cameron, Engineer-in-Charge.
(© DC Thomson & Co Ltd)

in 20 months. All had the ability and will to broadcast programmes either for local consumption or to a wider audience: the determining factor being status – whether a main or a relay station – and financial well-being. These were days of carefree experiment and the broadcasters cast their net wide as they sought ideas for their programmes. The public's initial fear of broadcasting – every station had its own story of a first-time broadcaster passing out in front of the microphone – was now giving way to native curiosity and boldness. Station waiting rooms – those that hadn't become extra office accommodation – thronged with hopeful enquirers: 'Ah wis wantin' a try on the wireless.' 'Yes. Are you a singer or what is your special line?' 'Aye. I'm a singer.' 'Have you sung in public?' 'Oh, aye. I hiv sung at a lot o' smokers and I aye get an encore.'

Mixed in with those seeking musical fame were others wishing to use the BBC's SOS message facility – usually misguidedly. The SOS service had been initiated for messages regarding dangerously ill relatives or friends and not, as many thought, to help those seeking missing pets and errant spouses!

Quite suddenly, to have broadcast was eminently desirable. It marked you as somebody of importance. When the Glasgow station persuaded Sir Thomas Lipton to come to the 5SC studio a photographer was on hand to record the occasion. Posing in characteristic attitude immediately after the broadcast 'Tommy' could not resist declaiming, 'If you want the best tea...' at which point the Control Room Engineer dived for the microphone switch, still live and feeding Sir Thomas's words to the transmitter.

Glasgow, being the first of the BBC stations in Scotland, had assumed the mantle of headquarters almost from the very start. Its seniority was reinforced by the size of its audience and the growing reputation for innovation enjoyed by its small staff, the latter a recognition that was hardly surprising in view of the nature of broadcasting but still nonetheless well deserved.

A little more than six months after the opening of 5SC the British Broadcasting Company Limited wrote to various educational bodies in Glasgow proposing a local advisory committee as part of a national scheme. There was immediate interest in the BBC's proposals and, at a meeting held in the Central Station Hotel, Glasgow, on 23 January 1924, John Reith, who had travelled north to Glasgow from London especially for the occasion, presided at the inauguration of the BBC's Glasgow Educational Advisory Committee.

Chairman, Sir Charles Cleland, Glasgow's Director of Education, was enthusiastic from the start and imbued with the thought that the broadcasting service might be used 'for the purposes of edification and even education as well' (Reith's opening theme at the meeting). He therefore quickly found himself in cahoots with the 5SC staff arranging a special broadcast that would prove to be a milestone in the history of British broadcasting – the first custom-built schools broadcast to be transmitted by the BBC.

Chosen for the experiment were the senior pupils of Garnetbank School who were to listen to a programme designed by the Glasgow station for schoolroom listening. Alex H. Swinton Paterson of the Glasgow staff was put in charge of arrangements for the broadcast, which was scheduled for 2.30pm on Tuesday 26 February 1924. V.A. Bulow, now Engineer-in-Charge at 5SC, supervised the technical details – a twin aerial about 20 feet long connected to a receiver described as 'a crystal detector with a two-valve amplifier to operate a loud speaking telephone' – and the programme was listened to in the school hall by close on 100 attentive pupils and interested spectators. Taking part in the broadcast were Professor Charles Martin, Mademoiselle Pierrette Grizel and Mr J.R. Peddie, presenting between them a violin recital, a talk on the ballad, a lesson in music and a short reading in French. The experiment was a success and a few months later, on Friday 9 May, Glasgow began regular schools broadcasts.

On the day that Reith had held his meeting of educationalists, he had also set about forming a Scottish version of his religious advisory or 'Sunday Committee'. Never one to tolerate waste, he used the same room in the same hotel and at 2.30pm in the afternoon, along with his Director of Programmes, Arthur Burrows, and 5SC's Station Director, Herbert A. Carruthers, he convened a meeting of interested theological representatives. The 'Sunday Committee' group that resulted from these deliberations consisted of representatives of the Church of Scotland, the United Free Church, the Congregational Church, the Wesleyan Church plus the Bishop of Glasgow. John Reith was disappointed that, in Glasgow, it had not been found possible to secure the Roman Catholic denominations and hoped this would not take long.

Unlike their education colleagues, the members of the religious group were extremely tentative when it came to arranging broadcasts. They had a basic fear that anything more than what was already being provided by 5SC – a regular programme of hymns and a religious address – might eventually empty their churches. However, after a great deal of discussion and reasoned argument it was finally agreed that broadcasting a full religious service would quite likely involve many listeners who would not otherwise have taken part in worship and they agreed to support the BBC's plans.

A little over a month later, in March 1924, the Glasgow station embarked on a series of regular broadcasts of religious services from local churches. Sadly the Glasgow 'Sunday Committee' has no further place in the record. It very quickly disappeared from view mainly because of the inability of its members to reach agreement on a time or place for future meetings. It shouldn't be forgotten completely, however, for its decision to support the BBC was, at the time, a courageous one. At the first meeting in the Central Hotel, Reith had put the Company's case simply and clearly saying that in broadcasting services and, in any of their religious work, the BBC were actuated simply by the desire to do the right thing. The Committee's considered reply was to say, in effect, that above all else Man needed some contact with God for his general well-being and that was paramount to all else.

New developments in broadcasting were now an almost weekly occurrence and innovation in Scotland was no longer the prerogative of Glasgow alone. Aberdeen, the second of the Scottish main stations, was also forging ahead. Within weeks of its opening it had written into its log the first broadcast in Gaelic (a religious address given on 2 December 1923), the first Gaelic song recital broadcast 19 days later and on 7 March 1924 the first regular sports broadcasts in Scotland, a series of talks given by Peter Craigmyle, an international referee.

R.E. Jeffrey, the Aberdeen Station Director, quickly gained the reputation of being a man who always spoke his thoughts at the microphone. He was a strong believer in the importance of listeners using a high aerial, mentioning this during broadcasts, and for years after, the aerial masts in the area were always thought to be higher than anywhere else. Jeffrey would also talk about the weather – a favourite subject – and one evening, having bemoaned a sudden change that brought the rain teeming down, he stepped out of the BBC premises at the end of the day to find both sides of Belmont Street filled with cars, all waiting to give him a lift home.

While innovation and increased output were for the moment welcome factors in the expansion of broadcasting in Scotland, it was obvious that some kind of control was going to be required to bring order to the local element of broadcasting. Stations seemed to be largely oblivious of each other. Too many programmes were duplicates of what was being done elsewhere and there was a pressing need to systematise the haphazard engineering methods that were being used. To remedy the situation, early in 1924 the BBC announced two new posts designed to deal with Scotland as a whole. J.M.A. Cameron, 5SC's Principal Engineer, and the man who had supervised the technical side even pre-BBC, was to become Northern Area Maintenance Engineer, responsible for all aspects of engineering in Scotland and, as it so happened, as far south as Stoke-on-Trent, and, to cope with programme and administrative matters there would be an Assistant Controller, Scotland. Both would be based in Glasgow and, as well as their Scottish responsibilities, would have an overseeing role in Northern Ireland.

THE GLASGOW RADIO HEADQUARTERS STAFF.

Glasgow radio headquarters staff

D. Millar Craig (*fourth from left, seated*) first Assistant Controller, Scotland (1924–1926) with subsequent responsibility for 5SC as its second Station Director replacing Herbert A. Carruthers, who became Head of Music.

(*back row l/r*) Miss J. Hunter; William Black, Maintenance Engineer; Miss B.M. Ferguson; Leslie Hotine, Chief Maintenance Engineer; William Rae, Maintenance Engineer; Mungo M. Dewar; Miss S. Grant; Alexander H. Swinton Paterson; J.B. Watson.

(*front row l/r*) Vincent A.M. Bulow (Engineer-in-Charge); Miss Kathleen Garscadden; Herbert A. Carruthers; D. Millar Craig; J.M.A. Cameron, Superintendent Engineer (North); Miss E. Bebbington; P.A. Florence, Asst Superintendent Engineer (North).

(© From an unidentified newspaper)

The creation of the Assistant Controller position – the 'Assistant' prefix was no more than a deferential nod to head office where 'Controllers' reigned supreme – was the vital first step towards the establishment of what was to become known as the BBC's Scottish Region and an acknowledgement that while on the one hand Scotland was a nation, it would still have to come under a common control like the rest of the UK. Indeed, in announcing the new post the BBC spoke openly of the need for someone to act as a liaison officer between the Scottish stations and London and to 'interpret BBC policy according to Scottish needs.'

What was not stated was the Company's wish to see some order created out of the burgeoning and boisterous conglomeration of stations that were forming in Scotland.

To fill the post the BBC chose D. Millar Craig, a man known in the Scottish capital as having an interest in music and education, as well as being the brother of the legal secretary to the Lord Advocate. He had other attributes that oddly fascinated the BBC.

'During the war he was a captain in the Fifth Royal Scots and was gassed and wounded. One of his most interesting duties at the Front was when he undertook the work of Officer Commanding in Charge of the literature-propaganda-by-balloons. This had a marked effect on the enemy's morale in the latter stages of the war.'

In the six months that followed D. Millar Craig's appointment there was a great deal of friction between himself and Scottish listeners. As he set about achieving some kind of co-ordination amongst the Scottish stations – three by the time he was appointed and soon to be four – he discovered that local loyalties die hard. At the start his plans met with considerable opposition both from listeners faithful to their own local station and those who resented the inevitable domination by Glasgow's 5SC. Letters in the press made the mood quite clear: 'The 5SC orchestra is very poor.' 'A shock!' 'The 5SC standard is that of a Saturday after-noon concert in a local corporation hall.' 'Edinburgh has demanded London – the BBC Glasgow staff should see the writing on the wall.'

D. Millar Craig persevered. He had little option to do otherwise as the proliferation of duplicate programmes from every station made a nonsense of finance and quality and there was very little direct co-operation between the stations. As many had feared, Glasgow's hours increased – brought about by the departure of R.E. Jeffrey from Aberdeen to London and the consequent move of drama back to Glasgow – and the increasing use of the 5SC premises as a line-routing centre for simul-taneous broadcasts resulted in 202 Bath Street bulging at the seams. As there was no room for expansion another home had to be found.

The new premises were at 21 Blythswood Square, a gracious Glasgow square not far from Bath Street. There was a great deal more room as befitted the Scottish headquarters and for the first time there were two

New 5SC premises at 21 Blythswood Square, Glasgow.
(© Steve Newman Photography)

studios, the main one being 40 feet long. Greatly improved equipment was installed in the Control Room and a new style of wiring had been introduced with plugs and jacks beginning to replace the notorious Glasgow double-throw knife switches.

For the opening on 7 November 1924, there was the now almost obligatory concert. The Lord Provost of Glasgow, Mr M.W. Montgomery, did the honours supported by Sir Charles Clelland. The programme was transmitted from the new large studio and broadcast simultaneously in Aberdeen and Edinburgh.

Radioptimists, 5SC Glasgow (1927)
Gordon Gildard (*left*); Halbert Tatlock (*centre, top*); Helen MacKay (*centre, middle*);
Marilyn C. Webster (*centre, bottom*); Nora Mitchell (*right*).

The announcer for the evening was the Assistant Controller, D. Millar Craig, and the orchestra was conducted by Herbert A. Carruthers, anticipating perhaps the short announcement that would appear in the press a few days later:

'The new premises move marks a management change. Herbert A. Carruthers is relieved of responsibility in connection with the business and administrative side and will devote his whole time to the musical part of programmes.'

From now on D. Millar Craig was to run the Glasgow station as well as shaping one overall service. An indication perhaps that 5SC was gaining control. The Glasgow press used the occasion to give a general nod in the direction of what he was doing.

'Programmes seem to be improving in quality,' reported a Glasgow weekly. 'The radio fare is becoming brighter and perhaps less highbrow than it was. Obviously the BBC is bowing to popular taste and trying to give what is wanted. The personal element seems to be somewhat subdued at most of the stations except in the case of *Children's Hour*.'

Radio's popularity was marked in another way that month when, less than a week after the opening of 2DE in Dundee, broadcasting acquired a place in the crime statistics of Scotland:

> During the absence of a family from a house in the city some person or persons entered and made a clean sweep of a complete wireless set. Nothing else was touched.

First Outside Broadcast (OB) van
Outside 21 Blythswood Square.

Soon 1924 was to come to an end and as the four stations reached their first New Year together, the two main stations were strangely quiet, choosing to join London at 9.30pm for a fairly muted welcome to the New Year. Dundee closed down at 10.30pm, but Edinburgh, unusually capricious, abandoned London, kilted her skirts and danced away the night to midnight and 'Auld Lang Syne'.

In a way they all deserved to catch their breath. Scotland's broadcasting milestones had been passing like telegraph poles on a fast train journey. Some were ideas that dispersed into the ether as fast as the modulator would allow, their inevitability consigning them to total disinterest. Others are more deserving of recall as notable moments in Scotland's broadcasting history.

February 1924: the special programme from Glasgow's 5SC heard by children at Garnetbank School.

March 1924: Aberdeen's 2BD starts the first regular sports broadcasts in Scotland with Peter Craigmyle, an international football referee, talking every Thursday.

March 1924: Aberdeen's 2BD explores the world of community singing with a broadcast from the Music Hall, Aberdeen and finds it has a runaway success on its hands that becomes a tradition.

April 1924: Glasgow's 5SC presents three plays performed by the Scottish National Players. Amongst the cast are Moreland Graham, Elliott C. Mason, R.B. Wharrie, Nan Scott and Grace McChlery.

May 1924: Aberdeen's 2BD presents the Repertory Players in *Macbeth* with R.E. Jeffrey, A.M. Shinnie, George Rowntree Harvey, R. Gordon McCallum, Christina Crowe, Eric Linklater and W. Dundas.

On 5 June 1924 the *Radio Times* reports:

The high-class orchestra the London, Midland and Scottish Railway Company have installed at Gleneagles Hotel will broadcast a programme of music... by means of a land wire connected with the Glasgow Broadcasting Station. Mr Henry W. Hall, Manchester, is conductor of the orchestra.

Three weeks later, Sir Harry Lauder makes his first broadcast from Glasgow on the eve of Scottish Scouts' Week.

July 1924: R.E. Jeffrey leaves Aberdeen to become the BBC's Head of

Drama in London and is succeeded as Station Director of 2BD by Neil McLean, a noted Gaelic singer.

On 7 November 1924: Glasgow's 5SC transfers to new studios. No longer would the announcer intimate a short break between programmes as the microphone was wheeled from one part of the studio to another.

It was also the year when Sir Charles Clelland spoke of his plans for broadcasting to Scottish schools and the Rev Dr White of the Barony embarked on a spirited defence of broadcasting church services to win round the Presbytery of Glasgow.

'I know the gentleman who is at the head of the British Broadcasting Company. He is the son of a Moderator of the United Free Assembly (Dr Reith). He has inherited the strong Sabbatarian principles of his father and he has been guided by these in all his broadcasting activities.'

CHAPTER TWO

The Rise of Edinburgh

WIRELESS BROADCASTING WAS developing at a speed that exceeded all expectations. Programme output increased, new techniques were established and refined, and staff numbers grew. Glasgow's 5SC, starting in 1923 with five people, now had a staff of 16 and a similar build-up was happening in the other Scottish stations. Glasgow had already moved into larger premises and, on 31 July 1925, 2EH moved a few doors along George Street to number 87. In Aberdeen the landlords, the Aberdeen Electric Engineering Company, always had room to spare. In July 1924, the BBC expanded into two additional rooms and less than a year later the Station Director, Neil McLean, R.E. Jeffrey's successor, found the accommodation still inadequate and three more rooms were taken over. At the same time a new entrance was constructed and the address changed from 17 to 15 Belmont Street.

The engineers of the BBC had completed a quite remarkable achievement with the opening of one new relay station every month and, as a result, the number of licences doubled during 1924. But relay stations were essentially an urban rather than a rural concept and their numbers were limited because of frequency problems and interference. Wishing to bring even more people within range (particularly important in Scotland with its scattered population and remote islands) the BBC applied for, and got, a licence to use a temporary long-wave transmitter at the Chelmsford works of the Marconi Company. The results were successful and a new transmitter was opened on 27 July 1925 at Daventry giving reasonable reception up to almost 200 miles away.

While the new long-wave station was out of range for most of the population of Scotland, listeners in the north quickly became familiar with its output and the obvious attraction of having an alternative station through articles in the press and the publicised schedules in the *Radio Times*. D. Millar Craig, already beset with difficulties trying to bring about a degree of unity in the programme output of the four Scottish stations, found himself increasingly having to find programmes to offer to England and the high power station. These entailed problems of organisation and supervision, something he was not very good at, and there was a growing feeling amongst head office staff that broadcasting had not advanced as rapidly in Scotland as it had been hoped. Because of this, Scotland's Assistant Controller may well have tried to assume a low profile. Certainly he didn't expect, nor want, the sudden publicity that erupted from Station 2EH and a certain Father Knox.

It happened on Saturday 16 January 1926 – a snowy day in Edinburgh with the promise of a sharp frost later in the evening. For those hardy enough to be abroad after nightfall there were various entertainments on offer. Rudolph Valentino's latest picture, *A Sainted Devil*, was showing at the Caley Picture House in Lothian Road and there were three popular pantomimes still filling the theatres. For the sophisticated the Embassy Club at 5 Queen Street was running an Evening Dress Dance, while the Palais de Dance at Fountainbridge extended an invitation to enjoy the 'finest dance band ever heard in Scotland' – Miranda and his Band.

If your choice was to stay at home the chances were you would listen to the wireless. Warm and snug at your own fireside you could enjoy a series of music programmes ranging from *Patrick Thomson's Orchestra* to the *Savoy Orpheans*, relayed from London. Sandwiched in the middle, at 20 minutes to eight in the evening, there was a talk from the Edinburgh studio. Given by Father Ronald Knox and entitled '*Broadcasting the Barricades*', it was something of a star attraction for it was being broadcast simultaneously throughout the UK.

The broadcast had been arranged by Edinburgh's Station Director, George L. Marshall, who had met Knox on more than one occasion and knew of his reputation as an author and humorist. Officially described as a 'Talk' it was in fact a lengthy spoof news bulletin, complete with effects, reporting an imaginary communist rising in London.

At the beginning of the programme some sixth sense made George L. Marshall warn his audience that it wasn't to be taken seriously but he under-estimated the listeners' unshakable belief in everything they heard. As grave and utterly unexpected tidings flowed out of headphones and loudspeakers throughout Britain a state of alarm bearing on consternation swept the country. The National Gallery was in flames. Big Ben had been demolished by trench mortars. A communist revolution was exploding in London and the mass forces of the unemployed had plundered the Savoy Hotel and set it on fire. Finally, as the programme ended, there was a report that 'unruly members of the crowd are now approaching the British Broadcasting Company's London station with a threatening demeanour.'

Listeners up and down the country sprang to their telephones, convinced that London had been laid waste. The Savoy Hotel was bombarded with calls from the excited relatives of guests while the Irish Free State made enquiries through diplomatic channels to discover whether it was true that the House of Commons had been blown up. Later that evening the BBC issued an apology, 'the BBC regrets that any listener should have been perturbed by this purely fantastic picture.'

Next morning the newspapers were full of accounts of the hoax and a leader in *The Irish Times* spoke of humour and satire as dangerous instruments, counselling the BBC to be wiser in future and to take no risks with its public's average standard of intelligence.

Although no-one was reported as having died as a result of the broadcast, many elderly and nervous people were prostrate with shock and a huge postbag of indignant letters were received by the BBC. Questions were asked in Parliament and the press could talk of nothing else for several days on end.

In London, John Reith called for a copy of the script and in order to save time attempts were made to dictate it over the telephone. Because of the character of the script this proved to be impracticable and George L. Marshall despatched Tony Cogle, the Edinburgh office boy, round the corner to the nearest post office to have the script telegraphed to London. Later the manager there said that it was the most expensive wire he could remember ever having been sent!

After the first few days of public concern and indignation the tide of feeling changed. Many of the letters now arriving at the BBC in London were of an appreciative nature while others were from individuals kicking themselves that they had not been in possession of a wireless set at the time of the talk and the number of licences increased considerably over the next three months. In Edinburgh the staff at 2EH were rather pleased with the broadcast. They regretted the alarm that had been caused but felt that they should be complimented on the high standard of their 'effects' which had obviously been remarkably realistic.

The uproar over Knox's broadcast had hardly died down before the BBC became heavily involved in a complete reversal of *The Barricades*, this time broadcasting information and reassurances at a time of genuine crisis and disquiet. The General Strike in May 1926 found the BBC in the unique position of being able to relay information instantly throughout the whole country and the strain and effort involved in retaining the Company's independence and growing prestige was monumental. Much of the burden fell on John Reith's shoulders and the management in London. In Scotland the outward signs were police protection at the studios and transmitters and, from the listener, yet more interest in what the wireless was saying. The local element of broadcasting received a sudden boost as far as news and information was concerned but it did little to stem the growing waves of dissatisfaction emanating from the public.

For some nothing would be right until Scotland had its own high-power station giving easy access to metropolitan-based programmes. Others were increasingly dissatisfied with the growing number of London programmes being carried by the local stations and also complained that Scottish programmes were being over-anglicised – pronunciation and dialect being smoothed out in favour of standard English. To London it was clear that, despite the appointment of an Assistant Controller broadcasting in Scotland had not settled down. The hoped-for unification, implicit in D. Millar Craig's appointment, was only a fragile arrangement at best. There was nothing for it but to make major changes in the management in Scotland.

John Reith's interest in Scotland gave the changes a passing mention in his diary:

> (Saw) Millar Craig from Scotland. I told him he would have to leave and could come here and join the Music department.' 'Saw Marshall from Edinburgh and told him he should go to Glasgow.' 'Saw J.C.S. Macgregor, wife (*sic*) of Kitty Craig that was. Gave him the Edinburgh job and she is very pleased.' 'D C T dined with us and we went to the office afterwards. I trust Thomson fulfils our hopes of him in the north. He is in many ways clever and presentable, but I trust he will not get a swelled head. I should not think tact is his long suit.

D C T was David Cleghorn Thomson, a young man from the *Radio Times* section in London who now found himself in command of the unit at headquarters in Glasgow, virtually replacing D. Millar Craig, though for the moment given the title Liaison Officer (Scotland).

1926 was to be the last year of the BBC as a 'Company'. Ahead lay a Royal Charter and the granting of a long-term licence for ten years. Thomson knew that broadcasting in Scotland, and particularly in Glasgow, needed some good publicity to help ease it into the New Year. He decided to arrange a major conference in Glasgow, lasting two days and culminating in a public meeting. Those two great pillars of Scottish veneration, religion and education, were judiciously conscripted to his cause and the theme was widely circulated – The Role of Religion and Education in Broadcasting. The BBC's Managing-Director agreed to be present (despite a pressing need for him to remain in London) and the dates of 12 and 13 October were finally agreed.

The outcome was surely never in doubt. John Reith was in sparkling form, quickly gaining approval for his Company's policy of Sunday broadcasting and, on the second day, delivering a rousing address.

The public meeting was held on the evening of the second day. Towards the end a message from Sir Harry Lauder was read out to the large audience: 'I am of the opinion that the Scottish voice is something that can be heard to advantage!'

There was loud laughter – but then everyone laughed at Harry Lauder – and the evening closed with the Secretary of State for Scotland giving fulsome praise to John Reith: 'A most admirable wet nurse!'

It was a statement that could have not been closer to the truth, for Reith had worked hard and was profoundly thankful to get the 10.30pm sleeper to London.

A fortnight later, David Cleghorn Thomson was appointed Northern Area Director. In the promulgation which went to the four Scottish

David Cleghorn Thomson
Northern Area Director then title changed to Scottish Regional Director (1926–1933).

stations, Reith stated that this was no reflection on Station Directors but was done for the 'advantage of the service.' So far, Reith's new Scottish appointment had fulfilled all expectations. As Liaison Officer, Thomson had achieved some excellent publicity and had helped to re-affirm broad-casting's commitment to religious and educational programming. Now, as Scotland's Director, he would be expected to draw together his four disparate stations, for financial and staffing reasons if for no other.

John Reith had already challenged the amount of people being employed in the provinces. Using the coming transfer of staff from Company to Corporation as an opportune moment he had asked his Station Directors to report whether all the members of their staff were adequately employed and worthy of transfer to the Corporation. The replies, particularly from Scotland, were unhelpful:

ABERDEEN	'We are not overstaffed here. I could never tolerate any inefficiency in any department.'
EDINBURGH	'I have no hesitation in saying that I consider all members of the present staff at this station are entirely suitable for transfer to the Corporation.'
GLASGOW	'The staff at this Station, including clerical, is not excessive, and I cannot see how it could be reduced without impairing its efficiency.'
DUNDEE	'The position here is satisfactory.'

Clearly there were to be rough times ahead but for the moment all were allowed a brief respite. It was time for the formal act of bidding farewell to the four-year-old British Broadcasting Company, and the BBC in Scotland metaphorically joined hands with its colleagues throughout Britain to ring out the old and ring in the new while the pre-arranged obsequies took place. There were to be no surprises as the final minutes ticked away. All Station Directors had been told to leave stationery that bore the name of 'Company' out on their desks. On the morning of 1 January 1927 specially detailed staff would replace it with 'Corporation' stationery. The public already knew the names of the new Governors who would replace the outgoing Board of Directors and the country was rife with the rumour of Reith's approaching knighthood. Staff and artists alike had been specially briefed to remember to refer to 'The Corporation' and not 'The Company' and that the abbreviation 'BBC' was preferable at the microphone.

Unlike the practice of previous years the final hours of the year's broadcasting came from London. Midnight's silence was heavy with emotion and there are still those in Scotland who remember the first stroke of Big Ben – in itself a miracle a few short years before – not as the harbinger of a New Year, but as the passing of a well-loved friend. Only for a moment though, for it quickly gave way to a feeling of pride in the new British Broadcasting Corporation, its newly designated Director-General and the ideals of public service broadcasting.

Thomson, like any good tactician, first strengthened his own resources. Andrew Stewart had joined on 16 December 1926 as his personal assistant. The Glasgow-based unit began to recruit additional staff and on 1 January 1927, Miss C. Scott Moncrieff was appointed to supervise Women's and Children's programmes. Suitably reinforced, and conscious that a similar recruiting policy was taking place in the Engineering Division under J.M.A. Cameron, he set about his task.

Unlike his predecessor, who had tried to cajole his colleagues into some semblance of unity, Thomson set about reorganising each of his stations individually and, in the process, tailoring them to fit his future plans. His method was simple – to pick out the best that each station could offer on an all-Scotland basis and label the rest as unwanted dross. Wisely he steered clear of one area of programming, *Children's Corner*, which, for the moment, he allowed to continue on a local basis.

Station routines and discipline were also sharpened up. A system was devised for noting programme errors – a form of blacklist – and insistence on the wearing of evening dress by announcers was rigidly adhered to. Soon Glasgow, both as the home of unit headquarters and as a broadcasting station, was showing every sign of becoming the dominant partner in the new co-ordination of broadcasting in Scotland.

Not everyone was pleased with this dominance. Controversy over the 'Glasgow Voice' sharpened into complaints, particularly in plays and Thomson was driven to a defence in the pages of *The Glasgow Herald*: 'English drama would be the poorer without the voice of the Cockney,' he wrote. 'So Scottish drama would be the poorer if we were to exclude the voice of the Cowcaddens and 'Wee Macgregor'.'

His plea fell on stony ground. He had still to learn that the dialect of the Glasgow streets was largely perceived as the province of comedy and the music hall and that most other forms of broadcasting should be performed in tones more suited to the West End and Morningside.

In Aberdeen the taint of metropolitan snobbery and urban competitiveness was thankfully almost unknown. The large agricultural hinterland with its long tradition of bothy life and entertainment seemed to have insulated the town. The familiarity that other Scottish stations had achieved through their *Children's Hour* programmes Aberdeen had accomplished right across the board. A visiting head office official described it as 'a unique station... doing unique and successful work in the broadcasting system. I think we do not make enough of it.'

Nearly every visitor to the station received an immediate impression of perfect unity, efficient control and general enthusiasm for the work of broadcasting. From the outset, 2BD had forged a strong and lasting bond with its listeners. The story of R.E. Jeffrey's seeking a lift home on a wet night could have been matched time and time again by other broadcasters at Belmont Street and Jeffrey's replacement as Station Director, Neil McLean, quickly became as well-known. His ability as a singer of Gaelic and Scottish songs made him a popular broadcaster and the community singing club, formed in March 1924, went from strength to strength under his guidance.

The Aberdeen listener liked, and got, a varied and entertaining service from his station, including light music, some drama and plenty of choral singing and local humour. One of the most popular programmes from 2BD was *Musical Romances*, a competition in which a romantic tale was unfolded by the station's own house orchestra playing well-known tunes, the unannounced titles of which dovetailed into a brief synopsis of a story. Listeners were then invited to send in their own version and quite often over 100 compositions were received. There was a 2BD repertory company with such stalwarts as Daisy Moncur and Grace R. Wilson appearing almost weekly, more often than not in a play written by Arthur Black. Arthur exemplified the close relationship between listeners and the station. One day in 1925 he had presented himself at Belmont Street, produced a manuscript from a capricious pocket and proceeded to entertain the whole staff for a space of more than ten minutes. After that, as many plays that he could write were broadcast, each one proving more popular than the last.

Here was the perfect station, wanting little or nothing from the other broadcasting centres and ready to supply Scottish humour, music and variety, to both its own listeners and the rest of the country as required. Perhaps that was its downfall. Too strong to be a partner, it was 'reorganised' in a truly tactless way.

On 1 January 1927 the station's house orchestra was reduced to an octet, while six weeks later, on 17 February, H.M. Fitch, an important part of Neil McLean's production team, was transferred from Aberdeen to Glasgow and not replaced. A pooling system was instituted for evening talks – Aberdeen and Dundee sharing one day a week. Local religious services were restricted to one a month and *Children's Hour*, school talks and publicity came under the general supervision of the staff at headquarters.

It was an impossible situation for the Aberdeen Station Director, made worse by Thomson's complete disinterest, refusing even to visit Aberdeen, far less speak to the staff. Whatever the merits of Scotland's reorganisation, the effect on Aberdeen was one of depression, discouragement and a considerable strain on loyalty. It began to feel isolated and cut off from head office in London. A new authority had been interposed between them – an authority not always exercised wisely or kindly – and it is not difficult to imagine the effect on both people and programmes.

If the decision to reorganise the Scottish stations had ever been in the balance, and despite Neil McLean's many appeals to head office, there is no evidence that it was, the next engineering breakthrough made what had been desirable, now imperative. The National Programme experiment, started in 1925 from Daventry 5XX on long wave and, depending on listeners re-equipping themselves with a two-wave receiver, had been a tremendous success. The listening public, those who could pick up Daventry, enjoyed having a choice of programme and the plan was, now, to build a series of high-power, medium-wave transmitters placed at strategic points throughout the country. Each transmitter would be a twin-wave station giving the listener immediate choice between two stations, both on medium wave. The new transmitters would replace the many small local, low power transmitters and would cover Britain in a very predictable way:

1   London and the Home Counties

2   Manchester and the Industrial North of England

3   Glasgow, Edinburgh and the Scottish Lowlands

4   South Wales and the West of England

5   Birmingham and the Midlands

Now there had to be separate BBC Regions. The Regional Scheme of Distribution was no longer just a proposal and work started in April 1928 on the first of the two programme twin-transmitter stations, Brookmans Park servicing London and the South-Eastern Counties.

Now there was more than just a modicum of sense in the Scottish Director's declaration that it was now a race and he would win it. While this certainly reduced the time available to him to sort out all the problems, Scotland had by nature and tradition a major unifying thread – it was a nation – and therefore should come together to create one broadcasting

General Assembly of the Church of Scotland in the Highland Tolbooth on 24 May 1929
The most important early Outside Broadcast of its type in Scotland, with the OB Engineer visible in the top left-hand corner and the microphones to the left of the speaker. It features the key report of the Committee on Union delivered by the Rev Dr White that virtually concluded the proceedings for the Union of the two Churches in Scotland. Behind the Moderator's chair is the throne with the Duke of York sitting as the Royal Commissioner, the Duchess, and members of their suite.

channel all that more easily. With even greater diligence than before a variety of popular programmes was scheduled for general transmission in Scotland.

OBS were favourites with listeners – particularly 'great occasions' – and in Scotland, Edinburgh had set a Scottish record for the number transmitted in 1927. As the capital it had a lead on the rest of Scotland as far as national ceremonies were concerned, particularly with royalty present, and it pursued them with vigour and aplomb, and a considerable amount of engineering and production expertise. Often these occasions did much to promote the feasibility of a single regional service, a telling example being the opening of the Scottish National War Memorial on the Castle Rock in Edinburgh by HRH, the Prince of Wales on Thursday 14 July 1927.

The BBC installation was complex to a degree. Ten microphone points were wired into a central Control Room and three extra engineers were sent from London to assist Edinburgh staff. The programme was heard in all parts of Scotland as well as being relayed throughout the United Kingdom to all stations, and also on Daventry long wave. The principal commentator for the broadcast was Major J.H. Beith – later best remembered as Ian Hay. Major Beith gave his commentary from the turret of the old Palace buildings, the oldest point in the Castle, and the strategically placed microphones, many of them being used for effects, picked up the colour and ceremony that marked the day.

The music of the bands as the Prince arrived, the Dedication Service with the Moderators of the three Presbyterian Churches and the Primus of the Scottish Episcopal Church and the arrival and departure of units from Scottish Regiments made it a powerful and emotional occasion. Scotland seemed to catch its breath. Thanks to their radios, so many more people than could ever have found places at the event were deeply involved in the ceremony and once again the BBC demonstrated its ability to reach out, overriding distance and seeking intimacy in a way that was at times quite profound.

Military occasions sometimes had their lighter moments. One of the voices supporting Major Beith at Edinburgh Castle was J.C.S. Macgregor who had replaced George L. Marshall as Station Director at Edinburgh. Macgregor frequently did duty as a commentator – not surprising as at that time Edinburgh was running to five or six OBS a week – and one of

Outside Broadcast, Scottish Tattoo, Dreghorn (1927)
Note commentary position with microphone.

his commitments was the Scottish Command Military Tattoo held at Dreghorn Barracks outside Edinburgh. In those days all essential communication between commentator and engineers was carried out by a complicated system of hand signals and grimaces. This meant that J.A. Beveridge, the Engineer-in-Charge of 2EH and his team were dug in to a slit-trench about 50 yards inside the arena with Macgregor 20 yards away lying in the mud and facing the microphone which was mounted only a foot from the ground.

As the show got under way each event seemed to come closer to the BBC party. Cavalry galloped past showering them with mud, the mock explosions spattered over both people and equipment and a display of tanks very nearly buried them for ever. Suddenly, during the break in the commentary, when it had been planned to listen to music and effects, Macgregor heard the band breaking into a Gilbert and Sullivan selection. Because of copyright problems, the music could not be broadcast. Failing to attract the engineers' attention and remembering that it was important that he keep flat and as close to the ground as possible, he had no alternative but to wriggle on his stomach across to the engineers' trench to tell them to switch off the band microphone. It seems he was successful as no mention was made of any copyright infringement but he did, when retelling the story, admit to having caught the worst cold of his life.

Another item popular for all-station scheduling was drama. Plays and casts were still largely 'bought in' and Glasgow found itself once again a major drama centre thanks to its close contact with the Scottish National Players and their producer, Tyrone Guthrie. Guthrie had already worked for the BBC as a producer at the Belfast station and had left there to come to Scotland to work with the Scottish National Players. It was an ideal association, but lacked the stimulus of new writing for radio.

A competition was organised to find new authors but it had limited success and there was general disappointment within the BBC at the low standard of the plays that were entered. Aberdeen alone seemed to be a shining light as far as sustaining local authors was concerned but most of their offers were not to the taste of headquarters who were less than taken by some of the area's mawkish whimsicality and matters were not helped by the regulation that required all plays to be seen by head office before they could be accepted by a local station.

Meanwhile new authors continued to surface in the theatre. A young Moultrie Kelsall – he would later become the BBC's Aberdeen Station Representative – was in the audience at the first Scottish production of a play by Mary Henderson, presented by the Scottish National Players at the Lyric Theatre in Glasgow. After the final curtain the author appeared on the stage. Moultrie Kelsall, along with many others, found the lady who stumped on from the wings less than convincing and it wasn't long before most people knew that the play had in fact been written by a Glasgow doctor, Osborne Henry Mavor, later to call himself James Bridie, who went on to become one of the leading British playwrights of his generation. But for the time being, Scottish broadcast drama was largely confined to standard works and authors – *Clydebuilt* by George Blake, *Campbell of Kilmhor* by J.A. Ferguson and the plays of J.M. Barrie were all staple fare for the listener.

Another extremely potent and effective way of uniting the Scottish audience – and used frequently by London as well as Glasgow – was to indulge in out-and-out sentimentality. Various key words and phrases could trigger instant waves of emotion. The radio was an ideal vehicle and who better to practise it than Scotland's best-known entertainer, Sir Harry Lauder.

Scotland's grand old man of music hall was now broadcasting on a fairly regular basis, although always from London, having eschewed the Scottish stations since his first broadcast in 1924 from Glasgow. He was adept at administering the emotional twinge that was a comfort to so many.

'I shall be heard in mansions and other places where the servant lasses are', he wrote in an article for the *Radio Times*, 'and my thoughts turn, too, to my own folk – the shepherds and crofters in the distant, silent glens in Skye, Harris and Lewis and Islay, Rum and Coll and Eigg, in far St Kilda and all the wee hooses among the heather, not forgetting the hoary fisherman on the dark tide and the lonely lighthouse keepers.'

What an emotional gazetteer, allowing everyone to identify with the land of the 'Ever-Young' – where all the sordid and grubby social problems of an embattled Britain faded away and, for a moment at least, the soul was free of all suffering.

The use of place names in programmes was known by broadcasters to be excellent public relations and while Lauder and others used them in a romantic sense, the BBC used them to allay local fears about regional broadcasting, putting as many places as possible 'on the radio map'. That great mainstay, the OB, was put to good use far outside the cities' limits and public concerts were held in what until then had been considered as out-of-the-way places such as Buckie, Arbroath and Anstruther. They proved to be invaluable in pacifying listeners who had complained of neglect.

For the same reason Gaelic programmes from the Aberdeen station were increased and Neil McLean initiated a *Gaelic Corner* 'for those in the North of Scotland who speak the Gaelic tongue'. There were also programmes featuring Mod winners and by 1928 the BBC had started to broadcast Mod concerts and prize-winners.

By now the BBC's engineers had fully mastered the system of landlines that comprised the simultaneous broadcast network and were in their element coping with complicated multi-centre broadcasts. When an anniversary loomed, such as the birth of Robert Louis Stevenson, or St Andrew's Day, it was celebrated by a joint programme, contributed to by all four Scottish stations. Often these depended on time cues to switch from one source to another with the producer counting off the seconds before giving his engineer a verbal command to switch to the next source. Hence the perhaps apocryphal story of the over-polite engineer who, on being given a cue to switch to a musical item, politely checked with 'I beg your pardon?' and missed the opening few bars.

Special attention was also being given to the more mundane requirements of Scotland. Market prices were now broadcast regularly for Scottish farmers, together with fortnightly talks arranged in collaboration with the Board of Agriculture and the Scottish Agricultural Colleges. A series of fishery bulletins giving the prices ruling at various ports were also transmitted.

On Monday 24 September 1928, a Scottish news bulletin was heard for the first time. Until then it had been the practice for the four stations to broadcast 'local announcements' every weekday evening after the London general news bulletin and topical talk. The new programme was compiled and then broadcast not only in Glasgow but also simultaneously on the other three stations in Scotland. It was for the most part welcomed by listeners, who seemed to want what was in fact a switch from local to national news.

Thomson had no fault to find with the way matters were progressing. Listeners seemed to be accepting the gradual changeover of programmes from local to Scottish, and there had been surprisingly few complaints after the initial wave of protest. The promise of a choice of listening in the future had mollified all but the most hardened devotees of the original multi-station system and he was confident that his reputation at head office was still reasonably secure – something that was important to him. But there was still a lot to be done, especially if he was going to keep his promise to be the first to achieve regionalisation and it seemed a good moment to slip the cable that held him to Belfast.

'It would ease my mind and free my hand in dealing with the more pressing problems of Scotland if Ireland ceased to be part of the Northern Area,' he wrote in a memo to the Director-General in May 1928. He went on to point out that while in the beginning the local management in Belfast was far from satisfactory (the first Station Director has been 'relieved of his post' in July 1926) the station was now very ably run and, as there was an increasing tendency on the part of various departments in head office to handle Belfast separately, the existing arrangement served little useful purpose in the Corporation's interests.

Reith was not enamoured of the proposal. 'I am personally not inclined for this,' he wrote, but others were and recommended that Belfast come out of Scotland's command. On 8 May 1928, the minutes of the Control Board Meeting agreed the proposal, though insisting that no publicity be given to the press as there was the possibility that this might be changed again. Just over four months later, on 30 September 1928, Thomson's official title was changed to Scottish Regional Director and it was the signal for a series of major changes within the BBC in Scotland that would finally bring in a new regional regime.

Thomson had set his mind on achieving full regionalisation by 30 September 1929 and the spring of the year saw the curtailment of local programmes proceeding with a vengeance. The overall reduction in output was accompanied by a shift of what was left to Glasgow and, at the same time, a sizeable number of staff were jettisoned. Of Scotland's four stations three became little more than names. Aberdeen – Neil McLean left to carry out the duties of Station Director. Edinburgh – Kennedy Stewart, now the sole non-engineering occupant, working as Station Representative and Publicity Officer. Dundee – closed as a programme centre, the Engineer-in-Charge becoming the BBC's Station Representative. Even Glasgow felt the draught. Its house orchestra, having been boosted to 27 players, thanks to a head office agreement early in 1928, was reduced to an octet and all drama productions were assigned to outside producers such as Tyrone Guthrie.

However, there were some gains for the old 5SC Station. It was the home of an ever-growing unit at headquarters and was clearly the centre of production in Scotland. The cherished *Children's Corner*, for so long a local commitment, had given way to a single *Children's Hour* that was transmitted from the Glasgow studio six days a week. The number of broadcasts to schools had increased substantially thanks to a decision to appoint a full-time producer in Glasgow responsible for education and drop all London-produced programmes.

It was a major re-drawing of Scotland's broadcasting map. Dundee had been completely erased as a programme-making studio, only retaining its transmitter until a new high power installation could be built in Scotland. Eric Heddle, Station Director of 2DE since its opening in November 1924, had displayed a pragmatic attitude to the whole reorganisation, not saying much more than that programmes for Dundee would now be mostly from London. He subsequently returned to academic life as a lecturer in physics at Leicester Municipal College.

Aberdeen, as Scotland's second main station, had succumbed less easily. It was here on 6 June 1929 that *The Press and Journal* had broken the news of the BBC's major cuts in Scotland. Whether by accident or chance, Neil McLean had been on a walking holiday when the news had broken and it took some time for his staff to locate him. There had been immediate and prolonged protests and two MPs, Sir Frederick Thomson (South Aberdeen) and James Scott (Kincardine and West Aberdeen), had corresponded at length with the Director-General, though to little effect.

Dislike for Thomson was growing. He had done little or nothing to soften the blow as termination notices arrived on people's desks and there can be no doubt that in some cases he was paying off old scores. A private letter from Neil McLean to head office, written week before the news of Aberdeen's approaching demise broke in the Scottish press, revealed that the Aberdeen Station Director had had no warning from Glasgow of what was to take place and that a private and confidential memo written to him from London had been the first inkling he had received.

Another anxiety came to haunt Thomson – a belief that, as Scotland decreased in size as a programme maker, so his own position was diminishing in importance. It was a reasonable enough fear. When regionalisation was complete throughout the country the wings of the Regional Directors could well be clipped at the expense of head office departments and specialisation. He started to make personal overtures to Sir John Reith asking him to call him back to head office in London: 'The centralising trend which is observable in all spheres of our activities is making it steadily more clear to me how much I wish to return to the centre,' he wrote to the Director-General. 'One's wings are being clipped and one is being debarred from flight in so many directions.'

At the beginning of October, Thomson publicly announced his future programme plans. Local broadcasting in Scotland had now ceased and the bulk of the programmes on the Scottish transmitter would originate in London, with only a representative selection of items coming from the Scottish studios. Any item that could be better done in the London studio would originate from there, the one exception being the afternoon periods. The unification of the output still depended on the use of landlines to distribute the programmes to the four Scottish transmitters – there was still no high power regional transmitter in Scotland – and the General Post Office discouraged the use of these lines during business hours. Then, and only then, was Scotland able to originate programmes that were not of a characteristically Scottish nature. As one Scottish newspaper put it: 'The Metropolitan taste will predominate in all stations whether the holders of wireless licences like that taste or not.' The Scottish items, although reduced in number, appeared to have been well thought out.

Concerts by the Reid Orchestra were planned for the winter months and arrangements had been made to include items by contemporary Scottish composers. Scottish plays and specially written radio adaptations of stories commissioned by the BBC were to be broadcast. There was to be a broadcast from the Scottish Military Tattoo. Rugby internationals and other sporting events would be covered as would the church assemblies, getting off to a fine start with the joint service in St Giles marking the Union of the Church of Scotland and the United Free Church of Scotland and the subsequent first meeting of the General Assembly. The results of the Scottish Municipal Elections would be broadcast as available between 10.45pm to midnight on Tuesday 5 November.

A feature programme on the history of Edinburgh Castle was planned and a radio adaptation of John Buchan's novel *Huntingtower* – the first of many BBC re-creations of *Mr Dickson McCunn* and the *Gorbals Diehards*.

On 30 November the listeners of Britain would be entertained by a St Andrew's Day celebration relayed from an Edinburgh restaurant and on 25 January, it was planned to broadcast a Burns Night Concert directly from the Farmhouse of Mossgiel near Mauchline.

Another important series was in the pipeline. Ten well-known Scots were to take part in *What's Wrong with Scotland?*, each one contributing his thoughts on the many ills of which the nation was alleged to be dying.

There was an attempt to assuage the feelings of those living in the North East of Scotland with an assurance that, 'it was never our intention to choke off this source, so depriving Aberdeenshire listeners, and listeners all over Scotland, of some of the most interesting Scots programmes available through the year.'

Arthur Black's garrulous pair of cronies, *George and Wullie* would be well to the fore and, to interest the Highlands, a successor to *What's Wrong with Scotland* called *What of the Highlands*?

The public listened and, ignoring the many changes that had given such a bumpy ride to the staff, wisely based their judgements on what they heard from their receivers. Some correspondents displayed a talent of their own and a very obvious distaste of traditional Scots songs: 'Will you please tell *Jock o' Hazledean* and Willie of *Melville Castle* that the next time they come from *Edinburgh Toun* and meet *Annie Laurie Comin' thro' the Rye*, ca'in the *Yowes tae the Knowes* and singing *Caller Herrin'* frae *Bonnie Dundee*, they are all to join in the *March of the Cameron Men Doon the Brae* tae the *Auld Hoose* and shut themselves and those old repeats in it for the next 50 years.'

Mostly, however, they were well pleased. The new mix of programmes instituted under the Scottish Regional Plan was an improvement for many listeners and, in any case, some of the old favourites were still around, including Kathleen Garscadden who, despite leaving the staff, was still heard two or three times a week and was delighted when a letter addressed to 'Auntie: Glasgow' was safely delivered to her at Blythswood Square after a local post office had written on it 'Try Auntie Cyclone'.

Plays had always been popular with Scottish audiences and the BBC embarked on a series of community drama broadcasts featuring many of the country's best groups – The Ardrossan and Saltcoats Players, The Kirkintilloch Players, The Lennox Players, The Labour College Players and The Carrick Players. It was a rich seam that brought forward many of the actors and actresses who sustained radio drama in Scotland for many years afterwards – some still performing 50 years later. There was praise, too, for the eyewitness accounts of sporting occasions, particularly football, which were now a regular Saturday feature, and yet another long-running tradition was established on New Year's Day 1930 with an eyewitness account of the match between Celtic and Rangers – a broadcast that attracted a huge audience. However, it was the OB of the launch of the Clyde-built *Empress* by HRH the Prince of Wales which gave Scotland its most widely heard broadcast so far. Some papers estimated the audience as 'over a 100 million people throughout the world,' based on the fact that the National Broadcasting Company of America were relaying the broadcast to an estimated audience of 60 million while 13 Canadian stations were sending it out throughout Canada.

It could have been a time for the Regional Director to draw breath – for consolidation, uniting his staff and licking his wounds. Instead he chose to keep up the impetus that had been gained. He still wanted to make Scotland a noteworthy contributor to the London programme and in so doing perhaps strengthen his position in the longed for desire to return to head office. But there were one or two hurdles in the way. Scotland's studios were old and outdated by comparison with what could be achieved and from an organisational point of view things were made more difficult by having them scattered between Glasgow, Edinburgh and Aberdeen. There was also a hardening of London's metropolitan attitude that indicated time was short if Scotland was to succeed with London. It all added up to one thing – establish a new Scottish head-quarters, properly equipped with modern studios and equipment.

The need for new premises was quickly established and agreed by London, but where would the future headquarters of the Scottish Region be located? The lease of Edinburgh's George Street studio terminated in 1930 and the landlord was not prepared to renew on a yearly basis. The lease in Glasgow might only last until 1932. The options for both cities seemed wide open. The Director-General made it clear he had no strong views, although he did see the need for a large studio (as there was in Glasgow) in both places. It all seemed to rest with Thomson and he had no doubts whatsoever – he wanted the headquarters in Edinburgh.

Once the Scottish Director's opinion was known, various committees picked at his decision. Orchestras could be broadcast from halls rather than a studio. There was more potential for drama productions in Glasgow than in Edinburgh. More speakers for talks came from Edinburgh. Edinburgh was the capital and the cultural centre.

Engineering Division also chipped in and their argument had a notic-eable effect. Apparently new underground simultaneous broadcasting lines would soon replace the overhead lines network and would probably run up the east coast via Edinburgh unlike the overhead system, which used a west coast route through Glasgow. Cameron and his engineering staff would be closely tied to the new lines switching centre and it would make sense to have it in the same place as the headquarters of Scotland's administration staff.

The weight of opinion was favouring Edinburgh and only one question remained – Glasgow's octet should be at headquarters. Would its leader,

Losowsky, agree to move? The answer to that was 'yes' and on 12 November 1929, a search for new premises in Edinburgh began in earnest.

Glasgow's rage was almost immeasurable and protests of every kind were made. A Glasgow-based newspaper instigated a campaign to form a council to oversee the BBC in Scotland and enlisted the support of the Lords Provost of Aberdeen and Dundee. While the main purpose was to stop the move to Edinburgh, this was concealed, and instead it was declared that there was a need to put forward a distinctively Scottish outlook on social and other problems. A Glasgow councillor, Paddy Dollan, invited to give his opinion, put his finger on a real problem: 'I think the idea is quite practicable and worth experimenting with. I question, however, whether you will get any Board that will devise a programme satisfactory to all wireless listeners.' The campaign petered out and the search for premises in Edinburgh continued.

It was the beginning of 1930 and the Scottish Director wanted to be in his new headquarters by June of that year. Early in the search he had been attracted by what he described as 'a Palais de Dance' at 5 Queen Street in Edinburgh's New Town. The BBC Chief Engineer, despatched from London to report, had turned it down largely because of the badly designed offices, few of which had access to daylight. Its one asset, a large hall which had been added around 100 years before, replacing a coach house, stables and hayloft, had not been sufficiently attractive to sway him. Time wore on and still nothing surfaced that was anywhere near suitable and likely to be available quickly. Increasingly Thomson kept returning to 5 Queen Street and finally he got his way. With the understanding that the next door premises (number 6) might soon become available and thus alleviate the office problem, the BBC in London were persuaded to start negotiations to lease the building.

5 Queen Street was one of numerous examples of early New Town buildings that had acquired a host of tenants and reputations over the years. Originally a 'house with cellars under pavement in front, back court and coach house and stable, and hayloft above the said back court', the addition of the large hall at the rear had resulted in frequent changes of fortune and occupants. It had housed the Philosophical Institution, been a meeting place for the congregation of St Luke's at the time of the Disruption, given accommodation to the Society of Musicians and also a firm of stockbrokers. The citizens of Edinburgh had flocked to the hall

at various times to hear David Livingstone, be entertained by Charles Dickens and witness the first demonstration in Scotland of the modern teleprinter, then called the tele-writer. Most recently, in the mid-'20s, it had become a Dance Club, the Embassy Club, running an Evening Dress Dance at a subscription of five shillings. It would have no difficulty in taking its next occupants in its stride.

The Edinburgh staff moved out of 87 George Street and into the new Scottish Broadcasting House at the end of May and six weeks later they were joined by most of the Glasgow staff, leaving behind only J.C.S. Macgregor as Glasgow Representative plus a handful of engineering staff.

The alterations at Queen Street were still in progress but it was already obvious that there was going to be serious congestion at the new head-quarters. The Scottish Director was asked to give up a portion of his office. He refused, saying that this would mean a lack of dignity in there being no committee room available and instead he increased the pressure on negotiations to acquire the premises next door.

Meanwhile the broadcasters were eager to be about their business. The first programme broadcast from the new headquarters was a violin recital given by Isaac Losowky on the afternoon of Sunday 15 June. It was a nice compliment, and if not intentionally contrived, it should have been. Since 1923, Losowky had played a major role in Scottish broadcasting and it was fitting, therefore, that he should 'christen' 5 Queen Street by being its first broadcaster, co-incidentally on the day that was his birthday.

The formal opening was arranged for the eve of St Andrew's Day, Saturday 29 November 1930. A considerable amount of structural altera-tion had taken place, transforming part, at least, of the building into the BBC's most modern studios. The main hall was now 'Number 1 Studio' – the largest broadcasting studio in Europe and the best equipped. The walls were covered with expensive fabric and the high-domed roof had undergone acoustic treatment. Decoration was in tones of deep gold which complemented the three great BBC symbols, one of each of the two stage curtains and a third, resplendent, high above the proscenium arch. The balconies had been fitted with audience seating so that performers could use the floor of the studio, as well as the stage, and a partition was built under the north gallery to create a large waiting room/lounge.

Conscious of the history of performances that had taken place in the hall in the past, the BBC obtained a licence for the giving of public

Right

New premises at 5 Queen Street, Edinburgh.

(© Steve Newman Photography)

Below

Grand opening 5 Queen Street, Edinburgh

29 November 1930 by Secretary of State for Scotland, Rt Hon William Anderson, MP (receiving book) with guests including the Duke and Duchess of Atholl and the Marquis of Aberdeen and Temair.

performance for which a charge for admission could be made. There were another two studios in the building. Studio 2 was in what was formerly a small meeting hall – in size slightly larger than the Glasgow studio. Studio 3 was the speech or 'talks' studio. The decorative schemes for all three studios and the waiting room had been designed by Mr J.R. Mackay, a well-known Edinburgh architect, and woven especially for the BBC by the Edinburgh Weavers. Studio 3 was adorned with a modern Scottish tapestry and, to further the suggestion of a small Scottish study, was furnished with a reading desk, lamp, gramophone and small bookcase, all specially designed for the room. Finally, and to some the *pièce de résistance* of the technical area, there was an 'echo room' – an essential part of good broadcasting which Scotland had not hitherto possessed.

The office accommodation was less sublime. Much of it was in the basement, adjacent to the main studio, and lacked any form of outside light. Perhaps it was this that prompted Reith to note in his diary a few weeks before the opening, 'Saw the new headquarters; a weird place, badly arranged as was to be expected of Thomson.'

The Director-General was in markedly better fettle on his next journey north, this time for the official opening. Arriving in the morning, off the sleeper, he embarked on a busy day which included a visit to the National Memorial, interviews with four announcers and an afternoon drive to Peebles Hydro for tea, before arriving at 5 Queen Street for the opening ceremony.

Studio 1 was the venue for the main part of the evening – a special programme, *St Andrew's Eve: A Celebration of Scotland in Poetry and Song*, devised by Thomson, assisted by Moray McLaren, Andrew Stewart, Martyn Webster and Dudley Stuart Whyte. Before the programme, due to start at 8.00pm, there was half an hour of speeches incorporating the formal opening. Reith viewed the proceedings with some pleasure and pronounced the studio to be 'quite fine, and the decoration successful.' His account of the evening is relaxed and revealing:

The Secretary for Scotland made the inaugural speech and then a dedicatory prayer by the Moderator, which it was very fine to have. After that the 2nd paraphrase was sung and the Glasgow Orpheus Choir sang the 121st and the 124th Psalms. Discovered that Thompson's mother is a daughter of McPhail of Benbecula; a very fine old man; and her uncle Simon McPhail, a very great friend of my father. The Moderator was in his full dress. He told me he would not have been able to come owing to a previous engagement had we not threatened to have the dedication performed by the RC Archbishop.

The St Andrew's Eve programme was in two parts – *Battles Long Ago* and *Anent Love and Hame* – and suffered from an overabundance of dirge and lament. This somewhat melancholy celebration evoked protests from listeners who had looked for native Scottish humour to figure largely on such an occasion and they were not greatly pacified by the explanation that the programme was designed partly for English ears. It was an interesting example of the then current thinking by the BBC's Scottish hierarchy – that the representation of Scotland for English ears must be religious, warlike and quasi-Hebridean but with a hint of jocularity when a minister wasn't present.

With the headquarters in Edinburgh publicly launched, interest switched to the new transmitter. Only when it was built and fully operational could the regional scheme be said to have arrived, providing a choice of two programmes on medium wave, one of which could be designed for Scotland.

Situated at Westerglen, near Falkirk, and roughly half way between Glasgow and Edinburgh, the new installation was well up to schedule. Its operational staff had already been chosen and were under training at Brookmans Park – the first of the twin-transmitter stations, built to service London and the South East. At that time transmitter staff were considered by many to be the elite of Engineering Division and they invariably turned out to be a happy and industrious bunch, a mixture of ex-Marconi Company staff with intriguing pasts spent on board ship as wireless operators, and locally recruited men. Intensely professional, Engineering Division promised nothing more than hard work. Tony Cogle, the Edinburgh Station office boy, remembered the letter he received when he transferred there at 16. It offered him a job as an assistant but stressed there was no guarantee of any future prospects. He also remembered that jobs were exceedingly hard to come by and in the winter the unemployed, many of them with no soles to their boots, were shovelling snow on to lorries in Princes Street for little more than free soup.

In the late spring of 1932 the regional part of the twin-wave transmitter was ready for testing and on 12 June it was put into regular use, broadcasting the Scottish Regional Service on 376.4m. Listeners re-tuned to the new wavelength and three of the city transmitters that had started it all 5SC, 2EH and 2DE – fell silent. Only Aberdeen stayed on the air. The BBC were still wrestling with the problem of coverage of the North and West of Scotland and, for the moment, Aberdeen retained its transmitter, albeit on a changed wavelength.

The opening of the new Scottish Regional Service at Westerglen was formally marked by a parade of BBC staff and visiting dignitaries on 20 June. Many of the Scottish staff wore the kilt including Thomson and Moray McLaren who headed the procession. For some this was seen as a resolute and colourful gesture that befitted the occasion. There were others, however, who were not so taken with the sight of so much tartan. One engineer wrote: 'The official opening I still look upon as a complete let-down by Scotland. The parade, headed by Thomson, Moray McLaren and other programme people, all clad in kilts, made our English collea-gues laugh and we Scots were thoroughly disgusted at the infantile display of parochialism. To the credit of "E" Division, all our chiefs carried out their duties in a respectable and responsible manner!'

It's an account that speaks volumes. Not only did it presage a seemingly never-ending debate on parochialism in Scottish broadcasting, it also demonstrated the inherent loyalty that was already making BBC engineering synonymous with high professional standards, regardless of what their programme colleagues chose to do.

Three months later the other half of Westerglen, the Scottish national transmitter, came into regular service, completing the final stage of the policy of centralisation and regionalisation begun in 1928. A choice of programmes was now available to 80 per cent of the population of Scotland and, as had been hoped, the service area of the new transmit-ters extended far enough to include Dundee. Admittedly, the old boast of bringing the service within 'crystal range' was no longer applicable but valve sets were fast becoming *de rigueur* and few people admitted to using such an old-fashioned piece of apparatus as a crystal set – techno-logical snobbery was rife even in the 1930s. One section of the listening public did have justifiable grounds for worry, however. It was still standard practice to issue crystal sets to blind listeners and it was some time before these were replaced by valve receivers.

There still remained the problem of serving the sparsely populated

Highlands of Scotland. Noel Ashbridge, successor to Peter Eckersley as the BBC's Chief Engineer, had caused a shiver to run down the collective spine of the Scottish headquarters unit when, in May 1931, he announced that the BBC could not provide a service for the Highlands and Islands even when the new Westerglen transmitter was in operation. Scotland had banked on its new service being heard throughout the country and it was a shock to learn that a considerable part of the North and West would not still receive an adequate service. The Scottish press and MPs protested vigorously and once again there were complaints of English bias. Their annoyance was understandable. It had been disclosed that the longer the wavelength the greater the distance covered and that the two longest medium waves available to Great Britain had been taken 'by England' for use at Manchester and Birmingham.

Suggestions that an additional transmitter be built near Inverness were quickly dismissed and little was made of the desperate need for companionship and communication that only radio could bring to this thinly populated area. The great triumphal ode written by Ronald Campbell Macfie for the opening of the new radio headquarters in Edinburgh seemed to have a mocking ring to it:

The fisher on the lonely beach,
The crofter in the lonely glen,
Hear sudden sound of far-off speech.
And songs, and thoughts of unseen men.

CHAPTER THREE

Programme Expansion

WITH TWO MEDIUM-WAVE channels operating out of Westerglen from September 1932, the time had come to consolidate the new service and possibly build up the Scottish element in the mixture of programmes that was now called the Scottish Regional Wavelength. London had made it clear from the start that they would never countenance an all-Scottish channel – an unnecessary dictate as few if any of the staff ever contemplated such an operation – but there was a tacit understanding that programmes made in Scotland would gradually increase in quantity and quality provided that one important rule continued to be observed – never attempt anything that London could do better. All the BBC Regions were regulated in this way and it was impossible to slip anything into the system unnoticed. Now that listeners had a choice of wavelengths the Corporation were anxious to see that there was never any conflict between the two services and a strict eye was kept on all regional schedules.

Limiting the Scottish development in this way did throw the bias of programmes towards particular national themes but for the moment at least these were totally acceptable as far as the audience was concerned and everybody was delighted with the new climate of expansion. Soon Scotland's various centres thronged with broadcasters.

Dundee had gone for good, or at least for 20 years, but the new Edinburgh headquarters, newly equipped premises in Glasgow and Aberdeen's Belmont Street burgeoned with extra programmes. There had been a moment when it had looked as if Aberdeen would suffer the same fate as Dundee when, a few weeks before the formal opening of the new Scottish headquarters in Edinburgh, Neil McLean had left Aberdeen because of ill-health. However, instead of the expected closure a strange BBC-type compromise was proposed. Aberdeen would have a new Station Representative, but on a part-time basis. Luckily for Aberdeen, and for the BBC, the young man appointed to the post was Ian Whyte, at that time organist to Lord Glentanar at Aboyne. Some years later a colleague spoke of his immense energy: 'He didn't so much make an entrance as rush on and get started with the minimum of preparation.' It was just as well. As the part-time Station Representative he was expected to travel to Aberdeen three days a week to present gramophone recitals, arrange and conduct one afternoon concert a week (and an occasional evening one), undertake all auditions and accompanying and, in whatever time he had left, act as a music adviser to the BBC's Scottish Region.

Apart from engineering, there was no established profession that was recognisably allied with broadcasting. Music probably came closest but even here there was little sign of any particular recruitment policy. People were 'attracted by' or 'drifted into' the BBC. At formal interviews such questions as 'do you play golf?' and 'what is your club?' were not uncommon and some staff felt that too much emphasis was put on who you knew rather than what you knew. Yet this apparently haphazard and class-conscious form of recruitment produced a profession that always found time for the enthusiast and never showed even a blink of surprise when it realised it had uncovered a genius.

The surge of activity in and around the studios, coupled with vastly improved reception and increasingly popular programmes, signalled a broadcasting boom but its principal contriver was not to be around to savour it. For some time the Scottish Director's lifestyle and pyrotechnic displays of management had wearied London colleagues in general and Sir John Reith in particular. Thomson's imperious manner first came to light when Regional Directors' salaries were under review in the late 1920s. At that time they were being paid around £1,000 p.a. and had submitted a claim for a 100 per cent increase (The Town Clerk of Manchester was getting £3,000) pointing out their insecurity of position and lack of pension arrangements. The lack of car allowance was also keenly felt. In their view car upkeep, apart from occasional private use, merited around £150 per annum. The case, eventually successful, trembled in limbo for a few brief moments when Thomson revealed an expenditure of £250 to his chauffeur-valet.

It was his short fuse when dealing with colleagues that caused the greatest concern. A contemporary recalled a difference of opinion between the Scottish Director and Kennedy Stewart, Scotland's able Publicity Officer: 'Within moments they were taking their jackets off to each other.' In those days retribution for such subordination was swift and inside a week the London Control Board Minutes reported the termination of Kennedy Stewart's appointment, stating that Mr Moray McLaren would be

Edinburgh Staff (1930s)

David Cleghorn Thomson (*second row, sixth from left*) Scottish Regional Director and (*to his immediate left*) Moray McLaren, Scottish Programme Director and Thomson's 'interim' replacement in 1933.

(*back row l/r*) n/k; n/k; n/k; J.B. Watson; n/k; n/k; n/k; Tony Coghill; n/k; n/k; Sgt Rutherford.

(*fourth row l/r*) n/k; Doris Skeal; M. Ross; Eva Quade; n/k; n/k; Catherine Wilkie, Scottish Programme Executive; Cecile Walton, Children's Hour; Betty Ferguson, Secretary to Scottish Regional Director; Mary Mitchell; Binnie Crawford; n/k; n/k; n/k; n/k.

(*third row l/r*) Andrew Bryson, Accompanist; John Dickson, Principal Cello; Jack Mouland Begbie, Leader BBC Scottish Orchestra; n/k; n/k; Ian Whyte, Director of Music; n/k; W. McInulty, Principal Cello; Fred Cole, Principal Double Bass; n/k.

(*second row l/r*) John Gough, Features; J.G.W. Thomson, Assistant Engineer-in-Charge; Gordon Gildard, Drama; n/k; Moray McLaren; David Cleghorn Thomson; Jacky Beveridge, Engineer-in-Charge; D.R. Low, Edinburgh Organiser; George Burnet; n/k.

Front row – all n/k.

transferred from *The Listener* to be Number Two at Edinburgh, and adding 'if DCT is resigning, he should do so as early as practicable in the New Year.'

Thomson clung on, however, and the growling in Reith's diary increased. Finally, in March 1933, the long anticipated entry came. 'Saw Thomson and told him he would have to go.' The public announcement of the departure was dated 10 April. It stated that a successor would be appointed shortly and in the meantime the duties of Scottish Regional Director would be carried out on a temporary basis by Moray McLaren.

There is no doubt that David Cleghorn Thomson's period in Scotland had been prolonged because of Reith's inability to find a successor. Amongst the Scottish staff there was a legend that the next Scottish Regional Director, Melville Dinwiddie, was spotted, assessed and signed up all in the space of a weekend when Reith heard him preaching in St Machar's Cathedral in Aberdeen. It's a nice tale and fits well into the style and background of the man but the post demanded more than a snap judgement, no matter how attractive a candidate might seem.

In fact, finding a successor took a considerable time and Reith saw and considered close to a dozen people before making his choice. They included Johnny Bannerman, later to become a frequent and much respected broadcaster in Scotland, and Herbert Wiseman, who did join the BBC but some years later as the Scotland's Head of Music. Throughout this time one man stayed in Reith's mind and he came back to him again and again. He was Joseph F. Duncan, first suggested as a possible candidate by Mrs Hamilton, a BBC Governor. Duncan was the leader of the Scottish Farm Servants Union and already known in Scotland as a writer and broadcaster. Reith described him as 'quite a remarkable man, very well-known' and was attracted by Duncan's outlook and knowledge of local characteristics but considered his trade union association and age – he was 53 – insuperable hurdles.

Dinwiddie first came to the Director-General's notice through Sir George and Lady Lilian Adam Smith in Aberdeen. A letter from them reminded Reith that he had heard the minister of St Machar's preaching a few months before – would he be worth considering for the Scottish Directorship? Reith replied 'Yes' and asked that he travel to London for an interview. Just two days later they faced each other across a table in the new Broadcasting House in London. Question and answer, probing here and a statement there, the meeting lasted over an hour and finally Melville Dinwiddie asked a personal question. Would Sir John Reith be in the BBC for many years to come? Reith did not hesitate and his answer was characteristically short and to the point. 'I expect to be where I am for some years yet.' The meeting ended and the next Scottish Director had been chosen. But five years later, Reith was gone. Dinwiddie stayed the course for a memorable quarter of a century.

There were strong similarities between the new Scottish Director and his Director-General. Both were Scots and sons of the manse, serving with distinction in Scottish regiments during the war – Dinwiddie in the Gordon Highlanders and Reith with the Scottish Rifles before transferring to the Royal Engineers – and they shared the same ideals and hopes as far as broadcasting was concerned.

In his Sunday morning address to the congregation of St Machar's, when he told them of his new appointment, Melville Dinwiddie had said: 'This appointment is bigger than even the biggest parish, for its vast influence will extend over the whole of Scotland and far beyond, and although I shall not be in direct touch with you I shall feel a very real and indirect contact with many of you at your own firesides.'

And just in case that vast influence became too intoxicating, a valedictory article in the Aberdeen *Bon Accord* urged him to hold the balance between entertainment and instruction: 'We look for "hailsome fairin" with an occasional bout of high feeding; and the sound judgement which has marked your work in the ministry.'

Dinwiddie, or 'Din' as he would soon be known, took up his appointment in Edinburgh on 2 October 1933, and it wasn't long before he realised that he had at his command an extremely quick-moving, lively group of people. He warmed to the spirit of enthusiasm amongst the staff and was gratified by their loyalty both to the BBC and to his predecessor, realising that the situation was a great deal more favourable than he had anticipated. Thomson had gathered together people with abilities that couldn't be bettered in any other equivalent station and the output of ideas and energy was remarkable. Everybody expected to work at high pressure and there was a refreshing vitality and freedom from red tape about the

Melville Dinwiddie
Scottish Regional Director, then much later title changed to Controller, Scotland (1933–1957).

station. All of which was very important in view of Dinwiddie's immediate task.

For some time the number of licences issued in Scotland had been well below the national average. In a letter to the Scottish Director written within weeks of his arrival in Edinburgh, Reith had clearly indicated his annoyance with the situation, grumbling away that from the earliest days broadcasting had never aroused the same enthusiasm in Scotland as it had elsewhere. The current Scottish total – just under 400,000 – was too low and he expected his new Director to do something about it: 'What about a half-million licences by December 1934 as a preliminary objective and don't forget all the licence dodgers who needed rooting out?'

Dinwiddie met the challenge and bettered it. A full month before the deadline an internal head office memo to Reith noted that the licences in Scotland had exceeded the target of half a million. The memo, written by Basil Nicholls, the BBC's Director of Internal Administration, suggested that the Director-General recognise the achievement in three ways:

1   His personal congratulations to Dinwiddie and an increased salary

2   Some method of general recognition for the staff in Scotland e.g. a bonus of one per cent

3   Setting another goal of, say, 750,000

Some weeks later Dinwiddie was thanked at a private interview and his salary enhanced in a modest way. However, the second suggestion had been immediately ruled out. Reith's heavy pencil strokes on the memo are quite explicit. Instead, Reith acknowledged by letter the part played by both Dinwiddie and his staff and asked that his congratulations be conveyed to them all, along with a signed photograph of himself despatched under separate cover. It was a token of esteem that had an enduring quality. More than 50 years later it was still hanging in 5 Queen Street, Edinburgh.

Reith's other requirement – to root out the licence evaders – was less of a success story in Scotland. It was a chore that was not always to Dinwiddie's liking and his strong sense of humour and fair play did occasionally get in the way as was apparent when he was publicly rebuked by his erstwhile local paper, *The Bon Accord*. It appears that what the paper referred to as a 'tell-tale creature' had sent a letter to the BBC's Scottish Director giving a list of neighbours who were operating unlicensed wireless sets. Dinwiddie decided that it was a dirty trick and refused to do anything about it.

'The height of foolishness,' chided the paper. 'We like Mr Dinwiddie's way of looking at the problems; it is characteristic of the fine, upstanding character of the man. But we are not satisfied that the thrifty villagers who are stealing the programmes for which we help to pay should be allowed to persist in their iniquity.'

Dinwiddie and his staff had now settled into a steady pace of work. The BBC displayed a confident look and the programmes originating in Scotland were on the whole deliberately popular – what the BBC referred to as 'overcoming the reserve of the hesitating listener'. Licence figures continued to rise as new listeners were attracted by a mixture of more lively and topical features and talks, an increase in the number of eyewitness accounts, extended sports bulletins and, most popular of all, many more relays from major variety theatres. Radio's ability to transport the listener to a public occasion was nowhere more appreciated than in Scotland. To the country listener, particularly those in remote areas, visiting a theatre or concert hall in person was only a dream.

The radio was a means of filling time in an enjoyable way. It formed a topic of conversation that almost rivalled the weather and it gave a common interest in the family. Despite the doom-laden arguments propounded in the 1920s that broadcasting would have an adverse effect on such things as reading and concert going, the very opposite proved to be the case. Even with sporting events – and the same argument still rages – broadcasting tended to increase interest rather than diminish it.

In London the huge range of programmes meant that specialisation was becoming almost obligatory and offices became departments specialising in drama, sport, talks and announcing. The trend would come north but not for a while. For the meantime, the old adage of turning one's hand to everything still applied.

Producers in Scotland revelled in the range of their work and with purely Scottish programmes they were largely free from the constraints of the 'London can do it better' argument. The now familiar framework of basic ingredients that made up a large part of the output was quickly established. Scottish listeners had their own schools and religious programmes (in each case backed by a representative advisory committee) and a strong element for children. Drama was increasingly well served with adaptations of Scottish works and there was now more than a hint that some writers were interested in radio as a medium on its own. Music, with its wide appeal and attractive flexibility in filling schedules, had a very broad base: Scottish folk songs, country dance music, Gaelic music and numerous outside relays from the major choral and orchestral organisations. It was easy to justify a Scottish theme in talks – *A Discussion on Slum Clearance in Scotland*

Drama recording in David's Tower, Edinburgh Castle (1937)

(l/r) n/k; Elsie Payne; Bruce Morgan; Nan Scott.

between Sir Godfrey Collins and Sir William Whyte; a talk on *The Work of the Scottish Development Council* by the Earl of Elgin and Kincardine – but sometimes the Scottish element was delightfully contrived as in *A Recital of German Ballads in the Scots Tongue* translated by Professor Alexander Gray and sung by Mona Benson and Robert Burnett. 'Just let someone try and challenge that as something London could do better!'

Variety posed no problems in justifying the Scottish tag. Nearly all the Scots comics were now regular broadcasters and the OB engineers were almost permanent fixtures at all the major variety and pantomime venues. To match the quickening interest in programmes, the Scottish operation was bolstered by two significant developments that increased its status and moved it deeper into public service. The first was the tardy but welcome growth of Schools department, for too long restrained by indecision and lack of support in Scotland. Full recognition of the importance of this branch of broadcasting came in 1935 when Ayrshire chose to mark the Royal Jubilee by giving a wireless set to every one of its schools and, a year later, in 1936, there were nine people in the department – Archie Adam, described as the Senior Schools Official, and three assistants, Douglas R. Allan, Harry Hoggan and Miss Helen Benson, four secretaries and a man whose job was to tour Scotland's schools recommending the best type of installation for good reception. At the time he was described by colleagues as the 'Radio Doctor', giving Scotland claims to another notable educational first. A total of 762 schools were registered as 'listening' and 83,000 pamphlets were sold for the autumn courses which covered literature, Scottish history, music, nature study, biology and French.

Second, and of equal importance, was the founding late in 1935 of the BBC Scottish Orchestra, replacing what was now Edinburgh's small studio orchestra. From the earliest years it had been the BBC's practice to broadcast a number of major concerts from Glasgow and Edinburgh. In the West of Scotland it was usually the Glasgow Choral and Orchestral Union (the 'Scottish Orchestra') and from the capital, the Reid Orchestra. At various times the BBC also promoted its own concerts, particularly in Glasgow, but these along with desultory attempts to stimulate interest in forming a National Orchestra had merely resulted in ill feeling between the BBC and the various music bodies in Scotland. Then in the summer of 1931 Thomson moved Ian Whyte from his part-time post in Aberdeen into a full-time job at headquarters in Edinburgh. Ian respected the by then well-established habit of drawing freely on outside resources for a great deal of the 'concert' output, but longed for something more sizeable under the BBC's own control which would help to consolidate and extend a musical programme policy. With the arrival of Melville Dinwiddie, he found a ready ear for his aims and, a few years later, along came the means.

The BBC Scottish Orchestra, numbering 35 players, met for the first time at 9.30am on 2 December 1935 and gave its first broadcast just over 24 hours later from Edinburgh Studio One. Led by Jack Mouland Begbie, its conductor was Guy Warrack. Ian Whyte himself, now formally elevated to Director of Music, was also at his happiest when composing or arranging and conducting. Kemlo Stephen, expected to assist Ian Whyte, also conducted.

As was the fashion with the other house orchestras, the BBC Scottish frequently sub-divided into smaller units. The 16 string players made regular Scottish dance music broadcasts playing many of Ian Whyte's own arrangements – not easy to play, but very cleverly done and some of them

The BBC Scottish Orchestra (1936)
The Conductor here is Ian Whyte, the Director of Music. The first members were
Guy Warrack, Conductor; J. Mouland Begbie, Leader; W. McInulty, First Violin No 2;
H. Carpenter, First Violin; W.W. Jupp, First Violin; C. Henke, First Violin; R. Bell, First Violin;
A. Burke, Principal Second Violin; W. Ivory, Second Violin; Alice Godfrey, Second Violin;
Esme Haynes, Second Violin; J. Fairbairn, Principal Viola; J. Linn, Viola; J. Dickson, Principal Cello;
J. McInulty, Cello; F.G. Cole, Principal Double Bass; A. Beers, Double Bass; A. Hedges, Principal
Flute; M. Knight, Flute & Piccolo; J.A. McGillivray, Principal Oboe; S. Barr, Second Oboe;
J.H. Clucas, Principal Clarinet; G.H. Green, Second Clarinet; G. Holbrooke, Principal Bassoon;
E.F. Worsley, Second Bassoon; J. Crocket, First Horn; J. Shandley, Second Horn; W. Bull, Fourth
Horn; F.C. Davison, Second Trumpet; T.C. Miller, Second Trombone; Sanchia Pielou, Harp.

very beautiful. Another sub-division – the Scottish Studio Orchestra under the charge of John Dickson – performed a vast range of popular tunes described as ranging from the *De'il's Awa'* to *O Sole Mio*, the devil to the blue sea.

Having only 35 players the new orchestra was not in any sense in competition with the other Scottish concert-giving organisations. Progressively their repertoire would become more serious and a decision at the beginning of the war that it should not have its numbers reduced would be a major factor in its eventual elevation to symphonic strength, but for the moment it was fully engaged broadcasting on all the BBC's services using the magnificent Studio One in Edinburgh, now virtually theirs alone. It was an ideal concert studio and, as an innovation, it was decided to allow an audience to be present during some of the music broadcasts. For many years audiences had been present during relays from outside halls but never at studio performances. Now there was an enlightened attitude that understood the importance of a tangible audience to most performers. It was some time, however, before the Edinburgh public could be persuaded to overcome their fear of the microphone and audiences had to be 'salted' with people ready to give a lead to the rest by clapping at the end of each item. Not so successful was the attempt to introduce 'promenade' concerts in the studio – an ideal arrangement as there were balconies on three sides. The Edinburgh audiences firmly rejected the idea of standing when listening to music and the idea of creating a casual 'Queen's Hall' atmosphere was dropped.

For the next quarter of a century Ian Whyte and the BBC Scottish Orchestra were tantamount to being the same thing and Ian, a most naturally gifted Scottish musician, began an outpouring of broadcast music which continued until his death in 1960. The radio audience found constant pleasure in his arrangements of Scots songs, his highly characteristic Scottish dance tunes and the huge radio series, *Music from the Scottish Past*. Everything he tackled was done with tremendous care and, when a friendship developed between himself and Sir Harry Lauder, he re-scored many of the old man's songs carefully preserving their original music hall touches.

Lauder had been one of the last traditional Scots comics to be brought into the Scottish broadcasting fold. After his many and popular broadcasts during the days of 5SC and 2LO he had appeared on radio less and less and by the 1930s he seemed, to the public at least, to be something of a broadcasting recluse. Finally it was a conversation between the BBC's Andrew Stewart and ex-Bailie William Thompson – a well-known Glasgow broadcaster – that led to the start of negotiations with the great Scots comedian.

Thompson was a member of the Harry Lauder Cronies Club and he would often ask why the BBC wouldn't put Harry on the air. One day Andrew told him, 'He wants an hour and he wants £1,000 – that's too long and too much.'

Thompson's reply was equally succinct. 'All he wants is to know that he gets more than Gracie (Gracie Fields) and that he's still head of the profession. You better come and meet him at Lauder Ha' over lunch.'

A meeting was arranged. Lunch was huge with vast helpings of potatoes and mince followed by semolina. Then the three of them ascended the great divided staircase to the long room that contained the old man's many mementoes and testimonials from all over the world. It was an astounding display, dominated by a large portrait of his son, Captain John Lauder. Mostly the talk was led by Lauder, dwelling sentimentally on the great debt he owed to the ordinary working man and then switching to his many great and titled friends with whom he spent many happy hours fishing. Around 4.00pm it was time for the visitors to leave. Lauder made to accompany them to the door and still nothing had been said about broadcasting. It was now or never, decided Andrew, and he launched into his opening gambit. Thanking the man for his hospitality he voiced the thought that he, Harry Lauder, knew well why they had come. It was clear, however, that he wasn't interested in any proposition that might have been made and despite his avowed interest in the Scottish working man, with over 100,000 still unemployed, even a week at the Glasgow Alhambra Theatre wouldn't help as they probably couldn't afford even the cheapest seats in the house. They could, of course, have enjoyed listening to him on the radio. William Thompson clutched Lauder's arm, saying that the young man from the BBC was right, and his old friend should reconsider. Lauder was visibly moved and, pausing only for a moment, said he would help the BBC all he could.

Seconds later, as if prompted by some sixth sense, Greta, Harry Lauder's niece, appeared bearing a tray with three glasses of whisky. They drank and the deal was done. In the car on the way back to Glasgow, Andrew was advised to treat it as a gentleman's agreement. 'No contract.' recommended the Bailie. 'Nothing in writing. You've shaken hands on it. Leave it there.'

A contract would have indicated the fee being paid but it wasn't easy persuading London to dispense with the formalities and ultimately Greta dealt with the paperwork. Sir Harry returned to broadcasting and as, on the face of it, he never saw a contract, had every reason to believe he was the highest paid performer on the books and for some time to come he probably was.

The chance to broadcast did not come quite so easily for another Scots entertainer – Jimmy Shand. Far from being wooed, he was practically turned from the door, although he was to become almost as popular as Lauder with Scottish audiences.

Jimmy Shand worked in a music shop in Dundee and was well-known throughout Fife and the East Neuk as a performer of Scottish dance music. Unbeknown to him his name had been put forward for an audition with the BBC and out of the blue he received an invitation to be heard at Queen Street, Edinburgh. A good friend offered to go with him and on a dismally cold day the pair set off for their nearest railway station, Kirkcaldy. Eventually they arrived at Queen Street – Jimmy had never been to Edinburgh before and they had walked from Waverley Station – cold, carrying the accordion case and feeling pretty miserable. As they entered the door of the BBC they were struck by the huge notices: *Silence*. It made them afraid even to draw breath. They spoke to nobody and eventually Jimmy was taken to a studio and told to play. 'I didn't have a chance', said Jimmy. 'I was frozen stiff.' He played anyway and before long the lilting music brought the life back into his hands. Life also came back to his feet and he was failed for stamping his foot.

It was an expensive day for the young Mr Shand. The return fare from Kirkcaldy was 1/6d and the BBC did not reimburse expenses. He always tapped his foot when he played but people no longer worried. He credited Andrew Stewart with arranging his second and this time successful audition and from then on he was a frequent solo performer on the Scottish airwaves.

Andrew Stewart is a name that appears increasingly. He was Melville Dinwiddie's Programme Director and as such was responsible for creating and organising the mixture that was prefaced to the listener by the words, 'This is the Scottish Programme of the BBC.' Andrew was what the BBC liked to call 'an all-round fellow'. He had come to broadcasting in the early days via the Scottish National Players to be 'Longfellow' with Kathleen Garscadden in children's programmes. Production work followed and then a spell as the BBC's Glasgow Manager. Imbued with a strong sense of Scottish purpose, he shared with Dinwiddie the conviction that Scotland was beginning to regain her national consciousness – he called it revived patriotism – and in the years that followed he endeavoured to give effect to this in Scottish programmes.

His job as Programme Director had been clearly defined.

'Regional Programme Directors are intended to have a comprehensive responsibility to the Regional Director for the Regional Programmes as a whole.'

While Melville Dinwiddie was expected to concentrate on what Reith had once described as 'the ambassadorial functions' – public relations, keeping up-to-date a network of personal relationships with key people and, by informal monthly reports, keeping head office informed of what the leaders of public opinion were thinking of the work of the BBC – the Programme Director was free to concentrate on the problem of planning programmes for Scotland – programmes that, as a mix, would reflect the character of the people, their tastes in entertainment and music, and their interests outside the country.

Planning was no easy task for it was ringed with restrictions and rules. It had to be clearly seen as an alternative to the National Programme offering speech as against music, light material when the other was serious and having majority appeal only when the alternative was of interest to a minority. Though named the Regional Wavelength it was largely London-based and if not under head office control was certainly under its influence. The matrix for the service was formed by the London Regional Programme, London's own alternative to the National Programme. This service was made up of a mixture of London-made programmes plus the best that was on offer from elsewhere, a kind of pool and available as a simultaneous feed to all the BBC's Regions. This allowed for material to be taken, a few programmes dropped, and the substitution of the Region's own material – 'opting out' was what it was later called, with a requirement, of course, to advise London of what was being done. So far, so good.

Where it became awkward was when a Region appeared to deviate from the pool too often, 'cutting out' they called it then, either unwisely in London's eyes or expressly against their wishes. In an effort to discourage this, programmes often appeared on the London schedules bearing a system of marking. Thus three '5s' indicated that a programme was compulsory, two meant you would be well advised to include it and one said that you better have a good reason for substitution. Gradually this system disappeared as Scotland (along with the other Regions) negotiated tirelessly for a more open attitude to their autonomy and Scotland was able to increase the number of programmes originated locally, finance and staff becoming the new criteria.

The need for contrast remained and brought some anxious moments, particularly on a Saturday when sport was involved. Such an occasion was the 1935 Boat Race and it generated some diligent correspondence between Scotland and London as well as evoking some interesting class-conscious attitudes.

At that time the contact in London was Lindsay Wellington and, early in the year, when planning for the Boat Race weekend was in its early stages he received a memo from Scotland. Not unusually, Boat Race day was also the date for another prestigious sporting event – the Scotland v England encounter at Hampden Park, and Scotland were hoping to persuade the Scottish Football Association to give their consent to a broadcast of the whole match. London planned a 'double feature' on the National Programme – the Boat Race at 2.30pm, followed by the second half of the football. The Regional Programme, as a contrast, was scheduled to have the Glasgow Orpheus Choir making a live broadcast from the Queen's Hall in London.

'I wonder whether you cannot possibly make an exception to the traditional rule,' wrote Scotland, going on to suggest that the whole of the match be transmitted on the Scottish Regional Programme. 'This, I admit, would omit the Orpheus Choir from our "Regional" in the afternoon but we have taken the Choir separately only a fortnight before.'

The argument seemed sound but to London any detraction from the Boat Race was a worrisome thought and there was the added concern that during the second half there would be no difference between the National and Regional transmissions in Scotland. As London agonised over the decision, Scotland pressed harder and soon was scoring direct hits.

'The number of people interested in the Soccer International in Scotland is almost incalculably greater than the number of people interested in the Boat Race.'

'The people who are interested in the Boat Race are mostly of the better-off class who are able to get the National as well as the Regional and therefore would not be deprived of the Boat Race.'

'I feel it would be very well worth the trouble... if we could take the popular and democratic move of giving the majority of Scotland the event in which it is far more interested.'

Eventually Scotland won the day, pleased its audience and demonstrated its nationalism without recourse to tartan and heather. But before pride swells in the bosom too much, later that same day, with full permission, Scotland dropped a programme from the evening schedules. It was the first of a series and was to have a phenomenal run. Called *American Half-Hour*, it was broadcast by a certain Alistair Cooke.

As direct London control of the local service eased, the next layer of restraint was uncovered – Programme Allowance, the amount of money allocated by head office to pay for programme costs. In broadcasting there was no concept of total costing. Instead staff, equipment and general administration charges were dealt with through central budgets, leaving the Regions responsible only for programme payments such as artists and scripts. Such programme expenditure was met by means of a weekly Programme Allowance which was averaged over a quarter. In the first quarter of 1936, Scotland asked for a weekly allowance of £525 and was allocated £500. Wales, who also covered the West of England, had the largest amount, £530 and Northern Ireland, as the smallest entity, made do with £300. The Regions were able to apply for a special grant for any particularly expensive programme and any programmes contributed to the National or London Regional Programme usually received financial assistance.

The Regions had freedom to negotiate fees with performers up to a certain level. Fifteen guineas was the limit for individual artists – it had stood at five guineas until a couple of years before – and a maximum of 30 guineas was allowed for combinations such as bands. Anything above these limits had to be agreed with head office. In practice, it was a rare occurrence for any artist or orchestra likely to command a high fee would either live in the London area or be on the London books.

Negotiations of this kind were anathema to some producers. It seemed to be in direct conflict with their creativity, spoiling the purity of relationships and in any case, they would, in embarrassment, probably offer too much. That at least was the feeling of the Corporation. Better that one person carry the responsibility in each Region and that there be little or no difference from the standard London routine. Thus were the Regional Programme Executives born, people who were to become legends in the BBC. The posts were frequently held by women and their particular attention to detail in contracts and copyright arrangements was well-known. Not always loved, but frequently respected, they had a practical and systematic outlook and were prepared to absorb a great deal of the Corporation's growing bureaucracy, thus allowing the many individualists around them to survive and prosper. They were also a way of ensuring uniformity throughout the organisation, something that the BBC set great store by. Too much perhaps, because uniformity meant rules – excessive official routines that could not suit everywhere and were often misinterpreted.

Public service was a noble and inspired status – high responsibility requiring a stern conscience – but reflecting this within the organisation sometimes made difficult things which would otherwise be easy. Even the simple wastepaper basket came under scrutiny in the mid '30s.

'An investigation has recently been made of the contents of wastepaper baskets in offices,' ran a memo from the Director of Internal Administration addressed to all offices. 'It is a definite instruction for the future that no paper should be thrown away without being torn in sufficiently small pieces to render subsequent reading impossible.'

As the BBC's commitment to centralisation was pursued by more and more departments, it was inevitable that it should rub off on to the programme makers. Programmes accepted from Scotland for transmission by London were often the criteria to which all else aspired and in such things as auditions and scripts standards were sometimes unrealistically high. The London requirement was uncomplicated and straightforward. 'Programme Directors are urged to maintain in their programmes the standards of performance accepted and required by the Corporation as a whole.' This left very little room for Scotland, for example, to have anything other than a modest supporting role for it made it very difficult to present ethnic and cultural characteristics that were other than stereotyped.

London expected from Scotland programmes that were mostly of a known quality and worth. The ubiquitous OB, particularly involving royalty or the aristocracy, was rarely turned down and any celebration of an internationally credited Scottish figure such as Burns or Sir Walter Scott was equally acceptable. Concerts by the BBC Scottish Orchestra and prestigious music occasions in Aberdeen, Glasgow or Edinburgh were usually agreed to 'on the nod', as were productions overseen by known producers whose work had been successful over the years. Occasionally, however, an idea would come unstuck and often the reason would be the alleged unintelligibility of the speakers. A programme on herring fishery from the North East of Scotland, for instance, brought the following observation:

I think that this type of programme, with its strong Scottish dialect, is frankly not worth relaying as I myself could literally not follow it at all... It is nobody's fault but it just is that it might well have been a foreign language.

Producers and Programme Directors became adept at juggling with the various ideas that came their way. Allegiance to the past and the glorification of Scotland's heavy industry were certainties for Britain as a whole, while broadcasting Scottish affairs, playing its music, speaking its ballads and expressing its thoughts – these were things that, if they were to be done at all they were best done in Scotland. Part of this sorting out process took place at the weekly Programme Board Meeting. Here Scotland's programmes, both in retrospect and in the future, were discussed every Monday morning in the headquarters in Edinburgh. Attendance was mandatory – 'a sort of master clock that regulates our lives' recalled one member – and those present consisted of all heads of departments and producers plus representatives from engineering and administration. Everybody was expected to contribute to the discussion and the meeting was thought of as an informed body of opinion representing Scottish taste. Nowadays that would be considered an elitist view but at the time the undoubted success of Scottish programmes and the versatility and ability of many of the staff and contributors swept all doubts aside.

Success came through a variety of programmes, all of them owing something to the very varied background and talents of those who had 'drifted' into broadcasting in Scotland. Complex OBs were still to the fore and on 26 September 1934, Scotland found itself handling its most important project so far. It was the launch of John Brown's huge Cunarder, *Queen Mary*, from their yard at Clydebank by the Queen accompanied by King George V. A hazardous project at any time, it was made even more difficult by the fact that the King was out of sorts with the BBC because of a badly handled broadcast at the opening of the Mersey Tunnel a few months before. Coverage from Glasgow just had to be faultless. The reputation of the Corporation would stand or fall through it.

Despite the vagaries of wind and tide, imponderable questions such as would His Majesty inspect the Guard of Honour and a heavy responsibility being carried by the commentator George Blake, the broadcast was a huge success. From the very beginning of the planning stage Melville

Dinwiddie had insisted that it was to be a Scottish operation, resisting the very great pressures that were put on him to allow London staff to supervise the day. The gamble, if it was a gamble, paid off. Within the BBC the Scottish Region's reputation soared and Andrew Stewart, who had been in overall charge, had no doubt that his competent handling of the day helped to make him Scotland's Programme Director.

The art of the OB was now being honed to a fine degree. The rather inhibiting, artificial atmosphere of the studio was demanding an increasing professionalism from performers and there was pleasant relief and an engaging freedom available 'outside'. Aberdeen used this to the full in December 1935 when it produced *The Farm Year, a Calendar of the Rural Round*, devised by John R. Allan and produced by Moultrie Kelsall, now the Station Representative. The programme set out to illustrate the farm year, month by month, in a uniquely ambitious way – as a live programme broadcast from John Strachan's farm near Fyvie. Every part of the farm was used. The dining room became the operations control centre for the engineers and the sitting room, the location for indoor scenes. Outdoor scenes took place in and round the farm steading and even the in-field was used to give the sound of a reaper.

As was customary in those days, everything in the programme was scripted, even interviews, and semi-professional artists were used throughout. Even so there were heart-stopping moments and looking back now the miracle is that it went without a hitch. As it was transmitted live at 7.45pm on a December night the yard and steadings were in Stygian gloom, relieved by an occasional pool of light. Inevitably one of the participants, Jimmy Kemp, slipped in the churned-up mud and landed on his back, although still managing to roar out his lines from what was undoubtedly a very uncomfortable position.

Programmes like this gave Moultrie Kelsall a tremendous reputation for having an abundance of energy and drive, and also brought to a high pitch his nail-biting habit of cutting a script on transmission by the simple act of leaning over an artist's shoulder and blanking out a sentence or more – even a paragraph – about three lines ahead of the performer's eye.

The successful multi-point broadcast from the farm was quickly followed by an ambitious use of multi-studio centres by another Scottish producer, Gordon Gildard. This time it was a historical re-enactment, *The March of '45, A Radio Panorama in Verse and Song*, written by

D.G. Bridson. Produced for the first time on 28 February 1936, the programme followed the progress of Prince Charles Edward Stuart from his landing at Loch Nan Uamh to the calling of a final halt outside Derby. It was in two parts:

> Part 1, *The High Endeavour* was produced by Gordon Gildard in Edinburgh, and Part 2, *The Turn of the Tide* was under the direction of E.A. Harding in the North Region studios in Manchester.

It was hailed as the most distinguished radio broadcast of the year. Its clever blending of dialogue, music and old Jacobite songs and readings taken from documents of the time was outstanding enough. To have it performed with the authenticity of style and accent afforded by the use of two studio centres marked it as something unique. Such was its success another production – this time in three parts – was broadcast later the same year in November. It was repeated again the following year as a special project for NBC of America and yet again in 1944, this time for the BBC's Home Service.

The March of the '45 committed Gordon Gildard to a career in broadcasting drama and his name quickly became one of those synonymous with 'on the nod' acceptance by London. Like many of his colleagues, he was still able to enjoy the regional freedom of doing other things and, in 1937, he produced Scotland's first major feature on Scottish football. In a sense this was a joint production too. Billed in the *Radio Times* as *Scottish Football – A Survey of the Season 36/37*, it stemmed from an idea of Peter Thomson's, the Glasgow office boy who would later become Scotland's principal sports producer and broadcaster.

Another of Gordon's successes, *The Trial of Madeleine Smith*, brought to the fore John Gough, born in Tasmania and now working in the Queen Street studios in 'balance and control', the BBC's equivalent of stage management. These members of staff were responsible for everything from sound effects to balancing and controlling sound levels and worked closely with the producer. It was a job that required a minimum of engineering knowledge and an extremely fertile imagination and for 30 years was considered the kindergarten for radio producers.

One of the attractive things about John Gough was the way he found everything in Scotland new and refreshingly different. For instance, he was amazed that he could walk along Queen Street in Edinburgh and pass the house where Simpson and his friends had experimented with chloroform and it wasn't long before he was turning some rather taken-for-granted facts into enjoyable and fascinating programmes. Notorious Scottish trials became a rich source of material for him, as did the histories of Scottish regiments. He was an important catalyst when it came to discussing programme ideas and his work as a producer showed a happy welding together of interesting subjects and clever studio craft, so much so that after six years as a feature producer he went to London as a senior instructor in the BBC's staff training department.

The variety of background and experience of the staff seemed to contribute to their imagination and versatility. It included James Ferguson, already deeply interested in Scottish history and the author of *The Letters of George Dempster to Sir Adam Ferguson* and a town councillor in the Royal Burgh of Haddington. Peter Keith Murray allegedly ran away from Harrow at 16 to work as a mining engineer in South Wales, then to India where he worked for a time as a journalist on a Calcutta newspaper before fetching up with the BBC in Scotland in 1934. His mind ran particularly to inventions and he had an alternative TV system to both the Baird and the EMI before any decisions were taken about either of them. One of his programmes, in a series called *Inside Information*, had him at a high pitch of complexity. It was a triumph of technical pluggery and skill with almost as many sources as there were minutes in the programme. A few days after the broadcast, a postcard from a listener arrived on his desk. It said, quite simply, 'By all means have your fun, but give the listener a chance.'

Radio's ability to re-create past deeds and celebrate sports triumphs, feeding the Scots' insatiable appetite for bygone days, meant a heavy reliance on nostalgia and tradition but it would be wrong to assume that this was the sum total of the output. Sandwiched between yet another adaptation of *Rob Roy* and a feature by John Gough on the Highland Light Infantry it was possible to hear *I Want to Abolish Burns Nichts*, jazz and an increasing number of irrepressible and irreverent revues, many of which originated from the new producer in Aberdeen.

Moultrie Kelsall became Aberdeen Station Representative in 1931 and his tremendous drive and resourcefulness had energised the old 2BD premises in Belmont Street. A law graduate from Glasgow University, his abiding passion was drama and he came to Aberdeen as former business manager of the Scottish National Players and an associate of Tyrone Guthrie. As the opening of the Westerglen transmitters had not brought the full choice of listening to the North East of Scotland, Aberdeen listeners still had to tune to the low-power local transmitter which served the city. In an attempt to give them as varied a service as possible it carried a complicated mix of material from the National and Regional Programmes and, as timings between the two networks were not always conducive to hopping between the two sources, the planners allowed Aberdeen the freedom to broadcast its own local programmes to bridge the more awkward gaps. This was manna to Moultrie Kelsall and his enthusiasm for broadcasting resulted in plays, a series of revues, *The Silver Citizens,* for which he wrote many of the sketches and songs, and a three-piano group which included a talented young Aberdeen 'jazz' player, Ruby Duncan, whom he married in 1934. For *Children's Hour* he created a group of animals, a far sighted as well as an entertaining idea as the BBC did its best to drop the designation *Uncle* and *Auntie* in 1934. The animals, along with *Granny Mutch* (Christine Crow) and Arthur Black's *Grandfather More* made a considerable impact during their lifetime and lasted until the outbreak of war. The benefit of a local try-out was immeasurable and helped greatly in preparing artists and material for a wide audience with rich pickings for both the Scottish Regional and the National Programmes.

Aberdeen was to maintain its reputation for programmes of ability and style for many years to come. When Moultrie Kelsall finally left in April 1937 to join the newly formed television department of the BBC at Alexandra Palace, joining a small but distinguished band of people which included Mary Adams, Eric Crozier, Reggie Smith and Royston Morley, he was replaced by a slightly bewildered young man from London called Alan Melville. There was just time to christen him as a *Children's Hour* animal then Moultrie Kelsall was off with Scotland the sadder for his going, leaving Alan Melville and Howard M. Lockhart, who had been sent from Glasgow a year before, to continue Aberdeen's tradition of friendliness and excellence. Alan Melville quickly latched onto the Kelsall legacy of revues with Howard M. Lockhart enjoying himself hugely on the many children's programmes.

Children's Hour in Scotland had lived through a number of changes since the first days of the local 'Aunties' and 'Uncles' cheerfully entertaining with impromptu stories and songs, birthday greetings and exhortations

Above

Aberdeen staff dance (mid-'30s)

(*back row – l/r*) Mr Watt (Engineering); Hugh Crawford, Engineering; fifth from left – George Mair, Engineering; eighth from left – Moultrie Kelsall, Aberdeen Station Representative.

(*front row seated l/r*) third from left, W.W. ('Pops') Inder, Engineer-in-Charge; to his right, Violet Davidson, local singer and entertainer; to her right, Ruby Duncan, wife of Moultrie Kelsall and 'Miss Squirrel' to his 'Rabbit' in Aberdeen's *Children's Hour*.

Left

Christine Orr
Organiser *Children's Hour*
(pictured 1942).

to look behind the sofa to find a birthday surprise. The intimacy of this radio family had seemed threatened first, when the Regional Scheme came into force and *Children's Hour* became centralised, and then when the Radio Circle membership, so huge it seemed likely to engulf the programme, had been abandoned.

There had been frequent and unsettling changes in leadership. Miss Scott Moncrieff had given way to Eva Kerr. She in her turn resigned in 1931 and was replaced for a short time by Winifred Callis, who had been in charge of Aberdeen's *Children's Hour*. She then left and was replaced by Cecile Walter, who was subsequently followed by Christine Orr. Another casualty was Kathleen Garscadden. After almost seven years as 'Auntie Cyclone', the presiding genius of the Glasgow *Children's Hour*, she had left the permanent staff to return to the career of concert singer and teacher, which she had interrupted to join the BBC. Happily she continued to take part on an occasional basis under contract, rejoining the staff again at the end of the 1930s.

Being *Children's Hour* Organiser was probably one of the most difficult jobs in broadcasting. With the disbandment of the Radio Circles and the end of Birthday Greetings, the character of the programmes changed. The years of 'Now Children, what shall we do next?' evaporated and were replaced by carefully planned entertainment. (Children were no longer listening under supervision but parents had an inclination to eavesdrop and woe betide any programme that might upset.) *Children's Hour* had also become a shared production – the various Regions pooling their programmes with London – and for children it was a sort of jigsaw, where a child might hear in one edition a play from London, songs from Edinburgh and a story from Manchester.

This didn't mean that the Scottish *Children's Hour* had ceased to be Scottish but it did give the Scottish child the chance to hear the widest range of items. Scotland, with its many traditions was found to be rich in material as it began to build its fine reputation for being a kinder-garten for writers and performers, always on the lookout for new ideas and fresh talent.

CHAPTER FOUR

The Renaissance of Glasgow

EVER SINCE THE HIGH-POWERED transmitters at Westerglen had come into service, there had been agitation for better coverage for the North of Scotland. Then, as now, the BBC had pursued a policy of providing for heavily populated areas first and it wasn't until the middle of 1934 that the Corporation announced that a site close to Burghead, on the north shore of the Moray Firth, had been chosen for its most northerly transmitting station.

It would be a single channel, operating on the same wavelength as the Scottish Regional transmitters at Westerglen and new technical know-how developed by the BBC's Research and Transmitter departments would synchronise the output of the two transmitters, thus overcoming the problem of having to find a new wavelength for the transmitter. The site was not ideal as far as the Highlands of Scotland were concerned but at least a large part of the North East would be covered and, mindful of the capital expenditure involved, it fulfilled other important criteria. Power lines were available to supply the transmitter and there was reasonably easy access to the GPO's telephone system which would carry the programmes to the site.

On 12 October 1936 the station was opened. Once again it was a well-attended affair and, as had been the case some years before at Westerglen, the tartan was much in evidence. This time, however, there was one man who wore the kilt as if he had been born in it and indeed, on his retirement 28 years later, many of his colleagues would testify that he was still dressed in the same garment, though by then faded and worn. The man was Hugh Macphee, the BBC's first Gaelic Producer, appointed by Melville Dinwiddie to initiate a properly structured Gaelic policy. His presence at Burghead was particularly appropriate for this was the transmitter that would penetrate some distance into the Gaelic-speaking domain and, as it was inexorably tied to the output of the central Scottish transmission, Gaelic programmes would now unite the northern areas and the city enclaves in Glasgow and Edinburgh.

The Gaelic tongue had been heard for the first time on the Scottish air on 2 December 1923 in a religious address conducted by the Rev John Bain from Aberdeen's High United Free Church, broadcast by 2BD. From then on, Aberdeen became the principal source of Gaelic broadcasts largely because of Neil McLean's days as Station Manager. The programme consisted mainly of religion and songs – the songs always announced and described in English – with the spoken word in Gaelic almost non-existent.

In May 1933 the first radio play in Gaelic, *Dunach*, was broadcast from the Glasgow studio. It was produced by Gordon Gildard who neither spoke nor understood the language but it represented a major change after ten years. Another step forward was taken at the beginning of 1934 and it merited a paragraph in the *Scottish Regional Notes* of the *Radio Times*: 'Yet another venture in Scottish broadcasting which will be of interest to a relatively small but important section of the community begins on Wednesday 10 January.'

It referred to a series of six fortnightly lessons in Gaelic pronunciation to be given by Mr John Nicolson and broadcast from the Glasgow studio at 6.30pm after the news. It was seen by the BBC as an experiment and, in case any offence was taken by listeners, it was pointed out that those who were not interested in Gaelic would, of course, find something more to their taste in the National Programme where the alternative was Eugene Pini and his Tango Orchestra!

As it happened there were no great howls of protest and the search began for a Gaelic-speaking member of staff. The man chosen, Hugh Macphee, was thought to be well qualified to be the first Gaelic 'assistant' (the title 'producer' was still comparatively unknown) for he had had some dealings already with the BBC in his previous job at An Comunn Gàidhealach and his brother James was a frequent broadcaster as a singer.

Hugh Macphee joined the BBC on 1 October 1935. He reported to the headquarters in Queen Street, Edinburgh, where he worked for three weeks before moving to the Aberdeen offices in Belmont Street where he joined Moultrie Kelsall and Howard M. Lockhart. His stay in Aberdeen lasted little more than six months and, on 1 June 1936, he was transferred to Glasgow – a sensible move for the Gaelic-speaking population of Glasgow was considerably larger than that of Edinburgh and Aberdeen put together.

He was a man of serious mien and dedicated to the preservation of the Gaelic language and culture. From the very start he sensed that the furtherance of Gaelic broadcasting would depend very much on the benevolence of his superiors and the encouragement of his colleagues and, mindful that his programme must in no way seem to obtrude on the service, he quickly consolidated what had already been done – there was a further series of Gaelic pronunciation lessons by John Nicolson at the end of 1935 – before increasing the range with some talks, ceilidhs and songs. Hugh Macphee understood the value of sentimentalism when dealing with the bulk of Scottish listeners, and when on 7 June 1936 the BBC transmitted its first OB from the island of Iona, it seemed only right and proper that it take the form of a Gaelic service from Iona Abbey.

The reverse of the coin – the social and domestic problems – were never revealed. Hugh Macphee's case was a cultural one and he was grateful for the little airtime that came his way. Perhaps he was too obediently respectful when he might have rocked the boat rather more but for the moment he wished to earn the approval of his broadcasting colleagues and the attention of the listener, both of which he did in no small measure.

By far the most popular part of the Gaelic output was its songs and it is ironic that it was also the most artificial. Every song had to be fully introduced in English and 'fully' meant a lengthy and detailed account of the meaning and content of the song. The influence of Marjory Kennedy-Fraser and her *Songs of the Hebrides* was still strong and, as a consequence, the themes were inevitably romantic and touched with Celtic twilight. As for the performers, the final arbiter in the selection of singers was the Music department – Hugh Macphee's contribution was to pass judgement only on Gaelic pronunciation – and the whole thing was treated much as if it had been a recital of German *lieder*. The day of the folk song was a long way off.

However, none of the foregoing meant that broadcasting was not listened to and enjoyed by the Gaelic community. Perversely, it was the exiles for the most part who could hear and contribute to the programmes. Those still at home in the far North West of Scotland and the islands were as likely as not still having to listen to the National Programme on long wave from Droitwich with its glimpses of an alien, unfamiliar world.

The money spent on the bricks and mortar of the new transmitter at Burghead was a welcome part of the BBC's capital development plans in

Scotland. It was a commodious building, larger than was necessary but commensurate with Reith's wish that all premises reflect the importance and prestige of broadcasting and, at night, the aircraft warning lights on the high mast added a mystical quality to its purpose. Within two years, in September 1938, another transmitter would be in service in the North of Scotland, this time at Redmoss and designed to cover the Aberdeen area, replacing the old city installation that had done duty for so long.

These were new major developments and important to the spread of broadcasting and the high standard of technical coverage that BBC engineers sought. There was also a major project taking place in Glasgow to replace the existing premises in Blythswood Square, something that would go a long way towards updating Scotland's studio facilities. But for many of the staff in Scotland there was still one important scheme that seemed a long time in coming – a change in headquarters in Edinburgh from 5 Queen Street into a larger and, if possible, custom-built building.

Melville Dinwiddie had been aware of Edinburgh's lack of space from the very start. Reith, having dispelled the euphoria that had engulfed him at the formal opening, reverted to his original opinion that it was 'a weird place' and agreed with his Scottish Director that alternative accommodation should be found. A 'Building Committee (Provinces)' had been set up in London almost coincident with Dinwiddie's appointment and at its inaugural meeting on 28 December 1933 it was told by the Director-General that Edinburgh should be placed first on the list of new premises to be built at the main centres. Meantime short-term relief from cramped quarters was achieved by renting temporary premises at 28 Queen Street and Schools and Adult Education were earmarked, with somewhat dubious distinction, as 'peripatetic' departments.

On 14 March 1934, the Building Committee (Provinces) held its fifth meeting and again the subject of Scotland was on the agenda. There was no change in the body's attitude. They would adhere to the priority stated at the first meeting. Edinburgh would be considered first and the BBC's Civil Engineer was requested to prepare tentative plans for a main building for the Scottish Region. Yet three weeks later, at its next meeting, a very different future was seen for Edinburgh. A new building was no longer considered. Instead the BBC would explore the possibility of improving the exterior of 5 Queen Street plus some moderate internal reconstruction. What had changed a seemingly certain case for new premises in Edinburgh? The root of the problem lay with Dinwiddie's dislike of what had happened to Glasgow since the move of so much of the people and paraphernalia of broadcasting to Edinburgh in 1930.

David Cleghorn Thomson had considered it imperative that the newly created broadcasting Region should be managed from Scotland's capital and within the BBC few, if any, were prepared to challenge his decision. The strength of Glasgow as the main centre of population and as the base of many Scottish performers was not thought to be as important as having the Scottish headquarters alongside government offices and the law, and close to the cognoscenti and literati of the nation. Within a year of Queen Street's occupation, and despite Edinburgh's obvious accommodation problems, the Glasgow premises had been reduced to two floors plus some temporary buildings at the rear.

To Dinwiddie this was an untenable position. Glasgow was a major city requiring a BBC presence large enough to develop its broadcasting potential. Almost from the start of his tenure with the Corporation he made his feelings known and, as he sought for a replacement in Edinburgh he never passed up an opportunity to lobby for two developments – two major studio buildings in Scotland.

Head office largely ignored his proposal, not surprisingly preferring to be guided by the Director-General who spoke only of a new Edinburgh Broadcasting House. A brief note to the Scottish Director made it clear that there would be only one building with full studio equipment and there the matter might have finished if hadn't been for a chance meeting that gave Dinwiddie an unexpected ally and a voice in the right places. On a private visit to Elgin in Moray, the BBC's Business Manager, Jardine Brown, called in to the Edinburgh offices on his way south. He listened to the Scottish Director's proposals, liked what he heard and, when he returned to London he reported that he and Dinwiddie had considered the matter as 'Scots' and had both agreed that it was very desirable. Immediately the Edinburgh building was put on 'hold' and the way was open for Scotland to investigate possibilities in both cities, putting its ideas to the Building Committee.

Dinwiddie's future plans were quite clear: to retain the headquarters in Edinburgh with the promised development of new premises in that city and, at the same time to provide in Glasgow facilities and accommodation that would properly reflect the sheer weight of population, the talent and the prestige that that city engendered. He was seeking something close to two headquarters – administration and planning in the East, and programmes in the West of Scotland.

Only one man appears to have challenged the wisdom of such a major separation. The Director-General, Sir John Reith, still had enough of the general manager in him to wonder what studios would be required for what activities vis-à-vis Glasgow versus Edinburgh. In a talk he had with Dinwiddie, he felt it would have been unfair to have pressed for exact details about the allocation of work. What he did do was secure from the Scottish Director, as he put it, 'his by no means unwilling agreement' that there were disadvantages in a dispersed staff and dispersed activities. Reith still supported the need for a change of premises in Edinburgh but had a fear that Dinwiddie would transfer a considerable amount of programmes to Glasgow. Once again he put his finger on it when he wrote to the BBC's Civil Engineer suggesting a visit to Edinburgh to investigate matters on the spot: 'Please bring the orchestra matter up, as obviously a good deal may depend upon whether our main orchestral activity is to be in Glasgow.'

Melville Dinwiddie knew how to play that one. The orchestra with its associated trappings was a 'capital' asset. It was important in his plans for the new Edinburgh building and therefore would remain there.

Surprisingly little time was spent on discussion before the Building Committee indicated its interest in the Scottish plan, or at least the Glasgow part of it, and one can only assume that, as Scotland's development had been given priority at the outset, it needed some movement on the Scottish front to allow other projects elsewhere to come through. All seemed to be set fair with only a slight hint of trouble ahead. Glasgow was to take precedence over the new headquarters building in Edinburgh, which was not to be constructed until the new programme headquarters in Glasgow were finished.

Attempts to find a suitable site for a Glasgow development started immediately and were carried out in an extremely clandestine way by members of the Scottish management and Jardine Brown. The Scottish Regional Executive, J.M.A. Cameron, played it so close to his chest he even used his own domestic law firm in Glasgow, writing as an individual rather than a representative of the BBC. This executive caution was not entirely out of place. Both Jardine Brown and Melville Dinwiddie knew the uproar that would result should there be any suggestion that Glasgow might once again dominate the Scottish airwaves. Cameron, expressing his fear of the Glasgow/Edinburgh antagonism in a letter to a colleague, wrote that he would even meet any fees incurred by payment through his own bank.

Various locations were considered. All were close to the existing premises at Blythswood Square and ranged from the Locarno Dance Hall in Sauchiehall Street (heaven knows what the acquisition of that building would have done to the Glasgow statistics of GI brides!) to the Lanarkshire Bus Company premises in Pitt Street. The location that appealed most was a block of buildings bounded by West George Street and Blythswood Square, virtually the other side of the road from the existing offices. Then, as often happens, within a few weeks of a memo from the Scottish Director indicating his preference, Jardine Brown received a note from the BBC's solicitors in Glasgow.

The reason for the letter was to clear up a point regarding the asking price for the preferred site. That done, it went on to enquire how far from the city centre the BBC were prepared to go. It continued, 'As you possibly know Glasgow University have discontinued classes in Queen Margaret College and I understand they are seriously contemplating selling the property.'

There followed a brief description of the site. It was protected on one side by the River Kelvin and included attractive grounds with fine trees. There were tennis courts and a bowling green (leased to a private club until 1938) and most important of all, the price was likely to be considerably less than that being asked for the Blythswood Square project.

Within days, the College had been inspected by Melville Dinwiddie and J.M.A. Cameron. Both were very taken with what they saw. Later, in their subsequent reports – Cameron to the BBC's Civil Engineer, Dinwiddie to the Controller of Administration – much use was made of words such as splendid, dignified and admirable. The distance from the city centre was not considered a drawback.

'A taxi hired by us to Queen Street Station was approximately eight minutes,' wrote Cameron. 'Some 12 minutes in a tramcar or bus,' reported Dinwiddie. He also made an interesting reference to the future. Pointing out that the site was, if anything, slightly lower than the surrounding district, he wondered if it might be unsuitable for the transmission of television.

Within weeks, the BBC was well on the way to purchasing Queen Margaret College and the transaction was finally confirmed in *The Times* on 27 May 1935. The Scottish papers had suggested as much a few weeks earlier, speculating that the BBC were once again moving their headquarters – a possibility that was quickly quashed by 'an official' who stated that the new premises would be used only for the same purposes as the existing Glasgow studios.

The Glasgow project was now safely in the bag. Melville Dinwiddie continued his crusade to improve conditions in Edinburgh, despite the Building Committee's warning that nothing would happen in Edinburgh until the Glasgow building was complete and occupied. Once again Jardine Brown, imbued with his success in the Glasgow venture, stepped into the ring suggesting that, taking a long view of broadcasting development, it might be wise to purchase a property in Edinburgh similar to Queen Margaret College. Dinwiddie needed no second bidding. Within days of Jardine Brown's proposal he had ready a list of 12 sites within the city and early in May 1936, the Corporations' Civil Engineer arrived in Edinburgh to inspect and report on them.

The list was as varied as it was long. Some of the suggestions were summarily dismissed as being virtually slum property, not a suitable position for the BBC. Others were occupied government buildings and unlikely to become available until the completion of the new Scottish Office building at the Calton Hill. When the survey was completed, top of the list was a proposal to purchase and develop numbers 4, 5 and 6 Queen Street, strongly supported by the Civil Engineer. The rest raised little support, although interesting in that they reflected Dinwiddie's wish to have a central location in Edinburgh:

- The Edinburgh Ladies College in Queen Street
- The National Bank of Scotland at 14 George Street
- Lothian House in Lothian Road
- Synod House, Castle Terrace
- The Calton Hotel, North Bridge

In fact, the survey had produced nothing new. The development and extension site stayed on the books as the first option and, still faced with an accommodation problem, Edinburgh continued to occupy various temporary premises – York Place, leased in 1935, given up in 1937 and 42

Queen Street, leased in 1937 and vacated in 1939. There were continual repairs to numbers 5 and 6. The roof leaked, an office required strengthening. Early in 1938, Dinwiddie spoke of resurrecting the building project and it came to the ears of the then Controller (Administration) B.E. Nicolls, who immediately wrote to the Scottish Director. His memo was sensitive, considerate but final. There would be no new premises built in Edinburgh during the existing Charter period (1937–47) as it was one of the cuts that had been made in the estimates for this period.

Melville Dinwiddie replied at once. He accepted the postponement – there was little choice – and asked if, in view of a further ten-year period of occupation, something could be done to improve the exterior of the building. This would help give the building a look of being cared for and perhaps alleviate the misery of lack of space and congestion. Almost by return he received a three-line memo from the Director of Office Administration in London: 'It is, of course, unnecessary for me to comment to the effect that the congestion at Edinburgh is always curable by the transference of more staff to the commodious premises at Glasgow.'

Edinburgh's tail was definitely down.

The new premises in Glasgow were certainly going to be commodious. The main building of the College had been built in 1871, designed as a country mansion and private gallery for the brothers John and Matthew Bell who owned the Glasgow Pottery. They had been avid collectors of mediaeval works of art and it was their intention that the collection should remain in the various galleries of their house after their death, becoming the property of the people of Glasgow. One brother, Matthew, died before the house was completed. John, who lived in the house for nine years, died intestate and, as a result, the collection was dismantled and sold.

In 1884 the house and grounds became the home of Queen Margaret College, an 'Association for the Higher Education of Women' which later became incorporated with Glasgow University. During this period the College built a separate medical wing some distance to the rear of the main building. This building, erected in 1884 and housing lecture halls, dissecting rooms and a mortuary, was the work of the architects Honeyman and Keppie, (Honeyman had completed the work on the original Northpark House). The design was ostensibly John Keppie's but the hand of a young draughtsman, Charles Rennie Mackintosh, was clearly discernible.

Adapting the site for the BBC began in earnest in the autumn of 1936. The principal architect was James Miller, RSA, FRIBA, working closely with the BBC's Civil Engineer and the extensive alterations planned for the two existing buildings plus a brand new four-level block that would be built to join them meant at least two years' work.

It was certainly an outstanding development and represented a substantial extension and improvement of the facilities available for the production of Scottish programmes. With ten studios – three for music, four for drama and features and three for talks, narration and gramophone recitals – it would increase the Scottish stock by almost 100 per cent. No wonder speculation regarding the final location of the Scottish headquarters increased and soon even Reith was drawn into correspondence on the matter.

The Lord Provost of Glasgow had been delighted with the new role for Queen Margaret College and, in a congratulatory letter to the Director-General, he proposed that the BBC headquarters now move back to Glasgow. Replying, Reith betrayed an uncharacteristic lack of resolve. 'One could almost write a book on the Glasgow/Edinburgh question', he wrote. The letter continued. 'I will content myself here with saying that whichever may be the titular headquarters of the BBC in Scotland, we are abundantly committed to a duality which should prove satisfactory to both cities... We are ourselves rather in the dark as to what the eventual distribution of programme activity will be.'

In the same letter Reith used an expression that he was later to regret. Referring to the duality proposal he wrote, 'It is in pursuance of this solution that we have taken Queen Margaret College and are there making the finest *provincial headquarters* in the country.' Within days Edinburgh was beating on his door. No amount of assurance from Reith could lessen the concern of the City's Lord Provost who had obviously been told by a gleeful Glasgow that Edinburgh would no longer be the centre of Scottish broadcasting. Reith agreed that they would meet in London, an arrangement that had to be cancelled at the last minute when the Sheikh of Bahrein decided to visit Edinburgh. Once again the Orchestra was seen as the key. Were it to move, it would be clear that Glasgow was, indeed, the new headquarters in Scotland. Despite the size and lavishness of the largest of the three music studios under construction at Queen Margaret Drive, it gradually became clear that the BBC Symphony

Orchestra would continue to be based at 5 Queen Street. Edinburgh's 'headquarters' status was assured and relationships between the capital and the BBC became less anxious and formal. Besides, there were more serious things afoot than city rivalry.

For some time Scotland's programme makers had been climbing the ladder of professionalism, certainly in the eyes of the London management. But the expansion of ideas and techniques associated with broadcasting was so rapid and continuous it was difficult for 'provincials' to keep up. Glasgow, it was hoped, would solve the problem. The size of the new Broadcasting House was not to be seen as an indication that there would be more programmes, but rather a chance of improving quality by providing better facilities for rehearsal, studios with differing sound characteristics and space to house the many new technical developments that were being devised to meet the growing demands of broadcasting.

The development of modern drama facilities was probably the most important factor in the new complex. Scotland had begun to carve a niche for itself in this increasingly popular output. Because of the London dictum that all that was best, and that included sophisticated, came from the metropolis, radio drama in Scotland had become over-burdened with historical subjects and those relating to its regional traits. A few of the staff were aware of the stultifying effect of this narrow prospect with its constant repetition of character and situation. They were eager to break away but the tradition of Scottish theatre did not help and creative writing for broadcasting was still hard to come by.

In 1935, as an experiment, the BBC had launched a Scottish Radio Drama Festival and it had attracted sufficient interest to merit a second festival in October the following year. The choice of plays is interesting and the Herculean effort required to pack them into two weeks shows why the new premises were needed. There were three historical plays: *Douglas*, an adaptation by James Fergusson of John Home's tragedy; *The Laird of Kininmonth*, by S.C. Russell, adapted for broadcasting by Arthur Black; and *The Queen at Lochleven*, which had been specially written for radio by Horton Giddy.

Giddy's play was markedly different from the rest in that it gave a picture of the personality of Mary, Queen of Scots, without attempting to tell her life story and it dispensed with all archaisms in the dialogue. The remaining three plays were *Old Music* by Neil Gunn; *The Romance of Steam*, a dramatic documentary that had been written for the James Watt centenary; and *If Charles Came Back Today*, a fantasy by Allan MacKinnon – not a historical play but a satire on the attitude of contemporary commercialism and the traditional sentiments of Jacobite associations.

As there was still no permanent recording facility in Scotland the plays had to be transmitted live. While the original concept of drama broadcasting – one studio, one microphone and one clockwork gramophone – had been improved upon, the Drama Festival still meant a very intensive period of work. For three weeks, every evening was taken up with either rehearsals or broadcasts. Fifty different artists were contracted and some were used in more than one broadcast. All three Scottish centres were used and arrangements had to be made to release the four producers involved from all other commitments. Multiple studio working of a kind was now possible at the various centres, provide there were no other programmes waiting to broadcast but even so, conditions were cramped and the studio's fetid atmosphere called for boundless enthusiasm from everyone from the principal players to the effects boy kneeling in front of the actors, thundering out the horses' hooves as the hero fled from danger.

Production departments were not the only ones looking forward to using the new premises. The existing Glasgow Control Room had the reputation amongst engineers of being the most compact in the BBC. Others called it just plain congested and certainly one-way traffic was insisted on. For them, the spaciousness of the new technical areas was as attractive as the new and sophisticated equipment that was being installed. The engineers had another reason to be anxious about the progress being made at Queen Margaret College. In the late spring of 1938, the Empire Exhibition would be opened in Glasgow's Bellahouston Park and without some access to the new Broadcasting House and its facilities the planned coverage would be impossible.

Great national occasions had always been the backbone of broadcasting and had done much to establish the prestige of the BBC. From the launch of the great Cunarder by Queen Mary in 1924, the Silver Jubilee celebrations, the death of King George V, the Accession and then Abdication of Edward VIII and finally the Coronation of George VI, the BBC had never failed to meet the occasion. Now, four years after the 'Queen

Mary' broadcast, it was to be Scotland's turn again. Melville Dinwiddie considered the Exhibition to be of consuming importance. In his *The Scot and the Radio*, written ten years later, he spoke of it as a turning point of years of poverty, hardship and idleness for Scotland:

> Scotland was well on the way to regain her national consciousness. She was determined no longer to be classed as a northern 'province' of England but, by the character of her people and efficiency of her industry, to be regarded with that respect due to a nation with a long history and high traditions.

He could have said much the same about the upsurge of broadcasting in Scotland. True there had been disappointment over Queen Street in Edinburgh but Glasgow was soon to be formally opened as the BBC's latest and best-equipped studio premises. The decanting of Aberdeen from Belmont Street to Beechgrove would greatly improve facilities in the North of Scotland and new transmitters had brought many more listeners into the fold.

Given time, Scotland's broadcasters could progress the new self-determination. Given time. But a few sensed that the time was required for something else. As the BBC moved in on the Empire Exhibition, other broadcasts were being planned, including talks publicising Air Raid Precautions, appeals for defence volunteers and explanations of the approaching international crisis.

Against this somewhat sombre background, Scotland scheduled a number of programmes designed to anticipate and publicise the great Exhibition. News bulletins followed the progress on site as building began and the BBC erected a small pavilion to house an exhibition on broadcasting and to serve as a focal point for the many OBs which were planned.

The opening ceremony, including the King's speech, was broadcast on 3 May and from then on there was a constant stream of programmes from and about the Exhibition. It was the largest OB commitment of its time with over 200 broadcasts in six months and, in addition, there were studio programmes, most of which came from the new Queen Margaret College building.

The success of the BBC's coverage of the 1938 Empire Exhibition, with programmes reaching huge audiences through the domestic networks and the Empire Service, brought approval and admiration. Broadcasting in

Scotland, celebrating its 15th year, had come a long way from the days of father dabbing the crystal with the 'cats' whisker', grateful for any sound that came his way. The homely ways, scouring Glasgow to find a minister who would take a religious service, pulling a singer away by the coat-tails to make room for the next artist at the microphone – these were now things of the past. There was a professionalism and a discipline abroad that was felt to be synonymous with the initials BBC.

The frenetic burst of broadcasting activity in Scotland had emphasised the need for disciplined routine to balance the vitality and creativity that was inherent in broadcasters. Programmes were built, clicked into place and were gone, all almost as a matter of course and with nonchalant ease for, by now, it was a fetish that the listener must never sense that any-thing untoward might have taken place in the preparation or execution of the programme.

From the welter of features, discussions, interviews and actuality broad-casts that took place, two events are worth recalling. The first illustrates the BBC's status within the community, the second the attitudes that were occasionally brought into play within the organisation to ensure an out-ward appearance of efficiency and respectability.

During the period of the Exhibition the Glasgow studios at Queen Margaret Drive contributed a regular programme of interviews and news items dealing with visitors to Glasgow – a version of London's *In Town Tonight*. Much of the research for the programme was done by journalist Jack House and, late one afternoon, he heard that the evening's principal guest had called off. The programme was live and with time running very sort Jack remembered a young girl who was fast becoming a local celebrity. Her talents seemed boundless: amateur actress with the Pantheon Club, an appearance on the *Carroll Levis Show* where her impression of the Scots comic Tommy Morgan had brought the house down, and a capacity to write shorthand at 300 words per minute. A quick telephone call to her place of work and within minutes Glasgow's Molly Weir – whose talents as a comic actress and writer subsequently made her one of Scotland's most popular performers – was on a tramcar heading for the BBC's studios.

In her book, *A Toe on the Ladder*, Molly gives an entertaining account of what followed. To demonstrate the incredible speed of her shorthand she was given a piece of dictation, watched by a panel of newsmen in the studio and, of course invisible to the listening audience. Then Molly read the dictation back. The exercise was genuine enough. Molly could and did take dictation with incredible speed and accuracy but, on a radio programme with everyone silent except Molly and the reader, how could the listener know that there was no pre-arranged cheating?

Quite simply, the integrity of the BBC was already such as to make any kind of abuse of trust unthinkable. To the many people listening at home the BBC was one of the country's most respected institutions, lying somewhere between the church and the royal family. If you heard something stated on the radio it was bound to be true and that was an end to the matter.

The second was an OB programme, one of Peter Keith Murray's extravaganzas in the series, *A Night Out*. It was one of his usual ambitious hook-ups, aiming to visit, 'live', as many parts of the Exhibition as possible as could be crammed into the allotted time and many of Peter's production colleagues rallied round to help, acting as interviewers and commentators and dashing from one broadcasting point to another. As was to be expected, it was a frenzy of signals and handovers. 'I'm just going to nip over to...' and 'I'll have to trot over to...' became the precursor of nearly every change of location.

To the many people taking part it all seemed great fun and, as nobody had missed a cue or failed to speak, it was thought to have been quite a success. Next day, everyone was summoned to the Programme Director's room. They waited for his opinion of their previous night's work. Excellent? Workmanlike? Entertaining? Diverse? A job well done? The verdict when it came was brief and to the point. 'No BBC commentator (*would*) ever 'nip', 'pop' or 'trot' – they just 'go'.' They had been guilty of an unbuttoned moment on the air, an unforgivable gaffe.

It was a fairly strict regime, even for the period. Office routines were precise and formal and every letter that was typed, in any department, had to pass inspection by the Senior Stenographer before it went to the post room. For the girls dresses with short sleeves were actively discouraged, even in the height of summer, and the men were expected to wear hats. Any form of 'liaison' between the sexes was reported immediately and the management would 'warn off' the offending parties unless an engagement was in the offing.

Of course there was a healthy resistance to all this. Many romances flourished despite the dangers of infringing the rules and, as the BBC developed its inevitable group of characters, getting round authority often became something of a hobby. Professional friendships developed between writers, producers and performers resulting in a stimulating quality to the programmes and this was reflected in the Scottish service. It was distinctive, welding together patriotism and a cosmopolitan outlook and doing its best to reflect the character of the people of Scotland by giving something of their taste in music, entertainment and drama. What a pity it was soon to stop, turned off like a tap in the autumn of 1939.

There was a warning of what was to come during the crisis at the end of September the previous year. Regular national news bulletins were increased to six each day. Output was scrutinised for unacceptable themes and ideas – nothing must strike a false note – and for a period of seven days a single programme was transmitted by all Regions to allow greater centralised control. Eventually the crisis passed and in the aftermath a semblance of normality returned to broadcasting. Separate programming

Farewell 21 Blythswood Square, Glasgow (1938)
(l/r) Andrew Stewart, Scottish Programme Director; A.H. Swinton Paterson; Miss Bogue, Secretary to PD; G. Burnett; Sgt Charles Gordon.

was restored and Scotland, at least for the moment, was free to busy itself in its own backyard and that included formally opening its new premises in Glasgow and Aberdeen.

The Glasgow opening was truly a grand affair. The date was 18 November 1938 and as was still the tradition with such occasions, the evening's celebrations were broadcast live.

Once formal obeisances had been made in the direction of church, state and city, the proceedings swung into festive mood with Guy Warwick conducting the strings of the BBC Scottish Orchestra in a medley of Scottish dances. The large audience gathered in the huge and impressive Studio One were treated to a 'turn' from Will Fyffe, followed by the Glasgow Orpheus Choir conducted by Sir Hugh S. Roberton – their sonorous harmonies extracting every last ounce of emotion as the studio filled with the sound of *Crimond*, *Scots Wha Hae* and the *Eriskay Love Lilt*. Still there was more to come. Broadcast from other studios in the building and relayed to the Concert Hall audience on loudspeakers, there was *The Kitchen Comedy* – a play specially written for the occasion with a 'popular' cast that included Jean Taylor Smith, Eric Wightman, R.E. Kingsley and James McKechnie – and a short recital of Gaelic songs sung by James Macphee. Finally, the audience having been suitably refreshed with a buffet supper, the complete ensemble of the BBC Scottish Orchestra –

New premises at Queen Margaret Drive, Glasgow
(Formal opening 18 November 1938).

this time conducted by Ian Whyte – brought the evening to a rousing finish with *Tunes for Everybody*.

The general opinion was that it had been a successful demonstration of the BBC's capacity to fully utilise the Scots' ability to entertain and that drama, music and variety programmes would all benefit from the new Glasgow centre.

For Melville Dinwiddie, the Scottish Regional Director, it was a keenly felt moment. He had achieved the first of his longed for twin headquarters in Scotland. The impracticable and congested premises at Blythswood Square, totally inadequate for broadcasting the talent and material for which Glasgow was noted, could now be forgotten. The conditions at Edinburgh's Queen Street still occupied his mind but he knew that budgeting for the next few years, even if the country did not go to war, made any change in Edinburgh unlikely and he was more or less resigned to that fact. The formal opening of the Aberdeen premises at Beechgrove, scheduled for 9 December, was only three weeks away. That, combined with the new Aberdeen transmitter opened two months before on 9 September and now servicing the Aberdeen area with good coverage of Scottish programming, would provide that part of the country with efficient and modern technical resources.

Euphoria all round. Yet one thing seemed missing – wrong – out of place. J.C.W. Reith, one time General Manager and subsequently Director-General, had not been in his accustomed place on the VIP platform. By

**Farewell
15 Belmont Street,
Aberdeen (1938)**
Howard M. Lockhart (*back row second right*); to his left leaning forward and smiling – John Mearns, Doric entertainer and raconteur; to his right at the front – Violet Davidson, singer and entertainer.

now most of the staff had become used to the fact that Reith was no longer the BBC's Director-General but particularly for Melville Dinwiddie, when faced with an occasion like this, it was difficult to adjust to the change. It was five months since Reith had left the BBC and almost his last action on behalf of Scotland had been a small favour for the Scottish Director. 1938 was not only the year of new premises, transmitters and the Empire Exhibition, it was also the 15th birthday of the BBC in Scotland. To celebrate, the Scottish Region published a small book and Melville Dinwiddie had asked John Reith to contribute a foreword. Characteristically, it was concise and to the point.

'This book has nothing to do with me', he wrote. 'I was instructed by Mr Dinwiddie to write a preface. I am always glad to do what he wants. Broadcasting is making good progress in Scotland and its value is more and more being realised.'

It was a well-timed, valedictory message to a respected friend. Despite its grandiose opening, Glasgow's Broadcasting House stayed disappointingly under-used during the early months of 1939. Indeed the new premises at Beechgrove, opened three weeks after Glasgow by the Marchioness of Aberdeen and Temair, was a hive of activity in comparison. Aberdeen's programmes had prospered in the care of Howard M. Lockhart and Alan Melville and Arthur Black, Addie Ross, Dorothy Farrell, 'Rab the Rhymer', John Mearns and many more were making regular visits to the new studios. Glasgow would come into its own eventually but for the moment it merely ticked over in the aftermath of the Exhibition at Bellahouston Park and betrayed little or no outward sign of the increasing reference being made to it as the BBC finalised its plans for Scotland should war come.

The government had decided that a wartime BBC would not be taken over but instead would work in close liaison with the Ministry of Information and already the BBC was preparing changes. Staff were being classified for availability – liable for war service, too old to be mobilised or 'reserved' for broadcasting duties – and some were allocated 'wartime' stations, often at diametrically opposed locations to their home base. Bemused Edinburgh engineers would soon find themselves hurrying off to parts of England while staff in the south would come over the border to replace them – a sure sign that the BBC was not immune to the fervour of wartime bureaucracy.

New premises at Beechgrove Terrace
Aberdeen opened 9 December 1938.

A number of studios would be closed down and, as it was known that the existing methods of radio transmission could give considerable guidance to enemy aircraft, preparations were made for a wholesale re-arrangement of wavelengths and the closure of the fledgling television service. Such was the discipline and single-mindedness of the Engineering Division, the time allowed to make all the necessary changes was only two hours.

On Friday 1 September, two days before the start of hostilities, the expected instructions were signalled to all BBC premises and the Corporation quickly moved on to a war footing. Well within the allotted two hours all out-of-London broadcasting ceased and a new announcement was heard throughout all of the country for the first time. 'This is the BBC Home Service' identifying a single channel for all listeners. Press notices were issued giving details of the new wavelengths and a telegram was sent for display in post office windows throughout the country. In Scotland, listeners found themselves cut off from their familiar programmes almost at a 'click' and, like the rest of the country, soon discovered that the new 'Home Service' was a gloomy mixture of official instructions and announcements, wrapped around with gramophone records.

The Scottish staff consulted railway timetables and packed their bags. Some were off to war, others were travelling to alternative studio centres. One significant move was the departure of the BBC Scottish Orchestra from Edinburgh to Glasgow. Not surprising, as part of the contingency plans for Scotland had included greater use of the new Glasgow complex, referred to as 'our battle centre in Scotland' because of the quality and strength of the work that had gone into the construction of the studios, and a belief that the east coast was more liable to air attack.

CHAPTER FIVE

The War Years

'THE DAY WAR BROKE OUT...' was the catchphrase of Robb Wilton's Mr Muddlecombe, a national favourite in wartime broadcasting. It was usually the start of some uproarious piece of reminiscence and the audience would laugh because they were on familiar ground. Everybody could remember where they were the day war broke out. Strange though it may seem now, it was a remarkable fact of the time. Until 25 years before, the country had learned of calamity and disaster slowly and over a period of time through newspapers, proclamation and word of mouth. Now, with close on 800,000 wireless licences in Scotland alone, almost every family in the land sat anxiously in front of their radio set. Nothing could have established the new Home Service more than when, at 11.15am on Sunday 3 September 1939, the transmitters of the BBC radiated the voice of the Prime Minister: 'I am speaking to you from the Cabinet Room at 10 Downing Street... This country is at war with Germany.'

The nation was united and the BBC had been the catalyst. Now the provider of a national service, it was important that the broadcasters hold the confidence of their audience. Yet in the immediate weeks following the September announcement, broadcasting was so dull and uninspired it verged on the ridiculous.

At first the lack of entertainment and the absence of favourite programmes went unnoticed. There were other things to think about such as evacuation, mobilisation and possible air attacks. People were hungry for news – there were now ten daily bulletins – and official announcements and government-inspired talks seemed to trip over themselves in their haste to get on the air. By chance, Scotland contributed within days of hostilities starting. On 5 September, the weary and exhausted survivors from the torpedoed ship Athena came to the Glasgow studios to speak of their ordeal and a few days later Edinburgh provided an eyewitness account of an air raid on the Firth of Forth. Eventually, however, the absence of entertainment became apparent and as the BBC persisted with a never-ending diet of music and official information – Sandy McPherson at the theatre organ made 45 broadcasts in the first fortnight – there were innumerable complaints from listeners. With most of the country's theatres and cinemas closed, people were hard-pressed to find some variety and a vista of nightly bouts of snap, charades and songs around the piano did nothing for the morale.

In Scotland Melville Dinwiddie viewed the broadcasting scene, or rather the lack of it, with some despair. His once thriving Scottish service had all but stopped and many of its principal people had gone. Andrew Stewart was seconded to the Ministry of Information on 31 August while Gordon Gildard, his senior producer responsible for drama output, was recalled to the navy. Others were either awaiting call-up or dispersed to distant broadcasting centres. He knew full well the importance of sustaining morale and the few items of orchestral music being played by the BBC Scottish Orchestra from their new home in Glasgow, plus such bits and pieces of news that were allowed by the censor, hardly constituted a Scottish presence on the Home Service. Not a man to be silent for long, he decided to approach London with a bid to get Scotland moving again. Scotland could produce two daily programmes that would minister to both the physical and spiritual requirements of the nation? These would be ten minutes of physical jerks, preceded by a brief and comforting expression of religious faith?

Over the years the BBC had considered various ideas for morning exercises. Indeed as far back as 1925 it had outlined proposals for such a broadcast to the Ministry of Health, who were then acting as the arbiter for Public Health talks. The reply was frosty and contemptuous: 'At that time in the morning the lady or gentleman ought to be engaged in dressing and ablutions.' The letter went on to condemn the idea on medical grounds saying that it looked a little like prescribing for the patient without seeing him – a very improper procedure. The BBC lost interest, although enthusiasts continued to write in asking for Keep Fit programmes. One correspondent conjured up a fearsome image: 'I have a couple of kids – a boy, ten, and a girl, nine, and given such a programme at 7.30am, I can see them on the line promptly in their nursery as naked as they arrived and as keen as mustard.'

Now with the country at war and fitness a priority, Dinwiddie not only got a hearing but speedy approval for his suggestion and the early morning exercise along with a daily five-minute religious talk were launched by Scotland.

Both programmes started on 4 December 1939. Contributors to the religious programme *Lift Up Your Hearts – A Thought For Today* were allowed a surprisingly free hand with both themes and content and within weeks of starting the programme had become an accepted part of broadcasting. *Up In The Morning Early* took longer to settle. It was more of an experiment and a variety of styles were tried including using the orchestra. Finally by mid-March an acceptable formula had been found: two presenters, J. Coleman Smith, a PT instructor at the nearby Glasgow Academy and May Brown, and music by a staff pianist. The Central Council of Recreative Physical Training formed an Advisory Panel and, perhaps the greatest accolade of all, the Variety department started devising comedy routines such as *Morning Capers, Came The Dawn – With a Jerk* and *More's the PT*! The programme would last throughout the war, with its final broadcast, by now called *The Daily Dozen*, on Friday 1 September 1945.

As both the programmes were transmitted live, they brought a great deal of early morning activity to Queen Margaret Drive, Glasgow. One of the BBC's two pianists, Andrew Bryson or Barbara Laing, would be on hand from shortly after 6.00am along with two producers (one for each programme), a duty announcer and a third producer whose job it was to man the censor key, ready to take the programme off the air the instant there was the slightest deviation from the script. The fact that the English were being uplifted, both body and soul, by broadcasting from Scotland may have puffed out some chests with pride but it fashioned a yoke of shivering despair for the producers and engineers who were scheduled for duty on freezing, fuel-starved Glasgow mornings!

Gradually the Home Service relaxed its regime of gloom and doom and a more liberal approach, particularly with music, began to infiltrate the day's broadcasting, keeping the Scottish music studios fairly busy. The orchestra seemed settled in its new home and there were rumours that the BBC's Military Band was about to be evacuated from London to the safety of 'Fortress Scotland'. In fact, this was fiercely resisted by the members of the Band and did not take place until October 1940.

Scotland's many excellent brass and silver bands were making numerous broadcasts and a wartime schools service, quickly off the mark with special programmes on 5 September, carried *Singing Together* presented from Glasgow by Herbert Wiseman with Harry Hoggan and Elliott Dobbie.

Some song recitals were beginning to find their way back into the schedules – German Lieder to be avoided – and choral programmes were eagerly welcomed by the entertainment-starved listeners. Still Dinwiddie wanted more. Supported by Moultrie Kelsall, who had returned to Scotland to take the place of Andrew Stewart, he strove to increase the Scottish output whenever an opportunity offered itself.

A very early success was, to everyone's surprise, in Gaelic broadcasting. The Scottish Director was deeply concerned that wartime broadcasting restrictions caused the greatest hardship to listeners in isolated areas and the Gaelic-speaking communities were, he felt, particularly at risk. The total Gaelic-speaking population was then thought to be about 100,000 and as a proportion of the UK, it did not rate much attention. Not that is until someone pointed out that the percentage of men from the Highlands and Islands in the services, especially the navy and the merchant navy, was well above average. The British sense of fair play found this irresistible and the Gaelic tongue was invited back on to the air.

Herbert Wiseman in Schools broadcast *Singing Together* (1941)
He later became Head of Music.

Its first wartime appearance was on the 216.1m wavelength along with a broadcast in Welsh and the first full-length programme was transmitted on 30 November 1939 – St Andrew's Day. A propitious start and, considering it was a mixture of music and news review, it was probably thought by the many non-Scots who heard it to be a form of national celebration. For the next few months Gaelic had an occasional airing, becoming a permanency in the spring of 1940 when, on 27 April, BBC Scotland broadcast the first five–minute weekly bulletin of news in Gaelic on the UK medium-wave Home Service.

Occasionally these incursions into an essentially English-speaking world caused some surprise, as on the occasion in London when a distinguished American radio commentator was in Broadcasting House listening to the Home Service. It was around 10.00pm and the well-known voice of announcer Frank Phillips was signing-off the previous programme. There was the statutory five seconds pause and then the next announcement – in Gaelic. The American leapt out of his chair. 'God Almighty – what's that?'

'The Gaelic programme', was the reply. He asked how many spoke the language and was told. For a moment he paused. Then, with a rueful shake of the head, said, 'It just couldn't happen in the United States.'

Writing after the war, Dinwiddie made a point of praising the contribution that the Highlands and the Gael had made to the diversity of Scottish broadcasting. He included in his tribute the songs and the music, the assets of the regiments and the unspoiled naturalness of the people themselves. He could have mentioned one more thing – the cunning of a certain Lieutenant Brock of the Belgian underground who used Gaelic programmes as a means of getting BBC news. It seems that the German occupying forces in his area believed that what he was listening to was Flemish and left him to his own devices as he happily distributed, by word of mouth, the various news items he had heard through the Gaelic services.

It would be wrong to imply that Gaeldom was completely satisfied with what Dinwiddie had achieved. Late in 1940 a meeting of the An Comunn Gàidhealach executive expressed dissatisfaction with what was being done. They wanted two news bulletins per week instead of one, and a *Children's Hour* programme in Gaelic. Shortly afterwards the matter was raised in the House of Commons. In a written reply it was stated that, since 1 October of that year there had been three and a quarter hours of Gaelic broadcasting in the Home Service programme plus a weekly 40 minutes of 'Highland' music. This, it was felt, was quite sufficient. It probably was, considering the 'blanket' coverage of the Home Service. The real surprise came at the end of the statement – the fact that there were no broadcasts in Gaelic in the Forces Programme. After all, the case put forward at the start of the war had been based on the number of Gaelic speakers who were serving at sea and in the Forces.

The Forces Programme had started early in 1940 designed as a service for the British Expeditionary Force in France and an 'alternative' service in the UK. The emphasis was on variety, light music and sport – a few considered it to be 'excessively light' – and very soon the BBC's Listener Research department was reporting a huge audience. As well as being a welcome alternative to the Home Service it was the harbinger of good news for Scottish broadcasting, for the substantial increase in broadcasting hours meant much greater output. Scotland welcomed the prospect of more to do but anguished that some provision must be made for broadcasting in the Scottish idiom, and Dinwiddie set about getting a regular spot on the Home Service as it would, as he put it, 'keep alive our native music and story.' Lest the London management prove stubborn he made sure that the matter reached ministerial level. Tom Johnston, shortly afterwards Secretary of State for Scotland in Churchill's wartime coalition cabinet, had consultations with the Minster of Information and the outcome was the introduction *of Scottish Half-Hour* in September 1940.

Into the programme went all the familiar ingredients of pre-war Scottish broadcasting, heavily condensed. It was a microcosm of Andrew Stewart's schedules – the leading figures of church, state and the universities and the familiar voices and songs that had become popular in the late 1930s. The programme was avowedly for Scots and, while contributors were encouraged to keep in mind the possibility of interesting and holding the English audience, they were instructed not to mar the programme in any way because of sticky patches for listeners in the rest of the country.

It was good advice and few of the Scottish producers disagreed. There was no reason why intelligible Scots should not be used provided it had something to say. The danger lay in those people who might confuse natural dialect with the patter of the music hall. The heavyweights of the Scots Comic Brigade were now well to the fore in both the Home and Forces wavelengths – Sir Harry Lauder, Will Fyffe and Harry Gordon –

and they and many more, complete with 'hoochs' and giggles, broad vowels and the rolling 'r', were becoming the archetypal Scot to many southern ears. Happily they were counterbalanced by an increasing flow of features and plays and soon other Scottish names were seen once more in the *Radio Times* – Edwin Muir, Neil Gunn, J.M. Barrie, James Bridie and Eric Linklater – presenting a different image of Scotland, using more cultured tones.

Natural accents, as distinct from the professionally wrought intonations of actors, were difficult to find on the radio. Although actuality broadcasts and interviews were on the increase again, people were often overwhelmed by the thought of 'being on the wireless' and would make wild, uncomfortable attempts to speak 'BBC English'. As nearly every interview was pre-written and then read, the result was often excruciating. What finally became accepted as the sound of Scotland was 'BBC Scots' developed by the BBC and a tight little band of semi-professional actors and reasonably faithful to its roots as well as being intelligible the length and breadth of the UK. Just as important, it was intelligible abroad, for by the end of 1940 the number of broadcasts made by Scotland on the External Services exceeded the total for home consumption – a demand that resulted in another Scottish series, this time for overseas.

Scotland had become particularly adept at using the strong emotional ties of 200 years of emigration. There were programmes linking towns and other cities with the same name and, remembering the many Scottish societies in America, Canada and Australasia, there were series about famous clans and Scottish regiments. *Children's Hour* arranged programmes for the parents of evacuees, uniting them with their children in Canada and America for a brief exchange of personal messages over the air, and colonial troops came to the studios to broadcast to various parts of the world. A contemporary account of such an occasion in Edinburgh recalls 'a young lady announcer in the best traditions of the famous Mary Slessor restoring order out of what seemed like an African riot in the artists' lounge in Edinburgh.'

Her name was Pamela Patterson and she continued announcing and keeping order until her retirement from BBC Scotland in 1979.

Here was another change, not just in Scotland but also throughout the BBC: the recruitment of women for a wide variety of jobs. Women had begun replacing men almost from the outset of the war. The Corporation

Elizabeth Adair (*front left*), Producer, *In the Country* and guests in studio at Coldside Library, Dundee (1951).

was not over keen to use them on the air as announcers or as producers working in London but the Regions were less inhibited. The first woman announcer in Scotland, Elizabeth Adair, was appointed in November 1940. A few months later, advertisements appeared in the press inviting engineering applications for the appointment of 'Women Operators' and the first four to be allocated to Glasgow reported for duty in the Control Room. Women were also considered for posts at some of the transmitters. Sometimes the first inkling of this, certainly as far as engineering at Fraserburgh was concerned, was a memo that read: 'It is probable that women operators will be posted to your station. Please obtain and forward to me a plan and price for the erection of extra toilet accommodation.'

When BBC Scotland chose Elizabeth Adair, the news of her appointment was greeted in the Aberdeen press with the headline, 'This woman has got BBC style.' A touch parochial, perhaps, for there was a strong Aberdeen connection. She was the daughter of H. Adair Nelson, who had been the first manager of His Majesty's Theatre, Aberdeen. But Elizabeth did indeed have style and she was a happy choice for Scotland. She had been recruited to replace Howard M. Lockhart who had been brought to Glasgow from Aberdeen and was now being released by the BBC for military service. The Aberdeen Broadcasting House at Beechgrove, like so many other small stations, had all but closed at the outbreak of war leaving only a small engineering staff supervising the technical needs of the Home Service as it passed on its way to the local and northern transmitters.

Howard M. Lockhart
Producer, with Jean
Taylor Smith reading a
letter in *Strike A Home
Note* for troops in India
(1944).

For her first year Elizabeth Adair worked in Glasgow. Then, in mid-1941, when the BBC relaxed its early wartime stringency, she was offered the chance to go to Aberdeen as producer to open up broadcasting again. She needed no second bidding. For the next few years Elizabeth carried on virtually as a one woman operation, out combing the North East for interviews and news stories and back in the studio putting together various programmes involving the stalwarts of Aberdeen broadcasting. Alan Melville, hearing of her new posting, had given her a host of performers and writers which she put to good use and the Aberdeen Station Representative, Alex H. Swinton Paterson from the early Glasgow 5SC days, along with engineers W.W. Inder and J.A. Beveridge, did everything possible to help.

One of Elizabeth's first missions from Aberdeen was to talk to some fishermen at Fraserburgh Harbour. Afterwards, as she made her way along the main street to the Saltoun Hotel, a solitary German plane dived out of the sky and proceeded to spray the street with bursts of machine gun fire. The bullets narrowly missed her as she dived for the safety of the Hotel's pillared doorway and it was with relief that she swallowed a glass of whisky later, watching from the lounge window as the plane eventually flew off towards the North Sea.

Elizabeth's visit to Fraserburgh had been partly because of two fundamental and related changes taking place within broadcasting. Mobile disc recording was now readily available and news had acquired a high profile and was demanding frequent eyewitness reports and on-the-spot interviews.

Recording had appeared in London at the start of the 1930s when the BBC experimented with three different systems – wire/steel-tape recording (based on the Blattnerphone), a new kind of film recording being developed by Philips and recording onto a lacquer coated metal disc, known as the Watts machine. The disc system won the battle for mobile work and, by early 1935, had been installed in the first of the BBC's mobile units, described by some as a cross between a bus and a van. It proved to be a success and shortly afterwards two more were ordered, this time for work outside London where Scotland and the English North Region would share one van between them, an arrangement that was to be repeated 20 years later when mobile television units were being allocated.

Unfortunately, the new regional vans suffered from 'improvements' which greatly increased their size and weight. They weighed almost seven tons when loaded and were over 23ft in length, and to make matters worse, head office decided that the news vans would be based in London, only making occasional forays to other parts. Later common sense prevailed and by 1938 one unit was based in Manchester to serve the north of the country. It was also realised that mobility was inversely related to size and that recording cars would be a more practical concept, particularly where news gathering was concerned.

Within a few months of the outbreak of war, gathering news became a priority and mobile recording gear and technicians were stationed permanently in Scotland. An early assignment was to travel to Haddington to cover the story of the first German aeroplane to be brought down on British soil. The ensuing interview with the farm grieve who was an eyewitness electrified the 1.00pm news with his description, 'Whiles we were runnin' in and whiles we were runnin' oot.'

News was all-important. A special unit had been established in Scotland and it broke some outstanding stories including first person accounts by the Ballachulish soldiers, captured at St Valery, who escaped and bluffed their way across France into Spain pretending to be Russians and speaking nothing but Gaelic, the incredible tale of the tanker *San Demetrio*, and interviews with the family and soldiers who captured Rudolph Hess after his forced landing near Eaglesham. This last story almost didn't materialise as far as the BBC was concerned and a fairly high-powered post-mortem ensued. It seems that when word of the event first came through, neither of the BBC's reporters could be found and, as a result, it was some considerable time before they, and the Scottish recording car, arrived to cover the story. They set about gathering some eyewitness accounts in an effort to retrieve the situation but the people who *had* been involved – particularly a farmer's wife – were now fed up with all the badgering and questions from the press. The resulting discs were almost unusable and required a great deal of editing to remove the strong language.

Because of the shambles Melville Dinwiddie decided that the time was ripe for some order to be brought to the news unit and he summoned back to Scotland a previous member of staff who had been posted to Bristol at the start of the war. The man he chose was Archie P. Lee, previously the press officer for the BBC in Glasgow for 18 months when he had replaced Robert Kemp who had departed to London, and now a war correspondent in Bristol attached to Southern Command. A recurring illness had just lost him his grade 'A' fitness categorisation and he was about to be replaced by Frank Gillard. Archie arrived in Glasgow to become War News Organiser – the first accredited member of the Scottish staff engaged completely on news matters – and although he was not to stay long before moving south again his brief tutelage stabilised the department and the number of stories from and about Scotland increased.

One problem that could not be overcome, and it was not just in news programmes, was the vexed question of censorship – the fear that something might be said, or implied, that would help the enemy. The 'switch' censors in the studio were there to make sure that no-one made a last minute deviation from the script but they were the last line of defence. The important measures were taken days, if not weeks, before the broadcast.

Most material was required to pass two inspections – the BBC's, who still maintained a rigorous watch on the output, and the Censor, who trawled for indiscretions, secret codes and heaven knows what. References to the weather were deleted and helpful hints on such problems as frozen pipes were very suspect. It was even thought that there were might be problems with the music used in *The Daily Dozen* and the tunes had to be cleared weeks before.

The idea that some transmissions might contain hidden information was not totally imaginary. Far from it, for the British authorities themselves were burying secret messages in some apparently innocuous programmes that were being broadcast by the BBC. One such vehicle – *The Radio Padre* – had a strong link with Scotland and the BBC's Scottish Regional Director.

The Radio Padre talks, transmitted on the Forces Programme on Wednesday nights after the 9.00pm news, were one of the most successful broadcast series of the war and at one time achieved a listening audience of ten million, something close to the figure for the famous *ITMA* series with Tommy Handley. The series, which ran from 1941 until the end of the war, was due largely to the friendship of three men: J.W. Welch, Melville Dinwiddie and Ronald Selby Wright.

J.W. Welch was the BBC's Director of Religious Broadcasting and a friend of Dinwiddie's to whom he turned when he was looking for a suitable speaker to present a short weekly series for men on gun sites as there were anti-aircraft units spread throughout the country, mostly on isolated and lonely stations. Dinwiddie immediately suggested Ronald

Selby Wright, a man who had done some broadcasting in Scotland before the war and was now a chaplain with a Territorial Battalion. He was, as it turned out, an ideal choice but proving the point took months of almost asinine negotiations with the War Office on the one hand putting up every conceivable kind of difficulty and the BBC absorbing them all like some great enveloping Mother Superior. Throughout it all, Welch kept up a flow of encouraging letters – 'Don't be disheartened, we shall drive this thing through if it means marching the ecclesiastical hierarchy to the War Office' – but in the end it was

Radio Padre
Very Reverend Ronald Selby Wright
(Moderator, Church of Scotland in 1972).
(© Church of Scotland)

Melville Dinwiddie who settled the matter in a time-honoured and gastro-nomic way by lunching the Army's Chaplain-General.

The *Radio Padre* gave his first broadcast on 1 April 1942 and from the beginning justified Dinwiddie's belief that he could create a new approach to religious broadcasting that would be easily understood. Ronald Selby Wright always felt honoured that he had been asked and made light of some of the trials and afflictions that came his way, visiting numerous lonely gun sites dotted all over the country, receiving as many as 60 to 100 letters a day – one broadcast produced over 1,000 – and often getting very little help in the by-going. There was also a hidden responsibility. Some time after the series got under way, his co-operation was sought, in secret, by MI9 at the War Office. Briefly the proposition was that he incorporate into his script coded messages that would convey essential information to Allied prisoners of war held in Europe, escapees and the resistance. His decision to go along with the scheme was not an easy one to take but eventually he agreed.

This special War Office task sometimes caused unexpected difficul-ties which were never fully explained until years later. The supervision of the talks when they came from the Edinburgh studios was frequently the responsibility of Pamela Patterson, the young female announcer based at 5 Queen Street. In reminiscent mood more than 30 years later she recalled her irritability on those occasions: 'The man was always late with his script. He knew it had to be passed by the censor, but even when I pressed him it was usually late.'

No wonder. For more often than not Selby Wright had to wait until the last minute before the coded message was woven into his talk. It is a tribute to the trustworthiness of those few people in the BBC who knew what was going on that Pamela and others like her remained oblivious for years after the war.

Whatever the outcome of its clandestine side, the success of the *Radio Padre* series was largely due to the fact it was something entirely new. In Dinwiddie's words: 'the creation of a radio personality who could speak to, and gain, the confidence of those on military service.' Broadcasting, almost unwittingly, was discarding formality and in the process getting even closer to its audience. A happy state of affairs, and in line with Melville Dinwiddie's intense commitment to using broadcasting to bolster confidence and he was never happier than when a Scot was involved.

As early as December 1939, W.A. Sinclair of Edinburgh University had started a series of talks, 'The Voice of the Nazi'. These were an exposé of German propaganda methods and were broadcast from London, an example of how centralised broadcasting became at the start of the war. Again Dinwiddie was particularly pleased with the series. He deplored the BBC's tendency to hush up any references to German broadcasts, feeling that this was head in the sand attitude that only served to give Lord Haw-Haw and other propaganda broadcasts an attractive air of mystery. W.A. Sinclair's broadcasts certainly helped to dispel the growing aura of bewilderment. In fact so effective was he in putting the German propaganda machine into proper perspective the notorious Dr Goebbels publicly vowed that he would be killed and as a consequence Sinclair was permitted to carry a firearm with which to protect himself.

Also counteracting German propaganda and putting the record straight, this time for overseas listeners, was another Scot, Alan Melville. The pre-war 'Mister Mole' of Aberdeen's Children's Hour had been moved south where, amongst other things, he wrote and produced Front Line Family, the first of the BBC's regular soap operas. It started life on the Overseas Service on 28 April 1941, portraying a middle-class English family coping with the war. Eventually the title was changed to The Robinson Family and at the end of the war it transferred to the Light Programme, where it ran until 1947.

As the BBC slipped naturally into its role of loyal support it became increasingly wary of anything in its programmes that might be construed as unpatriotic. It was determined to root out anything that could be even remotely considered as 'doubtful' and an early purge was, to many people's surprise, The Glasgow Orpheus Choir. The Choir had made its first wartime broadcast in December 1939 and had quickly become an integral part of the BBC's popular musical front. But its conductor and founder, Sir Hugh S. Roberton, was known to have strong pacifist views and the time came when the BBC, encouraged by the Ministry of Information, decided that pacifists should be prohibited from all forms of broadcasting. What was most surprising about the ban was its blanket application. No pacifists to speak was understandable but to forbid singers, actors, performers and conductors did seem a touch extreme. However, the rules were clear and Roberton and the Glasgow Orpheus Choir were shown the door.

Eventually, in March 1941, the Corporation's policy was questioned in the House of Commons and a reference was made to the absence of the Glasgow Choir because of the views of its conductor. The Prime Minister, Mr Churchill, voiced an opinion. 'I see no reason to suppose that the holding of pacifist views would make him play flat.' That was sufficient to lift the ban and Sir Hugh and his Choir duly returned to the Glasgow studios, their mellifluous harmonies, thought by many to be an important support of the public morale, one again surging over the Home and Forces wavelengths. Unfortunately, relationships between the BBC's Scottish Director and the Choir's Conductor, for long at variance, did not improve and they continued to circle each other like a couple of wily protagonists.

At the time much was made of the differing opinions of the two men. The implication was that Melville Dinwiddie had consciously sought to ban the Choir's founder because of their contrasting attitudes. One was an avowed pacifist, openly against the war and the other a one-time regular officer in the Gordon Highlanders, awarded the Military Cross in 1915 and the DSO for gallantry at the Battle of Arras in 1917. But it was easy, too easy, to assume that this contrast was the root cause of the antipathy between them when in point of fact their differences sprang as much from something much more closely connected with broadcasting.

Roberton's Choir had grown up with the century. Its first London concert had been in 1908. 1926 had seen it touring Canada and the USA, to be followed by a Command Performance at Balmoral Castle. By 1931 broadcasts were a regular occurrence. Sir Hugh always introduced the Choir and the selection of items and on matters of delivery and timing he would brook no interference. Gradually habit, an ever-growing reputation and Sir Hugh Roberton's appointment to the BBC's Music Advisory Committee in Scotland made coverage virtually automatic. No-one was prepared to question their style or the content of their programmes and the attitude of the Choir's founder became increasingly imperious. Others suffered in a similar way and in the autumn of 1937 the Northern Ireland Programme Director did not mince his words when writing to Scotland:

> While we have the highest opinion of this Choir, we do not feel that it is possible to maintain the prestige of the BBC while further submitting to the ruthless disregard of instructions and requests

which is now a part of Sir Hugh Roberton's make up... When any conductor, however, important, blandly and continually disregards the requests of the BBC, we can no longer employ him in this Region.

The response from Scotland was muted cheers: 'You will have done us a real service if this brings the matter to a head.' But deep down, it was known that Roberton enjoyed a privileged position vis-a-vis head office and this immediate reaction would be a direct approach to the Director-General.

For years Melville Dinwiddie had been able to do little but quietly seethe with anger as he watched Roberton ride roughshod over his staff. He appreciated the quality of the Choir's music and was more than willing to respect their conductor's skill with arrangements and tonal effect. It was Roberton's undisciplined manner and presentation that annoyed him.

'He comes to the microphone breathless after conducting the various items', he wrote, 'and his sentimental approach to the whole thing reduces its presentation value.'

When the BBC finally rescinded its ban on Sir Hugh, noting in a letter written by the Director-General that the Scottish Director had only been following instructions, Dinwiddie wondered if it would be possible to have the Choir back, but restrain Roberton from speaking at the microphone.

There was plenty of support from elsewhere, but head office vacillated to an alarming degree. Finally, in June 1941, Dinwiddie bowed to the inevitable and Sir Hugh Roberton returned to the air, introducing his Choir. In a written report on the broadcast, the Scottish Director could not resist once again drawing attention to the breathlessness of the introductions and the programme's bad timing. He finished with a sting in the tale: 'An "Alert" of ten minutes during the transmission would prevent many listeners in Glasgow and South Scotland from hearing the whole of the programme. The fact that this was the first "Alert" in the afternoon seems almost a judgement on Roberton.'

Ten years later the Choir was disbanded. The BBC made an album of their best-known songs and presented it to Sir Hugh. The note inside read, 'To Sir Hugh Roberton, with deep gratitude for all his fine broadcasts with the Glasgow Orpheus Choir.' The first of the signatures was that of Melville Dinwiddie.

The return of the Choir to broadcasting happened at a time when the amount of music coming from the Glasgow studios was reaching inordinately high levels. The BBC's Military Band had finally arrived in 'Fortress Scotland' in October 1940 and had settled into two years of sharing Glasgow's Studio One with the BBC Scottish Orchestra, bringing with them a lively professionalism that did no harm to the coteries of musicians already dug in at Queen Margaret Drive and more than few lasting friendships were formed. Inevitably the increasing number of regimental and service bands would eclipse the Military Band and result in its break-up in 1943, but for the moment it was a popular source of radio entertainment as well as being a handy income supplement for landladies in the West End of Glasgow.

Besides a busy Studio 1, music was taking up a great deal of time in another studio – Studio 2 in the old medical building, now the unofficial home of the Scottish Variety Orchestra. This Orchestra was a piece of wartime extemporisation designed to accompany variety programmes and perform a repertoire of light music and Scottish dance music. Formed in 1941 in the loosest of ways, the players were not even placed on part-time contracts until 1948, and it was the idea of Moultrie Kelsall and conductor Ronnie Munro, friends from the days of pre-war television at Alexandra Palace. They had seen the need for a musical combination to meet the increasing demand for programmes that were bright and lively and had easily persuaded the Home Service and Forces Programme to take its light music sessions.

Ian Whyte, as Director of Music, 'regretted' such an orchestra, so the conductor worked directly to the light entertainment producer. In later years this 'untouchable' position would work to the detriment of the svo but for the moment they were happy days.

Every Sunday morning, live, the showcase of the Orchestra's programmes, *Sunday Serenade*, would take the air. The red light in the studio would flicker and steady, a brief announcement and straight into Ronnie's signature tune *Highland Swing*. The precise voice of Madeleine Christie introduced a march, followed by vocal numbers sung by Ann Rich, Jae Fraser and Ian Gourlay. Then there might be a trumpet solo, Ronnie Munro at the piano, a Scots selection from the Orchestra, a couple of Scots songs from Janette Sclanders and before long the programme was over with the timing precise. A fine example of cool professionalism involving everyone from the conductor to soloists, players, engineers and house staff, and in the meticulous way that was then a characteristic of the BBC, even the payment cheques for the artists were awaiting their signature at the front door reception as they left.

With programme production again on the increase in Scotland, staff found themselves also caught up in various extraneous responsibilities caused by war. In Glasgow a local BBC contingent of the Home Guard had been formed and sentries were posted in the grounds. J. Mouland Begbie, the leader of the BBC Scottish Orchestra, caused more than a little consternation when he accidentally discharged a round from his rifle into the ceiling of the band room. Demonstrating that the bullets were real, it put the rest of the staff on their toes for the next few weeks and every challenge during the hours of darkness drew an immediate response. There was also a fire-watching rota at each centre with teams sleeping on the premises and taking shifts 'on watch', patrolling the roofs of the buildings. Eventually this need for vigilance was fully justified when Glasgow began to receive increased attention from the Luftwaffe, culminating in a crippling attack on Clydebank in the spring of 1941.

During the nights of 14 and 15 March 1941, enemy aircraft dropped over 1,000 bombs in the Glasgow area close to the River Clyde. The BBC premises at Queen Margaret Drive remained unscathed, although at 12.30pm on the first night it was, for a few seconds, touch and go. A large German land mine, drifting down attached to its dark green parachute, missed the top of Studio One by less than 50ft and a matter of moments later crossed the River Kelvin and exploded on the far bank from the BBC. A warden's post and police box were completely demolished, killing the occupants, and considerable damage was done to flats and shops in Queen Margaret Road. First reports were of six people dead with close on 50 trapped or injured in the surrounding flats, and it was the following evening before the last survivor was rescued and all the bodies recovered.

On the BBC site the damage was minimal – some broken windows along the north side where protective shutters had folded in like sheets of cardboard and the shattered nerves of those on fire duty who had seen the huge bomb gliding noiselessly above their heads.

The Scottish audience, in common with the rest of the country, had an insatiable appetite for this kind of news, and of course, any item that had a particular reference to Scotland was absorbed in detail. As the campaign in North Africa and the Far East developed, the fortunes of the Scottish Regiments became particularly important. The capture at St Valery of the 51st Division early in the war had verged on being a national calamity and now the new 51st fighting in North Africa and Italy was the focus of attention for all Scots at home. The recording of the Division's pipers parading before Mr Churchill in Tripoli could have been played over and over until it wore out.

Finding the background stories needed to amplify these items for magazine and feature programmes was not so easy. The Scottish BBC had no accredited War Correspondents of its own and improvised arrangements had to be made using journalists serving in the forces. Formal application could be made for some stories and in this the air force proved to be the most receptive. The navy, on the other hand, were usually most unhelpful and the 'old boy network' was often the only way to cover the senior service.

At home, the ever expanding foreign language broadcasts from London – by December 1941, the BBC was transmitting in 40 different languages – meant a host of strangers, usually with very limited English, scouring the Scottish countryside for material and Scotland had frequent problems with visitors from Oxford Street and Bush House, the two London centres for foreign broadcasting. Having set off to Scotland after stories, often with no authority or accreditation, the next that would be heard from these 'reporters' was usually a desperate cry for help, whereupon someone from BBC Scotland would have to go to John Brown's shipyard or the Naval Dockyard at Rosyth to vouch for the unfortunate individual and spend some time mollifying the security authorities.

Part of this interest in Scotland, especially by the European services of the BBC, was a direct consequence of the large number of Polish and Scandinavian troops based in Scottish camps. There was also the 'Shetland Bus', a dangerous and important contact route maintained between Shetland and Norway. Through this link BBC Scotland learned that many Norwegians listened to the output of the Burghead transmitter, particularly enjoying the music of Grieg and Sibelius, favourites of Ian Whyte and the BBC Scottish Orchestra. As an acknowledgment of this, in 1943, at the time of the Grieg Centenary and King Haakon of Norway's 70th birthday, Ian Whyte conducted the BBC Scottish Orchestra in a celebratory concert at the Usher Hall, Edinburgh in the presence of the King and Prince Olav.

For the broadcasters, 1943 was to be a year of eloquent landmarks. The war in Europe, at last on the turn, brought numerous successes to be reported home. It also marked the BBC's 21st year of broadcasting, an occasion for celebrations and much talk of what had been and what would be done. On 8 December an anniversary lunch was held in London attended by an impressive group of Cabinet Ministers, High Commissioners and broadcasting executives. The chief guest was Brendan Bracken, Minister of Information, who in his toast to the BBC touched for a moment on a then current rumour that the BBC was about to embark on advertising. Dismissing it out of hand as nonsense, he did allow himself a moment to suggest that a little healthy competition might be developed within the structure of the Corporation itself. He reminded his audience that the war had meant that an untimely reduction of regional broadcasting and expressed the hope that the regional staffs would be greatly strengthened in peacetime, with a measure of home rule.

It was the briefest of glimpses into the possibilities of the future and indeed occupied a very minor part of the Minister's discourse but if nothing else it acknowledged some of the work being done outside London and in Scotland where adventurous and lively experimentation was breaking the programme surface.

Of all the BBC's Regions, Scotland was undoubtedly top of the entrepreneurial list and any reference to even a vestige of autonomy had to relate to the Corporation's largest provincial operation. It had staged a strong recovery despite the absence of a Scottish service and was now holding a secure position in most of the programme areas. Drama and features were securely part of the Home Service menu. Both music and variety were heavily committed on the domestic channels and Scotland had re-established its pre-war reputation in education with a limited input to the UK schools service. Sensibly, with an optimistic eye to the future, it was also laying plans to increase its rapport with teacher training colleges. It had also achieved a considerable breakthrough in using UK time to cultivate the public service concept of regional broadcasting – programmes of special interest in the broadcasting area – largely under the guardianship of Robert Kemp in Edinburgh.

Robert Kemp's arrival in Edinburgh had been a timely shot in the arm. The wholesale exodus from the capital at the outbreak of war had left very little 'heat' in the Edinburgh studios, a situation hardly enlivened by building work at 11 Newbattle Terrace where two small studios were being prepared as a last-ditch bolt-hole for 'crisis' broadcasting in the event of an invasion. By 1942, however, restrictions on provincial broadcasting had relaxed sufficiently to allow an increase in production staff in all categories and Edinburgh found itself once again with a locally-based features producer.

His work as a producer was already known in the BBC and it was expected that he would bring to his new job a sense of care and appreciation for things Scottish, an expectation that was fully justified. Because of the limitations still being imposed on new programmes with a strong regional content he made use of the time already allotted to *Scottish Magazine*, once a month changing it into *Scottish Chapbook*, which he described as: 'A magazine of comment on current affairs, new music and poetry, sketches and review, contributed by Scots at home and overseas with a recorded impression of an event of the months from the Scottish news unit.'

From the start the programme fulfilled its fundamental obligation to Scotland, ranging widely over Scottish art and character. Amongst the first year's contributors were: Maurice Lindsay, writing from Staff College, Camberley; Ronald Falconer, later to become the BBC's Head of Religious Broadcasting in Scotland; Alastair Borthwick, serving as a lieutenant in the HLI; Lennox Milne, then an assistant in the department in Edinburgh; Dr C.A. Malcolm of the Signet Library – writing on *The New Testament in Scots;* Edwin Muir, later used as an assistant on the programme; Hugh MacDiarmid; Cedric Thorpe Davie; Alexander Reid; and George Bruce, who would later take over from Robert Kemp and continue to nourish the literati of Scotland with care and versatility.

Robert Kemp was a sympathetic, approachable craftsman, prepared to work hard and anxious to give airtime to Scots who showed imagination and originality. Thanks to him *Chapbook* was a success and became the progenitor of many successful arts programmes in the post-war years – *Poetry Notebook*, *Arts Review* and television's *Counterpoint* – although by then Robert had left the BBC to devote more time to writing.

Finally, and perhaps inevitably, the Scottish Region's growing enterprise flourished with considerable splendour and dash in *Children's Hour*, where Kathleen Garscadden was demonstrating the value of diversity in her many UK programme contributions. Through highly successful dramatisations of the classics of Scott and Stevenson, talks about the past by such notables as Walter Elliot, MP, and the Duchess of Atholl, music by Scottish orchestras, choirs and soloists and last, but no least, the fantasy and dialect of *Tammy Troot*, the loves and traditions of Scotland were becoming widely known.

The effect of Willie Joss's characterisation of *Tammy Troot* in Lavinia Derwent's stories was stimulating to say the least, and by 1944 the BBC was admitting with hand on heart that there had been reports of children in Southern England using words like 'scunner' and 'havers'. The Scottish vocabulary of these children experienced an added boost when in April of that year Kathleen Garscadden launched another programme that had an unmistakeable sound of Scotland – *Down at the Mains*, written by R. Gordon McCallum. This fictitious account of life on a farm, ending with a traditional concert held in the Mains kitchen, was a winner from

Down at the Mains (1950)
(l/r) Elsie Payne; Willie Joss; Grace McChlery; Isobel Robertson; Bill Jess;
R. Gordon McCallum; Eddie Fraser; Robin Grieve.

the very start and very soon the programme was a fortnightly regular on the BBC's Home Service. Few actors turned down a chance of appearing on the programme and for many it was the first step towards a career in broadcasting. The names that run through its history make it a microcosm of future broadcasting in Scotland: Elsie Payne, C.R.M. Brookes and Jameson Clark; Grace McChlery and Jimmy Crampsey as the original Mrs and Farmer Scott; Eddie Fraser, Robin Grieve, Miriam Owens and David Mowat; and cameo appearances by Molly Weir, Josephine Crombie, Tommy Morgan, Ian Sadler and Bryden Murdoch.

Down at the Mains was to run for over 20 years. It had the *Children's Hour* characteristics beloved by everyone – fun, yet with a touch of poignancy, wholesome and entertaining. Traits that could be detected in a lot of Scotland's broadcasting and likely to prove something of a stumbling-block when the time came to properly reflect the problems of the country's post-war regeneration.

As with many large organisations in the UK the BBC was keenly aware of the need to construct some kind of order ahead of the inevitable chaos of peace. With admirable optimism BBC engineers had started thinking about the problems as early as mid-1941, and by 1943 the mandarins of Broadcasting House were pondering the same question. As is usually the case when there is no definite 'action-date' on the table, discussion ranged over a multitude of headings:

- A continuing monopoly?
- Sponsorship?
- Costs?
- How many Home Services?
- The role of the Regions?

Early on it was decided that the post-war plan would provide three 'programmes'. For ease of planning they were initially referred to as the A, B and C services, later becoming the Home, Light and Third. More difficult to resolve was the role of the Regions and innumerable proposals and warnings were voiced. Some had no wish to see the return of this form of broadcasting, while others saw the dangers of a metropolitan-bound Corporation possibly hindering localised interests.

The Regional Directors were privy to much of what was going on. They attended monthly meetings in London and sensibly no attempt was made to hide anything from them. Early in 1943 the then Director-General, Robert Foot, circulated notes on the post-war possibilities and asked for individual and collective replies. The dialogue that ensued, both verbally and on paper, has in some measure continued ever since and even now it is difficult to properly evaluate the various points of view. Understanding and sympathy are so dependent on where your feet physically touch the ground.

The 'Regional Question' rattled around the offices and corridors of the BBC for over a year and a half with the respective Directors unanimous in their opinion that the combined resources of broadcasting outside London be used far more in broadcasting for the whole country. In fact the Director of North Region, John Coatman, was so critical of the wartime centralisation, he lobbied for the transfer of control, envisaging six Regions, power units of broadcasting, feeding their own areas as well as supplying programmes to two national networks on a competitive basis. Not surprisingly he met with considerable hostility, not just from London, but also from Bristol as he envisaged the disappearance of the pre-war West Region.

The man who came closest to what became the eventual plan, submitting the outline of a system that was to work in Region and Nation alike, was George L. Marshall, the Regional Director and later Controller of Northern Ireland. He had had a wide breadth of experience in different areas of broadcasting, starting with his stint as the first Station Director of 2EH in Edinburgh.

Marshall's recommendation represented a coherent and credible strategy: 'Regional self-expression will have to be maintained at all costs where it is justified ethnically. The Regions should obviously deal with such things as a local news service, music, including an orchestra which would be used for public concerts, local drama and the encouragement of dramatic societies, religion, appeals, talks, *Children's Hour* and topicality.'

Nobody put up any outward resistance to the plan. It suited London and the Regions alike, and Scotland and Wales who were now emphasising their Nation standpoint, were particularly attracted to it. In any case the talking had to stop, or at least become a degree less prominent, for the end of hostilities in Europe was fast approaching and as the Director-General had promised that a peacetime service would follow VE Day within 90 days, time was of the essence.

The BBC achieved its target date with a few days to spare and on Sunday 29 July 1945 – VE Day + 82 days – the broadcasters returned to a peacetime system. The first discernibly Scottish item on the new Scottish Home Service was at 11.00am, *Seirbhis Ghàidhlig*, a religious service in Gaelic. Later that evening the Scottish Director, Melville Dinwiddie, outlined his plans for the Scottish Service and how it would fit into the new scheme in a broadcast at 9.15pm after the news.

Regionalisation was back and, within the confines of a shortage of wavelengths, some new spots on the dial and ageing wireless sets, conditions were set fair to re-establish coverage of issues relating to local life and interests.

To begin with, the BBC operated two networks, the Light Programme, successor to the General Forces Programme, and broadcast on 1,500m long wave (the old National Programme wavelength) and the Home Service. The Third Programme, programme C in the engineering's early prognostications, was to be delayed until September 1946.

The Light Programme was purely a national service. It carried very few regionally produced programmes, mostly music-based or comedy, and its identity was easy listening. The BBC described it as: 'designed to appeal not so much to a certain class of listener, but to all listeners when they are in certain moods.'

It was to the Home Service that the Regions were directed for, in the words of the Corporation, 'It is the aim of the Home Service to provide the home programme of the people of the United Kingdom.' Using separate wavelengths, England was divided into four Regions plus Scotland and Wales. Ironically Northern Ireland had to share with the North of England.

The operation of the new Home Service was once again based on an option to 'opt-out' with local programmes still having to observe certain basic rules. 'Opting-out' was a term disliked in Scotland. At one point, Andrew Stewart, now returned as Scottish Programme Director, asked that it be dropped, pointing out that his job was to select the most suitable item for Scottish listeners. He was operating on an agreed policy, not exercising an option.

Whatever the way of it, the Scottish management welcomed the return of limited self-determination and openly acknowledged that they now enjoyed a greater measure of autonomy than had been given to them in 1939. If anything their euphoria was a shade too public. The war years had given radio an importance and reputation that was going to be hard to maintain and the listening public immediately expected more than the Scottish Home Service was able to deliver, not just in terms of hours per week but in style, variety and relevance to the Scottish scene.

Almost from the start the new service was lambasted in the Scottish press. Criticism even peppered the business of the House of Commons with a Labour member, Mrs Jean Mann, asking 'Who in Scotland is satisfied with the BBC?'

Scottish bodies seeking to promote a national culture were particularly scathing and The Saltire Society launched a campaign that was better orchestrated than most. They called for an end to what they described as the BBC's 'timidity neurosis' and circulated a questionnaire to their members seeking views on such things as 'were there enough Scottish items?' and 'are the Scottish officials up to the job?' Their campaign was conducted over a period of about six years starting with the publication of 'Broadcasting: A Policy for Development in Scotland' in 1944 (they had their eye on the fact that the BBC's Charter would shortly come up for renewal) and culminating in Saltire Society representatives meeting with Lord Beveridge and some of his Committee in Broadcasting House, Edinburgh, prior to the publication of the Beveridge Committee's Report on Broadcasting.

The complaints that rolled into BBC Scotland during the first few months of the new service did not fall upon deaf ears. Melville Dinwiddie was quick to joke that finding fault was a prerequisite of being a Scot – a sentiment supported by *The Scotsman* which described criticism of BBC programmes as 'almost a national pastime' – but with equal speed he identified at least one of the problems that beset the broadcasters in Scotland. In promising so much from the new service, they had quickly outrun the staff and facilities that were currently available. Too much was being attempted too soon and perhaps as a consequence there was a tiresome reliance on pre-war successes.

Wartime broadcasting had given listeners a host of new styles and values. They were attracted by the way items could be presented using recording and editing. They liked the cosmopolitan values that wartime radio had acquired and enjoyed greatly the new style of entertainment exemplified by ITMA, *Band Wagon* and American imports such as *The Bob Hope Show*.

When BBC Scotland launched into Harry Lauder, Will Fyffe and yet another account of the '45, there were concerted groans from many. To cap it all, listeners, having gained a wide knowledge of all BBC programmes during wartime listening, were quick to identify what was being missed when there was an opt-out to place something of 'Scottish interest'.

Dinwiddie had whetted the public appetite with his introductory talk in 1945, promising a Scottish Home Service that would be true to its name, but he also pointed out that the start would be slow, an important proviso that had been swept aside and forgotten in the clamour of criticism that followed.

At the Annual Meeting of The Saltire Society in Edinburgh in the same month the President, Robert Hurd, asked: 'Will the BBC staff be able to break loose from past habits of mind? Will they take risks? Will the new daily news bulletins continue to be a kind of appendage following London instead of a proper integration of Scottish news with world news?'

His speech was well-reported but quickly resulted in a backlash from those who feared control by 'the highbrows'. Soon it was a free for all.

The People's Journal echoed Hurd's views up to a point but maintained that Scottish listeners needed more light entertainment and not only from Glasgow comedians. Scotland should be combed for talent. There should be 'big and adventurous undertakings in music and drama'.

The Daily Record and Mail in Glasgow thought there was confusion between broadcasts of Scottish origin and broadcasts of Scottish interest. When it came to 'endless discussions of our own problems' the writer admitted he would opt for Tommy Handley.

In a letter to The Bulletin in Glasgow, the Marquis of Graham said that, on the whole, Scots programmes were poor and dull. He blamed the 'young Scottish intellectuals for their nationalistic bias; censorship by BBC officialdom in Glasgow, fearful of their London masters; the selection of Glasgow's BBC officials who, although Scots, had been chosen by Englishmen in London; lack of money; and lack of scouting for 'fresh talent'.

Hurd of The Saltire Society kept up his attack. The Society stood by its demands set out in 'Broadcasting: A Policy for Development in Scotland' and underlined its hope for a Scottish Corporation when the BBC's Charter expired at the end of 1946.

What of Dinwiddie and his management in this entire hullabaloo?

Tired? Broken men? Subdued and beaten? Not a bit of it. It was all grist to their mill. In a long article for the SMT *Magazine* towards the end of 1945, Andrew Stewart declared his Reithian principles: 'To us Scots, the measure of success by our broadcasting service should lie in the ability with which it takes its unique place as an index of our vital interests.'

Some months later, Melville Dinwiddie put it in a slightly different way when he spoke to the Glasgow Publicity Club: 'Wartime restrictions on broadcasting have resulted in many Scottish listeners becoming more anglicised and, due to the films, more Americanised in their tastes.'

He then explained that one function of broadcasting would be 'to restore a satisfactory balance of listening between cosmopolitan items and the purely Scottish material of which people had been starved during the war.'

As *The Bulletin* said a few days later, 'We may not have a Radio Scotland but, by golly, we do have Melville Dinwiddie.'

Gradually changes and adjustments were made. Valued staff continued to filter back from war service and new staff were recruited to fill vacancies and expand departments. The three elements of the BBC, production, engineering and administration, were re-established in the Scottish headquarters and their heads, respectively Andrew Stewart, F.W. Endicott and Peter Dunbar, did what they could with the limited funds available to them.

In the production division alone, the number of staff transfers and appointments was considerable. A promulgation signed by Dinwiddie as Scottish Director and dated April 1946 listed 16 names, all of them destined to become synonymous with the best of radio broadcasting in Scotland during the next 15 years:

Name	New Position
R.G.T. Gildard	Assistant Scottish Programme Director
A.P. Lee	Features Producer
H.H.E. Wiseman	Scottish Music Director
I.D. Whyte	Conductor
R.S. Calder	Music Assistant
Miss C.B. Laing	Accompanist
R.H. Gray	Recorded Programmes Assistant

Name	New Position
G.D. Runcie	News Assistant
R.H.W. Falconer	Religious Broadcasting Assistant
F.J. Macdonald	Gaelic Assistant
D.A.K. Stephen	Conductor (Light Entertainment)
R. Russell	Talks Producer
J. Crampsey	Schools Assistant
T.S. Allan	Schools Assistant
R.F. Dunnett	Publicity Officer

On this list alone nine of the names were new appointments, joining the dozen or so old hands who were scattered in Glasgow, Edinburgh and Aberdeen and in a remarkably short time all were poised ready to make a serious attempt at constructing a post-war Scottish Home Service along the lines proposed by their Scottish Programme Director, Andrew Stewart.

CHAPTER SIX

Radio Rules

IN THE 1946 BBC publication, *This is the Scottish Home Service*, Andrew Stewart quoted from *The Scots Review*: 'The future of broadcasting in Scotland is entirely bound up with the future of Scotland itself. If a revival of our national life is on the way, then broadcasting will play an important part therein. But if Scotland descends to the status of an English county, our broadcasting will show a similar trend.'

Andrew Stewart added:

> If you know the way you have come, you may know something of the way you are going... some enduring qualities of character have brought the Scots through centuries of adversity and crisis to this 20th century, still recognisable as a people: and ever since a Scotland existed it has refused to be made into a province... The 12 months which ended in August 1946 were, in fact, a year of resettlement and restarting... the teething troubles arising from such changes are almost over, and most of the jobs are filled. The feeling now is one of settling down for the first full year's endeavour to provide 'good listening' from the Scottish Home Service.

The extensive recruitment and resettlement programme had brought together a diverse group of people and for some of the new staff 'settling down' into the BBC's regime was an experience in itself. Ronnie Falconer, the newly appointed Religious Broadcasting producer, wrote that his 'first day in the BBC was a disaster' in his autobiography, *The Kilt Beneath My Cassock*. For one who later became an internationally recognised figure in religious broadcasting and led his department in Scotland for 26 years, it seems a strange beginning but being in the BBC did take a little getting used to.

The Corporation thrived on 'order' and a meticulous attention to detail. While never openly referring to its infallibility it did everything possible to ensure that there was little chance of making a mistake and indeed on the engineering side a strictly observed daily routine of checks and tests had all but eliminated technical breakdowns. Policy, for producers, was as precise as the control within engineering and programmes were planned, built and assessed using a 'code of practice' that brooked little deviation from the rules. The public reaction to this was to see the BBC as a cross between a favourite uncle and a kindly saint and the duty announcer, sitting in his small continuity studio alongside the Glasgow Control Room, would often field late-night telephone calls on subjects as diverse as unsolvable crossword clues, inscriptions for engagement rings or the plight of missing children.

Absorbing the detail of BBC policy could take a little time, hence Ronnie Falconer's bewilderment on his first day. Instruction was sparse. The Corporation believed that it was sufficient if you understood their prime tenets, which were simple and straightforward:

- Avoid misunderstanding – the BBC stands for honesty and authenticity
- Be impartial – hence the ban on expressing a BBC opinion
- Make sure all selection processes are based on merit – not easy as merit in programmes was often largely a matter of opinion

Within departments there were distinctive codes:

- Drama was warned off surgical operations and anything that smacked of 'Grand Guignol'
- Features faced the same strictures
- Light Entertainment had to be reminded to be British and to disregard that Americanisation sweeping in across the Atlantic
- Religious output was to maintain a degree of denominational balance while staying within the mainstream of historic Christianity

For the planners there was a 'Sunday Policy' to be observed and amongst the programmes refused a Sunday transmission on the Scottish Home Service were modern dance music, sport, variety and 'party politics' – restrictions that were balanced by the principle that Sunday programmes should be the 'best' of the week.

As topics, party politics and Parliament were further restricted by the 14-day rule: 'No discussions or statements may be broadcast on any issue which is within a fortnight of debate in either House.' It was acknowledged that politics was the supreme test of impartiality and that the reward for success was usually simultaneous complaints from both sides. Party and election broadcasts and all allied matters were strictly regulated in London and even the National Regions considered this head office control to be right and proper.

Inevitably the rules and restrictions proliferated as performers sought to widen their scope and range of subjects and producers and writers of light entertainment were expected to be particularly vigilant. Coarseness and innuendo were dealt with under the heading of 'Vulgarity'. There must be no jokes that referred to lavatories, honeymoon couples or commercial travellers. Ladies underwear was taboo and a remark such as 'winter draws on' was considered to be a suggestive reference. All impersonations required the permission of the person being portrayed and the Corporation was unwilling even to consider such a thing when it involved elder statesmen and leading political figures.

All departments were constantly reminded that advertising in any form was anathema to the BBC and not even the slightest whisper of identification was allowed on the air. Some trade names were just permissible, being regarded as generic and in everyday use, e.g. aspirin, thermos, nylon and a few others, and very occasionally, it was accepted that mention of a sponsoring body was a necessary courtesy. These occasions apart, any reference to a commercial undertaking was forbidden. Great ships were launched from a 'yard on the Clyde' and 'a leading industrialist' was a useful pseudonym to avoid close identification with a product.

The BBC's regime was strict, and the slightest deviation from the centralist view was considered at best to be administratively unwise. Yet no-one minded too much provided they were allowed some freedom in terms of production ideas and programmes. Yes, the allocation of money, staff and equipment were all centrally controlled and even the simple act of raising the flag every morning on the roof of Glasgow's Broadcasting House was regulated by instructions from head office, but to most of the staff there was nothing unusual in this. They saw themselves as part of a large UK organisation and the job in hand was what concerned them most, providing the listener with 'good listening' and a Scottish Home Service that would meet his or her needs.

The period of very public dissatisfaction and open criticism soon passed and listeners in Scotland, no longer showing an obvious preference for the Light Programme, returned to the Scottish Home Service in droves.

'We believe that only the best of its type, wherever it is to be found, is good enough for our Scottish audience,' said Melville Dinwiddie, and to prove it the Scottish programme schedules erupted with new productions of the most excellent kind.

Many of them quickly became part of the broadcasting day and would last for ten or more years before falling before the onslaught of television:

Scottish Survey, a weekly discussion programme, chaired by Alastair Borthwick.

Over the Sea to Skye, written by Jessie Kesson (her first script).

Robert Kemp produces an anthology of voices entitled *The Guid Scots Tongue*, later to become a major series.

A young John Wilson has his first feature script, *Clyde Pilot*, accepted.

Arts Review makes its appearance with speakers Ian Whyte and Joseph Macleod. Under the guidance of Robin Richardson, and later George Bruce, this would be BBC Scotland's major outlet for artistic discussion and review well into the late 1950s and in 1949 it would be joined by a stablemate, *Scottish Life and Letters* – a monthly miscellany edited by Maurice Lindsay and George Bruce.

The small team under Charles Anderson expanded the illustration of the news by using more recorded material. Their output, *News*, *Scottish News*, *Sports News* and *Topical News*, now had a staff of five – Charles Anderson, 'news observer' George Runcie, news assistant and sub-editor Madeleine Strong and two shorthand typists. It also had an engaging motto – 'If you feel at any time you have done well, try to do better next time.'

A Scottish Digest, edited by

Robin Richardson (*left*), Producer, and John Arnott, Producer and Announcer (1960).

John Wilson and Archie P. Lee, presented selections from current publications in Scotland and there was a new monthly programme, *Science Review*, edited by Harry Hoggan. Hugh MacDiarmid introduced *A New Approach to Burns* and later gave a talk, *The Deterioration of the Scottish Face*, which suffered last-minute postponement, ironically having to give way to a government ministerial statement.

The Country Mouse Goes to Town by Robert Kemp received considerable acclaim after a national broadcast and on the Scottish Home Service there was a small but appreciative audience for Sydney Goodsir Smith's dramatic poem, *The Death of Tristram and Isolde* while in *A Scottish Digest*, the actor Andrew Keir made his first broadcast using his own name, Andrew Buggy.

There was a semblance of a Scottish Repertory company beginning to form, much needed and a welcome aid to broadcasting for there was very little professional theatre in Scotland. The Wilson Barrett Theatre Company were playing the three major Scottish cities but with only a sprinkling of home-grown actors. Some of the company were imports from the south. James Bridie had started the Glasgow Citizens' Theatre and this was proving to be at least bread and butter for some. Hopefully they would get their 'jam' from broadcasts. However, difficulties arose with evening work which suited those with daytime occupations but not those working in the theatre.

Once again it was *Children's Hour* that supplied a large part of the answer with help from the Schools department. Children loved dramatic stories. They'd always been the backbone of *Children's Hour's* output and were immensely popular. Writers such as Angus MacVicar with his exciting features and subsequent forays into science fiction serials, and frequent dramatisations of the more exciting books of Scott, Stevenson and Crockett were in constant demand. As a result, Kathleen Garscadden was probably the largest employer of actors in Scotland and with a constant output and flexible planning she was able to combine 'pros' and 'amateurs', while at the same time bringing through a commendable list of new names.

Schools department, with its essentially daytime programmes, was also providing a useful haven for the young and impecunious. Fees were pitched on the low side and the importance of emphasising 'teaching points' often obscured the chance to properly extend an actor's range but they

Schools, Intermediate French (1946)
(*l/r*) Marcel Stellman; Andrée Durançon; Jean-Jacques Chemlin; Yvonne Oberlin.

did offer regular work on both the National and Regional Programmes. *Nature Study*, *Intermediate French* and *Singing Together* were being produced in Scotland for the whole country, and locally *Exploring Scotland* and *Scottish Heritage* were settling down to becoming a permanent part of the Scottish curriculum.

A.D. Adam was the forceful head of the Schools department, now the mainstay of operations at Queen Street, Edinburgh. It shared the studios with a small *Children's Hour* unit run by Margaret Walker, some features produced by Robin Richardson and talks under Alastair Dunnett. It was a large department in Scottish terms with five assistants (some strange tradition decreed that its producers were still known by the old nomenclature) and many of the Glasgow-based actors had cause to bless both the Glasgow/Edinburgh train service and the benevolence of people such as Harry Hoggan, R.E. Rogerson, Tom Allan, Mrs F. Lyford-Pike, Ian Wishart and Jack Gillespie, their benevolence suitably moderated by the department's administrative assistant, David Livingstone.

Drama had been a prime ingredient of Scottish broadcasting since the early imaginative productions devised by R.E. Jeffrey. Tyrone Guthrie had helped it to progress while working in Glasgow with the Scottish National Players and Gordon Gildard had advanced it a stage further, certainly in the minds of the London hierarchy, in the year or two preceding 1939. Now Gildard was back and again working for the BBC in Scotland. He

Drama recording for
Scottish Home Service
(1946)

(*l/r*) Lennox Milne;
Nan Scott;
C.R.M. Brookes;
Peter MacDonell;
Jean Fitzpatrick;
Grace McChlery.

was no longer a producer as such but was setting his feet on the grey
ladder of programme administration. No bad thing as it happened, for it
put him in a strong position to support the changes still needed if Scottish
radio drama was to continue a progressive improvement.

The drama producer post in Scotland had gone to Moultrie Kelsall
when he relinquished his wartime duties as the stand-in Programme
Director and almost immediately he had written a critique which bemoaned
the fact that few, if any, of the major playwrights had been induced to
give serious thought to broadcasting. Writing for radio offered a relatively
small reward when compared with the commercial theatre and films and
he saw little chance of changing that. The future would have to lie with
new writers and that would mean almost immeasurable care and effort
by producers giving guidance and encouragement to any who showed
promise.

The listener in Scotland had an appetite for a story, be it real or imaginary, and little cared whether it had been conceived and written with
broadcasting in mind. Yet the radio drama and feature producers knew
that broadcasting had the potential of transcending theatrical and visual
limitations and was wide open for exploitation if only more writers would
take advantage of it. But so far, finding manuscripts that showed real
promise was a slow process.

Some fresh names were coming through: David Forbes Lorne with

Days of Grace; Tom Hanlin's *Come Joy Come Sorrow*; and Moultrie Kelsall himself with an outstanding play, *Who Fought Alone*.

A radio play competition held in 1947 brought close to 200 submissions and was won by an architect in Dundee, Sinclair Gauldie with his play *Lives o' Men*. In second place was *Storm over Brackenridge* written by Douglas Baird.

However, the kind of writers that Kelsall was really after, authors such as George Scott Moncrieff and Robert McLellan saw their work as essentially stage productions in spite of the fact that *The Wund in the East* by Moncrieff and *The Carlin Moth*, a verse play by McLellan, both subsequently and successfully transferred to the microphone.

In 1947 Moultrie Kelsall resigned from the BBC. His reason for going was perhaps partly frustration. He had a growing concern for the way bureaucracy seemed to be pervading what was now a vast hierarchy but at the same time he wanted to spend more time writing and as an actor. Soon he was making frequent appearances on radio, television and in films (his debut as a television actor was in *The Trial of Madeleine Smith* where he established a record for the longest speech on television with an address to the jury lasting 45 minutes) and happily continued to meet and enjoy the company of his colleagues for a further 30-plus years. Beneath the gruff theatrical manner was a caring person with strong beliefs, always ready to remind you that there were decencies to be observed in broadcasting for you had been bidden to enter people's homes. He was replaced as drama producer by Jimmy Crampsey from the Schools department. He, too, was at heart an actor and a very fine one but would choose to remain a producer until his retirement in his mid-'60s.

While Moultrie Kelsall and Gordon Gildard had been hammering out the pattern of Scotland's radio drama, substantial changes already made in the Region's Music department were beginning to have effect. Ian Whyte had relinquished his position as Music Director and had replaced Guy Warrack as Conductor of the BBC Scottish Orchestra, which had been increased to 57 players and was considered now to be second only to the BBC Symphony Orchestra in London. It was only three players short of the magic '60' which would have allowed it to be officially regarded as a symphony orchestra. The pressure to correct what was an anomalous situation would continue for many years but meantime the Orchestra was busying itself increasing its repertoire of symphonic works and contemporary Scottish music. To help with the Orchestra, Ian Whyte had an assistant, Robert Irving, who was to head a long line of outstanding musicians who would serve an apprentice-ship in Glasgow's Studio One. The Orchestra was a marvellous train-ing ground and in music from Scot-land it reigned supreme.

The administrative problems of music broadcasting had been shifted to the shoulders of Herbert Wiseman, brought in from Educa-tion and appointed Scottish Music Director on 1 February 1946. A month later he was joined in the department by Ronald Calder

Ian Whyte, Conductor
BBC Scottish Orchestra (1955).

and together they were to make a considerable mark on broadcasting.

The vacancy filled by Ronnie Calder had been caused by the previous holder, Kemlo Stephen, being made the new Conductor of the Scottish Variety Orchestra in place of Ronnie Munro who had returned to the south. Like its big brother along the corridor, the Variety Orchestra still fretted over London's unwillingness to commit itself to all-out support. The players still lacked permanent contracts and it would be 1949 before they received some form of established status and augmentation to 21 players.

The music output achieved by Scotland was now quite exceptional. Mindful of the need to uncover new talent the department had carried out over 1,000 auditions in 1946 and 'passed' 300 new performers. While this certainly exposed quite a number of new broadcasters, it also had an adverse effect which the BBC came to regret. Any artist who was audit-ioned by an adjudicating panel was told whether he had passed or failed. This immediately presupposed in the mind of the passed candidate an offer of a prompt and frequent engagement, a misapprehension that caused a great deal of disappointment and ill will. The huge bank of people succ-eeding at auditions became quite preposterous and the number of sessions had to be drastically cut, ending up with no more than one a month at most. Even with this reduction the work was arduous and Wiseman and his staff were long-suffering and patient. What amazed them most was the lack of variety of songs. When asked what they proposed to sing most would offer *Comin' thro' the Rye'*, *Turn ye to me* or *Macgregor's Gathering* depending on their range. If the staff accompanist on duty was Andrew Bryson, the more tedious performances would be enlivened by his own personal assessment, conveyed in the accompaniment. Just how it was done was never clear but you were rarely in doubt as to his opinion.

A limited repertoire was also the curse of many of Scotland's choirs. The Glasgow Orpheus still held sway on the Scottish airwaves with the Kirkintilloch Children's Choir coming a close second. The many that failed to pass the adjudication were usually too imitative, offering a pale imitation of Roberton's *Bluebird* or an item from *The Messiah* that ignored completely the power and talent of the great Yorkshire choirs that could be heard on the air.

The BBC had always looked for new talent but now its search was for better talent. The Music department made major contribution to this task in Scotland as their high standards promoted an excellent style and consistency of performance. Within the BBC this department's area of responsibility was wide – religious music, variety (they now controlled the Scottish Variety Orchestra) and the people's music of Gaelic songs, Scottish dance bands and brass bands. Inevitably there was criticism of their rather high-handed ways, opportunities and talents missed because of small, silly foibles, but on the credit side they achieved a miracle of order and competence where previously all had been near chaos.

Their co-operation with one particular department, Religion, was a particular pleasure for its new man in charge, the Rev Ronald Falconer, who was an enthusiast who welcomed assistance from all quarters. Again it was largely a process of winnowing out the chaff, this time so that studio services might have a reasonable standard of singing. Advising on broadcasts from churches was more difficult. Stepping on the toes of well-meaning choirmasters was a hazard and often a compromise had to be reached for the sake of broadcasting a particularly outstanding preacher. Bit by bit, however, the singing of the hymns, psalms and paraphrases of the Scottish Kirk gradually improved. Ronnie Falconer's avowed aim was to present through broadcasting the great truths of religion – to persuade the careless, enlighten the ignorant and to confirm the convert.

Music's influence was also felt in Gaelic broadcasting, where a large proportion of programmes were Gaelic songs. Native singers were auditioned using the same criteria as would be applied to professionally trained singers fresh out of college. The audition panel did include a representative of the Gaelic department but his function was to assess the singer's proficiency in the language, nothing more. As a result many distinguished prize-winners and medallists were banned from broadcasting except in Mod-related programmes and *Children's Hour* and Gaelic department chose not to challenge the rules. Hugh Macphee had slipped into a role of quiet acceptance and seemed anxious not to rock the boat too much in case his limited access to the air was further interfered with.

The autumn of 1946 brought further responsibilities for the music staff. The BBC's third peacetime service, the Third Programme, was finally launched in September that year and immediately Scotland offered itself as a major contributor.

The new service was not confined to music. Its bill of fare also covered discussions, drama and serious literature, all of which were confidently provided. It was in music, however, that Scotland really made its mark. The first broadcast by the BBC Scottish Orchestra took place on 11 October and thereafter Scottish music contributions were frequent and varied and well respected. A snag was the unsatisfactory transmission range of the new service, particularly in Scotland. Based on a high-power transmitter at Droitwich, south of Birmingham, it had to supplement its rather poor coverage by operating small city transmitters. In Scotland these were placed in Dundee, Edinburgh and Glasgow with Aberdeen being looked after from the Redmoss transmitter. There were also problems caused by the severe winter that year. The BBC were asked to reduce their consumption of electricity and took the decision to close the new service during a large part of February.

While the more erudite parts of Scottish output were settling comfortably into their greatly expanded territory on the air, the popular and run-of-the-mill programmes were also on the increase. They, too, were part of the new vitality that was being openly talked about in relation to Scotland and they demonstrated most clearly that the country did have some common bonds of interest. Their aim was to cater for the regional need without seeming 'hick' or narrow-minded; to reflect a heightened consciousness that Scotland could, and was 'making good'; and to demonstrate that there was plenty happening within its boundaries that was of interest to everyone.

Sources for these programmes were as varied as the subjects they covered. Aberdeen inevitably was a significant contributor and it proved to be a microcosm of the Scottish trend. 'Our people have brains and like to be made to use them,' had been the testament of the Aberdeen *Bon Accord* when the new Beechgrove studios were opened in 1938. Now, with the dust covers removed and an assurance of a much greater output than had been possible during the war, Aberdeen set about making a name for itself.

As part of the post-war development Scotland had assigned a second production post to the North East to work alongside Elizabeth Adair. It was filled by George Bruce, born in Fraserburgh and fresh from 12 years of teaching at Dundee High School, and together he and Elizabeth channelled a great many programmes into the Scottish Home Service.

George was a craftsman of poetry and documentary programmes and sometimes he would combine the two in one production and, if only to demonstrate that he believed that broadcasting should have the best of everything he could do, he would appear regularly as a sports broadcaster and an authority on football.

Quite how Elizabeth would describe herself is difficult to say. She had developed a great love of gardening, the countryside and natural history and this promoted the planners to commission a cluster of programmes on these subjects. Through them, she brought to the microphone a host of 'names' – George Waterston, James Bruce, Ben Barrett, Henry Douglas Home, Christopher Mylne, Betty Gordon and Morton Boyd.

George Bruce
Producer.

Inevitably she was also the *Children's Hour* agent in the area and one proposal accepted with alacrity by Glasgow was a series that visited small primary schools where the children filled the programme by singing, acting and entertaining. At Monymusk, one of the schools chosen by Elizabeth Adair, the headmaster's small son stood on an orange box to reach the microphone while reciting *The Owl and the Pussycat.* His name was Jon Whitely and after the broadcast he was snapped up by a film company in London and subsequently starred in the film *Hunted* in 1952 followed by *The Kidnappers* with Duncan Macrae in 1953.

Discovering new people, 'talent' – as it was constantly referred to in the press – was not the sole prerogative of the North East. With broadcasting expanding and the public at large now less fearful of the microphone, it would have been surprising if new names had not surfaced elsewhere. But the nature and size of Beechgrove, small, intimate and friendly, a relic of the first day of radio stations and something the BBC would come back to years later, often meant that more time could be spent encouraging and stimulating people with recognisable ability. Such a person was Jessie Kesson. It was Elizabeth who finally persuaded her to attend a drama audition at the Beechgrove studios, no mean feat for Jessie was filled with a mixture of trepidation and offhandedness. Thankfully she came, and subsequently she and Elizabeth enjoyed a long broadcasting collaboration that spanned at least 30 features and plays on the Scottish Home Service.

Through Jessie Kesson another voice was heard – singer Kenneth McKellar. Kenneth was a student at Aberdeen University and heading for a career in forestry. It was early in 1947 when he applied to the BBC for an audition as a singer and Elizabeth Adair, who had been on the listening panel, immediately gave him a contract for a part in a programme she and Jessie Kesson were preparing called *Till a' the Seas Gang Dry.* In charge of the audition panel was the BBC's Head of Music in Scotland, Herbert Wiseman, and Elizabeth, impressed by what she had heard, suggested to him that Kenneth's name be put forward for a Caird Scholarship. This was eventually done and a few years later Kenneth went to the Royal College of Music in London, by now a seasoned broadcaster. While in the south he continued to broadcast for the Scottish Service, usually by going to a studio in London, and in this way he kept up his association with Scotland and its producers. Nor did he forget that two of the three people who sponsored him for the scholarship were Herbert Wiseman and Ian Whyte.

As well as putting together the specialist programmes that were being devised by Elizabeth and colleague George Bruce, Aberdeen was feeding a great deal of general material into Glasgow, re-affirming its pre-war tradition of being a major centre for 'country' entertainment. Numerous Scottish dance bands flocked back into the studio, often performing in front of an audience or with a group of dancers from the Scottish Country Dance Society and that great mainstay of radio, John Mearns – one of the greatest exponents of bothy ballads, actor and storyteller – practically took up residence so great was the demand for his talents. To service it all the busy engineers shuttled their way between Beechgrove studios and various OB locations covering everything from *Carols at Haddo House* to football commentaries and the launching of ships in Aberdeen.

Within the confines of what it was able to do Aberdeen was a success, and success, particularly in terms of popularity, was something that everybody in the broadcasting business coveted to some degree, including the senior figures in Scotland. 'Recognition' and 'acclaim' were important but there also had to be the popular approval of large audiences somewhere in the Scottish schedules to reinforce their claim to good listening and regional self-expression.

Like all good 'planners' they knew that Saturday evening held the greatest potential audience of the week and had set out to capture it for the Scottish Home Service, pulling many people away from the Light Programme, with three early evening programmes. Each one was different but had its roots in the Scottish character. Football, music that was plain and simple and a working-class situation comedy proved to be an irresistible mixture attracting an audience the size of which made Scotland the envy of the rest of the BBC.

The opening salvo came from *Sportsreel* which ran for 40 minutes following the 6.00pm news. It was the brainchild of Peter Thomson, one-time office boy and effects operator, who had had the idea for the programme during the war and had been allowed to make a first attempt on 11 August 1945. Week by week the programme improved. It was fast, bright and for its time amazingly complex with Peter assisted by another one-time sound operator Harold Gray, using all the new-found technical wizardry that had developed during the war.

The main emphasis was on football and, during the afternoon, commentary on a major fixture would be recorded for use in an edited 'sound picture' lasting around 12 minutes. Recordings were still made on disc, approximately 24 for one football match, and fitting together ten or so different excerpts kept everybody on their toes. By the time the red light signalled transmission time little more than half the programme was ready and typist and reporters continued to prepare and edit material right up to minutes before the end.

Practically every sport played in Scotland had a place in *Sportsreel*. Even shinty, struggling to re-establish itself after the war, had eyewitness accounts and a brief results service. The shinty results were often read out by actor Jameson Clark and, one memorable Saturday, egged on by his great friend Archie P. Lee, Jimmy chose to deliver them in a gentle Highland accent. It seemed to suit the moment and the information, and no doubt quite a few of those listening recognised one of his famous characters – the policeman, mainstay of many Ealing comedies. However, one man failed to appreciate the humour of the situation. Hugh Macphee, the senior Gaelic Producer, was listening in his home on the outskirts of Glasgow. Feet hardly touching the ground, he summoned a taxi and sped off to Broadcasting House, quivering with rage. By the time he arrived, there was of course nothing he could do, but it was many months before he would acknowledge, far less speak to those involved and Peter made sure that in future shinty, like football, was treated with respect.

Football was Peter Thomson's great love and he was determined to fight the vestige of middle-class prejudice that still existed amongst a few listeners against the round ball. He was a good organiser and had a natural ability for commentary. His likeable personality, tinged with a native shyness, quickly attracted a strong team that stayed with the programme for many years. Dunky Wright, Andy Cowan Martin, Malcolm Turner, George Davidson, John Wilson and Jack Inglis all became familiar voices to a large number of Scots and by late 1957 Listener Research were reporting an audience of close to one million for the programme every Saturday.

As the closing signature tune of *Sportsreel* faded out and the second hand on the clock moved to 7.00pm, there would be just time to announce 'This is the Scottish Home Service' before the strains of *Kate Dalrymple* ushered in the next programme, 25 minutes of Scottish dance music, successfully pushing the listening audience well past the one million mark. This was Scotland's folk music whatever the pundits might say and there were few households where feet weren't tapping in time to the fiddle and accordion men. There was also an air of expectancy, eyes turning to the clock to gauge its progress to 7.25pm, the time when Scotland en masse would pay its weekly visit to *The McFlannels*.

The McFlannels, produced by Scotland's Variety department, was Scotland's longest-running radio family serial. At its peak early in 1948 it attracted a nearly half the listening audience in Scotland and it proudly boasted of being as popular as Tommy Handley's ITMA on the Light Programme. It was a saga in the true sense of the word and by the time the series ended in 1951, the author, Helen W. Pryde had written 252 scripts.

Like many another successful radio programme, fame had been by no means instant. Helen Pryde first wrote about Willie and Helen McFlannel in 1939 after hearing a talk on the wireless describing a family living in the country. She thought her own childhood days in the tenements of Glasgow had been much funnier and sent a couple of short stories on this theme to the BBC. They landed on the desk of Robin Russell, then producer of variety programmes in Glasgow and at that time respon-sible for an afternoon show called *High Tea*. He liked the idea and sugg-ested to Helen that she re-submit the stories, filling out the dialogue and writing them as a short play or sketch. 'Like you see at the pantomime,' he explained.

This created a problem. Helen Pryde, already within sight of middle age and the product of an extremely puritanical upbringing, had never been to a theatre, far less a pantomime in her life. Nothing daunted, she

The McFlannels (1947)
Jean Stoddart (*Maisie*)
and Arthur Shaw (*Peter*).

went to her local library and read some plays. The stories were rewritten and Robin Russell was delighted. On 28 March 1939, *The McFlannels Rub Along* was performed in *High Tea*, sandwiched between a couple of brass band numbers.

Other commissions followed. The war brought an end to most regional material but someone saw an opportunity for wartime humour using a Glasgow family trying to cope with rationing and the black-out and *The McFlannels in Wartime* made occasional appearances. Helen enjoyed writing and began to expand the number of characters, sticking faithfully to her original idea of naming them all after fabrics: The McFlannels, warm and comforting; The McVelvets, a touch superior; Ivy McTweed, very durable and Scottish; and Mrs McCotton, forever masquerading as something other than what she was.

Wartime staffing problems meant there was no regular producer and it wasn't until Howard M. Lockhart returned to Glasgow, newly invalided out of the Army, that anyone took more than a passing interest. He enjoyed their honest, homely style and at the end of the war, casting around for something to bolster the rather frayed variety output available at the time, suggested a trial run of six weekly episodes of *The McFlannels*. At first it was touch and go. There were complaints but there were also a number of appreciative letters and as there was little else available to fill the spot, Howard M. Lockhart got the go ahead for another series.

As it happened it was the right decision. Soon the steady progress of *The McFlannels* up the listening barometer seemed to be unstoppable and when they returned to the air after a summer break in 1948 their now traditional Saturday evening spot was recorded off transmission and repeated twice during the following week.

Of course not everyone could bring themselves to love the antics of Sarah and Willie, endearingly played by Meg Buchanan and John Morton, as they provided an oasis of pre-war traditions and apparent good sense in the room and kitchen up a Glasgow tenement close. 'Too common', sniffed some, 'a surfeit of Glasgow accents,' said others. There were also mixed opinions available on a loftier plane and Melville Dinwiddie reported that the family was 'anathema to The Saltire Society' but that at the same time he had to live with the fact that the then Under-Secretary of State for Scotland loved it.

The McFlannels' popularity was quite phenomenal. It packed in an audience until it was virtually 'standing room only' for the rest of the evening on the Scottish Home Service. It achieved this success with scripts that were truly commonplace and characters who always reacted as expected, something that is now accepted as essential in any family soap, but at the time bewildered many in the BBC. The series also caused some initial concern in the way it created its own 'stars', fictional radio characters suddenly idolised by the public. However, there were some who could see in this a welcome reversal of Scottish radio's habit of borrowing characters from literature. They may have deplored the downright adoration that took place but were pleased that broadcasting now had enduring characters of its own making. A small indication perhaps that Scotland need not always escape into the past, and that there could be a continuing tradition in the future.

A notable trait in some of what Scotland was now offering to its listeners was concern with the present day and an examination of the future. There seemed to be less need to escape into the past, although of course traditions and a climate of patriotism still pervaded a great deal of the output and while variety and popular music clung to a fair measure of long established styles Scottish broadcasting did seem to be increasingly concerning itself with talking to a nation.

Nationhood in these terms had been anticipated early on by the BBC. In 1943, when it first started discussion internally of the likely pattern of post-war broadcasting, Moultrie Kelsall had prophesied the growth of nationalism in Scotland.

'In past wars we have seen the fusion of Scottish feeling into the United Kingdom's struggle. In peace, these ties gall and seem to become bonds.'

It was a shrewd observation and two years later peace did indeed bring a rumbling call for greater Scottish identity and the patriotism of the war years channelled itself into, as far as Scotland was concerned, something more nationalistic.

This call was answered, however faintly, by the government's *White Paper on Broadcasting* which appeared in 1946. It was a document that was largely taken up with the BBC's central matters – commercial broadcasting; the funding of the BBC; and the period of the next Charter (finally established at five years instead of the traditional ten). However, there were a couple of brief points. The BBC were urged to increase devolution to the Regions and afford them a large measure of autonomy in programme matters. As a result the Scottish staff had almost complete control over their programme output in the Scottish Home Service and the Regional Director was given quite remarkable powers within his own bailiwick plus a substantial voice in head office deliberations and when he and his counterpoints joined forces they were a potent body. The second and equally important recommendation was that the BBC establish advisory councils along the lines of the existing General Advisory body in London.

Many of the Regional Directors were unsure of this further step towards much greater autonomy but in Scotland Dinwiddie favoured the idea. He considered it a progressive step forward. He had always found value in listening to advisory groups and he was attracted by the spirit in which the new bodies were being set up, 'to ensure that the directorates of the Corporation are in close touch with movements of thought and opinion in their areas.'

The first meeting of the Scottish Advisory Council (SAC) took place in Edinburgh, still favoured by the Scottish Director as the administrative headquarters, on Monday 27 January 1947 at 2.30pm. It was a sizeable group, consisting of 25 people, including representatives from the Scotland's five existing specialist committees – Religion, Agriculture, Schools, Appeals and Group Listening. The Chairman was Sir Hector Hetherington and during that first meeting he outlined the body's function as he saw it: to appraise past and present programmes from the point both of policy and of performance, and to suggest possible developments in broadcasting in Scotland.

The SAC lasted for six years. During that time, within the confines of 'appraise' and 'suggest', it was an experiment that worked well. It would have been naive to have expected any substantial changes to have been brought about but it did manage to 'persuade' the BBC to adopt quite a few fresh ideas. It also represented for the first time some kind of contact with the listener even though its membership was such as to make this more than a touch biased towards the academic and middle class.

It built up a close and friendly relationship with the Scottish manage-ment and in the case of a couple of members early antagonism to the BBC gave way to respect and admiration, albeit grudgingly, and sometimes for the strangest reasons. One such person was Douglas Young, lecturer in Greek at St Andrews University, bitterly anti-BBC and a man of strong nationalist views. Despite this, or perhaps because of it, the BBC had worked hard to persuade him to become a member of the advisory group and although Young finally agreed, he still made it clear that there was little to be said in favour of the Corporation. That was until the day at a meeting when he met for the first time the BBC's Director of Home Broadcasting, Benjie Nicholls. What impressed Young above all else was the realisation that Nicholls was making notes of the meeting on his agenda paper in Greek. If a Greek scholar could be in charge of BBC programmes then, in Douglas Young's view, there couldn't be much wrong with the Corporation.

The last meeting of the SAC took place in Glasgow on 25 November 1952, for, as it turned out, the body had foreshadowed the creation of a more executive entity – The Broadcasting Council for Scotland brought into being as a result of the Beveridge Committee. At its final meeting the Chairman, now Sir John Falconer, spoke briefly of some of their recommendations and the way they had been acted upon by BBC management.

A call for more plays by Scottish writers had brought about a considerable improvement in the efficiency of the Play Reading panel and had increased the number of productions taken by the Third Programme. Suggestions that lessons in Gaelic were important brought a further three series and a request for improved coverage of Scottish affairs in discussion programmes resulted in a new series *A Matter of Opinion*. This programme, produced by George Runcie and chaired by Nial Paterson, was a well-nigh instantaneous success. It almost trebled its audience in the first five weeks and continued to be popular for many years, demonstrating Scotland's growing appetite for current affairs.

Where possible the SAC had also busied themselves with the nuts and bolts of broadcasting. They had added their weight to pressure from Dundee listeners for access into programmes, resulting in the opening of a small BBC studio in the Coldside Branch Library. The BBC couldn't resist the attraction of an anniversary and brought the studio into service exactly 25 years after the opening of 2DE, on 12 November 1949. Poor reception in rural areas seemed to them to be a particular problem in Scotland. Well briefed by the Scottish management they had lobbied hard for some improvement, particularly in Angus, the Borders and Dumfries and Galloway. Capital projects of this kind were difficult to force through but even so by the end of their term new transmitters were scheduled for Brechin/Montrose and Dumfries.

BBC studio in Coldside Library, Dundee opened 12 November 1949.
(© Dundee Central Library, Photographic Collection)

The BBC in Scotland had been well served by the SAC. As a farewell, they arranged a reception followed by a visit to Studio One to listen to a broadcast being given by the BBC Scottish Orchestra. It was a splendid occasion and the departing members were not slow in recognising the management's hand in the proceedings as they enjoyed the main work of the evening, Schubert's Unfinished Symphony.

The new Broadcasting Council for Scotland (BCS) owed its existence to the Beveridge Committee on Broadcasting whose report had been published in January 1951. A monumental couple of volumes with a myriad of recommendations, it included a great deal of evidence culled from Scotland and had quite a lot to say about broadcasting devolving power from the centre.

But by the time the report had been through the parliamentary process to emerge as the basis of the BBC's Charter for the next ten years, the focus was mostly on central matters – competition, finance and the expanding role of television. These were topics of considerable importance to the Corporation for broadcasting was being buffeted by change and, although the BBC once again emerged as broadcasting's single public service corporation, for the first time the licence was referred to as 'non-exclusive', a hint that in the future there might be some element of competition.

The volume of regional opinion had not been totally forgotten but much of it had been watered down and for the many shades of devolutionists the principal point of interest had to be the role of the new BCS and the fact that the number of Governors of the BBC had been increased to nine, to include designated National Governors for Scotland, Northern Ireland and Wales respectively.

In a straightforward lift from the Beveridge recommendations the BBC was required under its new Charter to set up two National Broadcasting Councils, one for Scotland and one for Wales, 'as soon as reasonably practicable'. Each National Council would consist of a Chairman, who would also become the Corporation Governor representing the Region, and eight other members.

Selecting the new BCS was not a particularly enviable job and perhaps so that everyone could appear to distance themselves from it the burden fell to a panel from the BBC's General Advisory Council, in practice, the handful or so of Scottish members. Their instructions were to select five members after consultation with 'such representative cultural, religious and other bodies in Scotland... as the panel of the General Advisory Council felt fit', and to pick the remaining three as being representative of local authorities.

Not everyone was happy with what was happening and a few people were distinctly at odds with the planned role of the new body. The departing SAC had not liked Beveridge's recommendations and it is possible that at times they were doing no more than voicing the opinion of some of the BBC's Scottish management. The main thrust of their hostility was the belief that the new arrangement would encourage parochialism. BBC Scotland would, it seemed, be cut off from the key executive body in London, and although the new BCS Chairman was to have a seat he would be but one delegated voice. Under the old system, the argument ran, the whole Board of Governors could more easily be drawn into Scottish matters.

There were others on the staff who were critical of the insistence that three out of the eight new members must be representative of local authorities. Such people would regard themselves as delegates, as would others appointed with an eye to sectional groups, and the net result could well be 'spokesmen' only interested in their own narrow interests.

Eventually the complicated process of picking the members was completed and the eight men and women were ready to take up their executive role. It was an important change to the basis of management of programmes for the BCS was charged with the function of 'controlling the policy and content of the programmes provided primarily in the country concerned.' But the Corporation was already well skilled in checks and balances. Written into the function were two provisos.

The first related to Party Political Broadcasts, broadcasts of national importance and interest, and schools broadcasts.

The second required that the new body be subject also to 'such reservations and direction as may reappear to the Corporation to be necessary from time to time for reasons of finance or in the interests of due co-ordination and coherent administration of the operations and affairs of the Corporation.'

As the BBC delicately put it, this indicated a balance of control between the central and the local authority.

The first meeting of the BCS took place on Wednesday 14 January 1953 at Broadcasting House, Edinburgh, and in the chair was the newly

Programme Planning (1946)
(l/r) Andrew Stewart; Gordon Gildard; Robert F. Dunnett;
Hugh Macphee; Robert Kemp; Herbert Wiseman; Moultrie R. Kelsall.

designated National Governor for Scotland, the Rt Hon Lord Clydes-muir (a BBC Governor since 1950). The eight members of the newly formed body were: Mr A.D. Buchanan-Smith, Bailie T. Orr, Lord Provost John M. Graham, Sir Cecil Graves, Dean of Guild, J.L. Kinloch, Mrs Rhona Mavor, Rev T.M. Murchison, and Mr A.E. McKenna.

Waiting to greet them in the Edinburgh Board Room were three members of the General Advisory Panel which had selected them and a group of BBC officials mainly from London, including the Director-General, Sir Ian Jacob. Also present was Melville Dinwiddie and at future meetings he would, of course, be the sole BBC representative in attendance.

Dinwiddie, by now designated Controller, Scotland (all 'Director' titles had been taken for head office use when the BBC formed its first Board of Management in 1948) had found himself in something of a quandary when preparing to face the new BCS. His natural instinct was to be as helpful and co-operative as he had been before but the previous body had enjoyed an advisory role, something that the Controller was well versed in dealing with. The role of its successor was very different. In its executive capacity would they tinker too much with the Scottish output? Or could he persuade its members that programmes were best left in the hands of the professionals? They were welcome to join him on a visit to the bridge at any time but it would be better he felt if they kept out of the engine room.

Beyond the confines of the BBC there was also concern, though here the critics split into two very different camps. Those set on a path of nationalism quickly dismissed any thought that the new executive might be a first step towards independence and instead voiced their frustration over the complete absence of any revenue-raising powers for the new body. Others, no doubt the successors of Reith's London babies of the late 1920s, expressed woeful predictions that any measure of independence in the framing of broadcasting policy would mean that soon the kailyard would reign supreme and that Scottish broadcasting would descend into narrow restrictive thinking.

In fact, the BCS very quickly found an exceedingly useful and impor-tant role for itself. Broadcasting in Scotland had the outward appearance of success but there were worrying cracks deep in the foundations and the advent of the BCS and its subsequent help and support came not a minute too soon.

The hard work of the Scottish broadcasters had been rewarded with a Scottish Home Service that had weathered expansion and now provided a developed and comprehensive output. It had the distinction of being the only BBC service to have a larger audience in its own area than the hugely successful Light Programme, while the number of contributors from Scotland to other London-based BBC services was the largest of all parts of the UK. Even the recent arrival of a limited television service from the new Kirk o' Shotts transmitter had failed to draw people away from their radio in the numbers expected.

Against this background of traditionally centralist broadcasting the BBC had contrived what it felt was a reasonable reflection of the changes and spirit now abroad in Scotland, and while it continued an underlying theme of 'here's tae us, wha's like us' in its music and entertainment, it cautiously dipped a toe into other waters. The signs of devolution seemed comfortingly respectable. A Minister of State had been appointed and additional Under-Secretaries. The Covenant Association continued to gather

Announcers meeting (1946)
(l/r) at window – Jimmy Crampsey; Hugh Macphee; Pamela Patterson; n/k; Gordon Gildard; n/k; n/k.

numerous signatures and there was an increased tendency for nation-
alised bodies to form Scottish committees with as much independence as
possible.

The BBC was endeavouring to deal objectively with these and other
matters with items in its news bulletins, by regular discussion programmes
and with talks and parliamentary reports. Sometimes its efforts were frus-
trated by outside opposition, such as at the time of the General Election in
1951 when it was the parties that refused to have any special broadcasts
for Scotland.

It was an immense variety of output and it was now causing concern.
While it added up to a very creditable performance it meant that broadcasting in Scotland was running well beyond its design capacity and had
been doing so for almost two years. Contributions to other services were
still being maintained at peak level but the programme hours for Scotland
had started to drop. A weekly Scottish total of almost 29 hours achieved
in 1950 had already reduced to a fraction above 26 hours.

Controller, Scotland decided that the sooner the BCS knew the true
position the better and as the bouquets for successful programmes were
still passing round the Board Room table he told then the sobering facts.
Under the general heading of 'The Policy and Content of the Scottish Home
Service' he gave them details of programme hours and the financial
position and outlined the reasons for the decline.

For the previous five years the Corporation had given Scotland almost
complete autonomy to initiate as many items as money and talent would
permit. But the Scottish staff were still working on an establishment agreed
in 1946 with only small increases in numbers since then. Engineering posts
had not been part of the devolved package at the end of hostilities and
the number of people allocated to Scotland was rigorously controlled by
London almost regardless of programme commitments. Expansion had also
been conditioned by the number of studios available, office accommodation and technical facilities. The most depressing news of all was the state
of Programme Allowance – the money that paid for the programmes.
Dinwiddie revealed there had been only small increases during the
previous four years. At the time of the BCS's inauguration the amount
available was £2,000 per week plus £120 for travel and duty expenses.
Of the programme monies only some £200 was a fluid asset, the remainder
being committed for common services, orchestral and other contributions

and expenses. That £200 per week was currently expected to meet the costs of features, plays, OBs, orchestral soloists, talks and short features.

With commendable swiftness a small sub-committee of the BCS gathered together the various strands of emotional and factual information that were available to it. Aided by the Scottish management who willingly guided them through the intricacies of the Corporation's logistics and traditions, they set out the general principles that they would be willing to stand by.

First, there was a reminder of the politics of the situation. Beveridge had said that there was case for the BBC receiving 100 per cent of the licence revenue but the subsequent White Paper had reduced the figure to 85 per cent. Beveridge had also spoken of 'devolution, if it is to be real, involves financial responsibility' and the Corporation had indeed subsequently provided for the transfer to the BCS responsibility for programme allowance, but at the same time making finance one of the reservations in reference to the BCS's activities.

Passing on, there was a moment to toy with something akin to separatism. This was rejected outright on the prima facie case that Scotland was getting a very fair share of the present licence revenue and that if there was a completely separate broadcasting service, financed entirely from revenue from Scottish sources, the present licence fee for sound broadcasting would need to be at least doubled.

The BCS then laid down the rules as they saw them.

The programme hours of the Scottish Home Service should be stabilised at a weekly average of a minimum of 26 hours and the emphasis should be on improving the quality of the different items.

Every effort should be made by the BBC in Scotland to offer engagements to broadcasters of experience and of established reputation in an effort to retain the best artists in Scotland.

Some additions to the production staff were necessary if the desired hours and standards of output were to be maintained.

In view of the present situation it was inappropriate to recommend any augmentation of players of the BBC Scottish Orchestra, but necessary provision would have to be made for any award of salary increase to the present players.

It had not taken long for the BCS and Scottish management to be as one, and from now on the annual estimates submitted by Scotland would have firm and resolute backing, demolishing the fears of those who had prophesied a weakening of purpose and a lack of cohesive drive. But there would be a great deal more to come out of the new partnership. Broadcasting, as usual, was on the move and Scotland, with an increasing awareness of its national status, wanted to be in the vanguard of change.

If all the latest material in Scotland were to be fully tapped it was clear that the existing facilities were insufficient. The BCS's 'agreed principles' were but a breathing space. Scottish broadcasting had to move forward once again. There must be an end to frustrating delays in the installation of new equipment. The Scottish Programme Allowance required a substantial increase. Programme quality both technically and in content must move closer to that of London-made programmes. Beyond the studios there were other problems to be dealt with. Improved transmitter coverage in Scotland was badly needed and though not yet approved by parliament, hopes were high for the future based on the introduction of VHF (Very High Frequency) broadcasting sometime in the next period.

These were the parameters of national broadcasting and once the BCS had found its feet a substantial part of its work was concerned with development. Dinwiddie by now had warmed to the body realising that, if he got their approval on some point that, combined with the ear of his National Governor, gave him considerable leverage. Of course, the Board of Management must reign supreme and all Regional Controllers were answerable to its Directors but there was nothing wrong in having another route to the top. Had they but known it the BCS had marked out the tenant of its dwellings with London for the following 30 years. Television would replace radio in terms of importance and the number of zeros at the end of financial estimates would rise substantially. But the insistence that Scotland must be given a large measure of responsibility for its own broadcasting plus the wherewithal to support it on a common standard would always be paramount.

For the BCS there was also work to do in supporting the management in their business of making programmes. The early spectre of the members getting too close and too involved had quickly receded, not so much through their own doing but rather because they soon found that the way to the heart of the output was in many cases already occupied by an advisory committee.

Advice had always been a feature in broadcasting almost since its inception. In the beginning the BBC had turned to individual experts but gradually panels and committees had been formed. The fact that the committees functioning in Scotland had been in operation for so long, and were now very much part of the established organisation of the BBC, gave them a standing which the BCS chose not to challenge. Instead it worked out a system of close liaison with regular contact and reports. The various advisory committee chairmen were invited to speak at BCS meetings, the members of the BCS were given sight of committee minutes and it was clearly defined that in future the names of those nominated for membership of the committee would be submitted to the BCS for final selection and approval.

Other areas attracted BCS attention, including the relationship with the School Broadcasting Council for Scotland (SBCS) and the vexed question of political broadcasting. Both were listed in the Charter as being subject to overall BBC control 'as may appear to the Corporation to be necessary from time to time', but, as this was a safeguard of transmission time rather than anything else, the BCS saw no reason to refrain from getting involved.

They were particularly conscious of the important part education played in maintaining Scottish traditions and they were anxious that not only should this continue but also that emphasis should be made on the need to develop the national culture. What is more they wanted to be associated with it as they felt that this was very much part of the terms of reference. However, the SBCS was already well wrapped up in its own constitution

It's All Yours (1951)
Jimmy Logan and
Stanley Baxter.

and enjoying a close and important link with the United Kingdom Council. Eventually a reasonable working relationship was established whereby the BCS would be given sight of the annual list of proposed programmes immediately after it had been presented to the United Kingdom Council, at which time it could make comments on what was being proposed. There was an added involvement, never even put to the test. Schools department in Scotland formed part of the overall budget of the Scottish Home Service. This, nominally at least, was now the responsibility of the BCS.

Political broadcasting was a subject that had been flooding off the walls of BBC Scotland offices for close on 20 years. It was at its sharpest when allocating time for pre-election broadcasts and Scotland had first become involved when at the run-up to the 1935 General Election it had urged that time should be allotted in the Scottish programme for representatives of the different parties to broadcast on Scottish election topics. The Scottish National Party applied for such a broadcast but was refused on the ground that they had fewer than 20 nominees. The following year the Islewater Committee Report recommended that the allocation of time between government and other parties should be arranged by agreement between them, but this left out small parties who had no members in the House. A more equitable basis for allocation was suggested as the number of votes cast at the last election, but this was not favoured.

In the 1945 General Election the same general rules applied. Broadcasts by small parties were again considered before the 1950 election but the agreement now in existence with the principal parties gave 50 candidates as a minimum qualification, and still the Scottish National Party did not receive a broadcast.

A complaint was lodged that the allocation was an unreasonable one because the party had no interest in offering candidates for constituencies outside Scotland and the proportion of 50 out of a possible 71 was too large compared with 50 out of a total membership of the House of Commons.

Again, in 1951, the 50 or more candidate rule applied.

The need for pre-election broadcasts designed specifically for Scotland and including Nationalist interest would rumble on. The BCS spoke out in its first year: 'This Council, having considered the question of pre-election broadcasts, asks that the parties be requested to agree to additional talks on the Scottish Home Service only by speakers who would deal with Scottish programmes.'

But nothing changed, not for the moment anyway. But the BCS did enjoy one minor triumph in political broadcasting a few years later, in 1958, with the reporting of the Kelvingrove by-election.

Kelvingrove was the first occasion on which the BBC reported a campaign in its news bulletins and also presented radio and television programmes featuring the by-election candidates. It was also the first occasion on which the BBC and a commercial television programme company (Scottish Television) collaborated in jointly produced programmes as a matter of public service to help the electoral process.

A perceptive comment on the television coverage appeared in *The Glasgow Herald* on the day before polling: 'Though it may put new life into British democracy... it puts a new and severe strain on (the candidates). It is not only that a new technique has to be acquired and a platform manner abandoned but also the knowledge that the result may depend on the impression of the candidate's personality conveyed during a few minutes of tension and strain.'

For the moment, however, in the mid-'50s, broadcasting and politics did not enjoy an easy or close association. The straight Party Political Broadcast, confined to 12 a year, had no direct Scottish participation except when Scottish members were chosen by their parties to give these talks. Ministerial broadcasts did take place from time to time on purely factual or administrative policy or in appeals to the nation to co-operate in these policies. So far as Scotland was concerned, in cases where there was a separate ministry, a broadcast for Scottish listeners only was arranged, usually at the same time as the ministerial broadcast from London. In fact, political comment was almost entirely confined to *Scotland in Parliament*. These were talks broadcast about once a month. The speakers were chosen to maintain a rough party balance and at the same time to deal with items of special importance to Scotland, e.g. the Scottish Grand Committee and debates on Scottish Affairs. Scottish members also participated from time to time in the London broadcast, *The Week in Parliament*.

And to really stunt the growth of political broadcasting there was the 14-Day Rule which ensured that any issues about to be debated by Parliament within that immediate next period could not be discussed on air.

While the BCS and the senior management did their best to secure some promise of financial aid for what was fast becoming an embattled Scottish radio operation, it was impossible not to cast an envious eye in the direction of television. The estimates being prepared for the Scottish Home Service contained some very necessary increases for rising costs and development. But capital expenditure was still subject to government control and the major part of what was being permitted was allocated to expanding television throughout the country. Television was the dripping roast and though constitutionally outside the scope of BCS influence, Scotland's Controller had already and legitimately, tried to extract some benefit for Scotland.

Early in 1950 the first public rumour of the approach of television had appeared in the Scottish press. It was a report stating that Edinburgh Town Council had been asked to provide a site on Blackford Hill on the south side of the city for a television development. It was, in fact, the General Post Office starting work on their chain of relay links to connect Scotland with the Holme Moss transmitter near Huddersfield. The site for the first television transmitter in Scotland was to be at Kirk o' Shotts, roughly halfway between Edinburgh and Glasgow and the projected finishing date for the contractors was to be around mid-1952.

When this had become known, Dinwiddie, aware of television's rapacious appetite for space and mindful of the fact that the lease for Edinburgh's 5 Queen Street was about to run out, had decided it was time once again to make a bid for new premises in the capital. Regardless of the fact that the major part of Scottish broadcasting was now firmly rooted in Glasgow, or perhaps because of that, Scotland attempted to prise open the television development coffers wide enough to pay for a new headquarters located in Edinburgh. Once again, Dinwiddie allowed 'premises' to float to the top of his correspondence tray. With his usual enthusiasm he offered a multitude of possibilities and proposals.

Two of the suggested locations enjoyed a brief flicker of life – the Dean Orphanage and John Watson's School, both on the west side of Edinburgh and within a stone's throw of each other, but the hoped-for Edinburgh development was, in truth, untenable, and most of the discussions with London were, in fact, short off the record chats, a sure sign of head office disinterest. The resources of the Corporation could not stand a second headquarters in Scotland and once again Controller, Scotland was told this. The BBC's existing plans for capital expenditure had been cut by the Cabinet Programme's Investment Committee. For 1952 alone, £1,300,000 had been removed and Edinburgh, to all intents and purpose, was a non-starter.

Dinwiddie reluctantly accepted defeat, this time asking only that London assist him in preventing 'the old bogies of Edinburgh versus Glasgow and Scotland under London domination again rearing their ugly heads.' The lease of Queen Street was renewed and Scottish programme management, who had occupied twin bases in the two cities since 1946, kirtled their skirts and moved permanently to Glasgow ready for the new venture of television and radio under the same roof. At the same time, everyone agreed not to mention Edinburgh again, not that is, until the next time, which would be a year after Dinwiddie's retirement.

CHAPTER SEVEN

The Arrival of Television

An attempt will be made tomorrow, Friday, February 15, to join the station to the television network, so that Scottish viewers can see at least part of the broadcast of the funeral procession of His Late Majesty, King George VI.

BBC Press Announcement, 14 February 1952

IT WAS A SOMBRE start for the new television service from Kirk o' Shotts. Earlier in the year it had been announced that low-power transmissions (5kw as opposed to 50kw) would begin on Friday 1 March. However, with the need to let as many people as possible to watch the King's

Kirk o' Shotts
Television comes to Scotland (1952).

funeral, the BBC cast aside its traditional caution. With the agreement of the GPO, plus many crossed fingers under various desks, the BBC's television service arrived in Scotland on the morning of 15 February 1952.

The transmission was successful and many Scots viewed the complete ceremony, but as the new vision link with the south was only operating in one direction and establishing the two-way system still required more work, it was decided that the original opening date should stand. Thus at 7.30pm on Friday 14 March, the service formally opened when *Television Comes to Scotland* was seen throughout the UK network.

The programme took place in the large music studio in Broadcasting House, Edinburgh and started with Mary Malcolm, a familiar face to viewers in the south, welcoming new viewers to television. Then, Lord Tedder, the Stirlingshire-born Vice-Chairman of the BBC Board of Governors, rose to introduce the Rt Hon James Stuart, Secretary of State for Scotland, who was invited to declare the new service officially open. Following polite applause from the invited audience there was a Prayer of Dedication from the Dean of the Thistle, and a Vote of Thanks from the Lord Provost of Edinburgh. Finally, and for an all too brief ten minutes, Scotland shook off its torpor and a kilted Alastair MacIntyre, BBC Scotland's Senior Announcer, introduced ten minutes of Scottish country dancing. Not surprising, the performance created an air of almost unrelieved boredom. With television, something a touch more sophisticated had been expected.

The most pungent criticism came from Reginald Pound, writing in the BBC's own magazine, *The Listener*. In an article headed *Scotch Without Splash* he wrote: 'Showmanship can be overdone. Headlines can be too bold. Loud voices can repel. 'The gift of the gab' is not invariably admired. Even so, need the Kirk o' Shotts opening ceremony have been so impeccably dull?'

There was worse to come. Cecil McGivern, Controller, Television Programmes, lambasted the programming in a memo to Gordon Gildard (Gildard, now the Head of Scottish Programmes was alleged to have been largely responsible for the programme's content).

'Speeches dreadful. Really dreadful. Dull and boring with the Provost coming off best. This sort of television dullness is most depressing...'

Such direct criticism was very different from radio's style. This had an urgency and candour that was foreign to those steeped in the traditions of the wireless. Television was exciting, yes, but at the same time surprisingly vulnerable and it dreaded anything that might be judged as unsuccessful. Around the time of Scotland's opening, another mandarin, George Barnes, was illustrating this in a report to the Board of Governors:

> Even a single failure is a considerable failure in television with its limited transmission hours and no alternative programmes. At least two million viewers see it and as they turn down their thumbs they howl for blood. Or that is the way it seems during the next several days.

It had been hoped that the next programme transmitted from Scotland, coverage of the Scotland v England rugby match at Murrayfield on the Saturday, would lift the general air of gloom. But the Scottish Rugby Union, despite strong BBC pressure, refused permission and the next broadcast seen in the UK was an Evening Service on the Sunday from St Cuthbert's in Edinburgh. Finally after a few days to draw breath, the television audience watched the third of the special opening programmes from Scotland – broadcast from the Citizens' Theatre, Glasgow.

With both drama and religion, Scotland recovered some of its footing. The service from St Cuthbert's, directed by a London OB producer, Aubrey Singer, who would later come to work permanently in Scotland, drew praise from London. So too did the play, J.M. Barrie's *The Old Lady Shows Her Medals*. This time, the verdict from McGivern was an unreserved 'thumbs up' and he wrote: 'The leads excellent (Madeleine Christie and Andrew Keir)', adding 'one of the best, if not the best, rep company transmissions I have seen.'

It had been an exciting and traumatic six days for the BBC in Scotland and things would never be the same again now that they had met television face-to-face. McGivern, summing up the first visit by television cameras to Scotland, chose to be hopeful: 'A small but most encouraging start. I look forward to Scottish programmes growing to a healthy, exciting stream'. Then, rather like the first exploratory probe by the Romans, the television visitors fell back to the south and no more programmes originated in Scotland until four months later.

Although the television cameras had gone, Scotland remained as the newest ingredient in the television 'mix'. Scots and Scottish interests, pseudo or otherwise, leapt out of the pages of the *Radio Times*. Mostly they cradled the old images of tartan, mist covered mountains and northern fortitude. The City of Glasgow Police Pipe Band crowded on to the small stage of Liverpool's *'Television Music Hall'*. Heading the bill in *On Show in Manchester* were Alec Finlay, Margot Henderson and Robert Wilson. A young Fulton McKay took part in J.B. Priestley's *Music at Night,* from the Alexandra Palace studios and a six-part adaptation of *Kidnapped* used such actors as James McKechnie, John Fraser and Russell Hunter.

Picturesque bits of Scotland began to be seen in London-made film programmes and Richard Dimbleby's *About Britain* series visited the Firth of Clyde doing a useful public relations exercise for the Clyde coast.

Throughout the Central Belt of Scotland, electrical retailers hopefully built up their stocks of television receivers and the various manufacturers increased their advertising in newspapers and magazines. Both the industry and the BBC were determined to take television into the homes of Scotland, although by the end of the first year the number of television licences issued, just over 60,000, would be considered to be disappointingly low.

There had been no lack of welcome for television, certainly, as far as the Scottish BBC had been concerned. As the largest BBC operations outside London it had chafed at the slow progress northwards, caused mainly by government stringency and there had also been a question of national pride involved. Everyone knew of John Logie Baird's part in the early tentative experiments with vision in 1929 and, although the Corporation later abandoned his mechanical system in favour of electronic methods, people in Scotland considered television to be a Scottish invention.

Then there was the important matter of revenue. Television licences brought more money into the BBC than radio alone and while there was no direct quid pro quo between an area's revenue statistics and its development, being an earner gave you a better seat at the negotiating table.

So far, so good. But television was an extra, an add-on, to radio which now had a well-developed management structure committed to servicing its highly praised Scottish Home Service. That same management may have been entranced by what had at last arrived over the border but for them the serious business was still radio broadcasting.

Even before the opening of Kirk o' Shotts a certain amount of re-jigging of the Scottish Home Service had taken place to minimise the effect of the new competition. Evening television did not start until around 8.00pm and, aware of this, Scotland had moved most of its popular programmes into the early evening period starting around 6.30pm and making use of what had become known as the 'high tea' strategy.

'High tea' had been devised by Andrew Stewart when, as Programme Director at the beginning of the post-war period, he had been anxious to hold off the challenge of the new Light Programme. Andrew had long since left Scotland to become the BBC's Controller, Northern Ireland – and would soon move to London to take charge of the Home Service. But his opting-out plan for the start of the Scottish evening was still a model of its kind.

The scheme was simple and effective and made full use of the routine in most Scottish working class households where the evening meal was not dinner but high tea. The man of the house would arrive home from work around 5.00pm or 5.30pm and as the children's programme finished he would listen at 6.00pm to the news and Scottish news while washing and shaving at the kitchen. By 6.30pm he was sitting at the tea table while either Scottish dance music or Scottish comedy filled the room. Thirty minutes later the dishes would be cleared away and father was finally in his chair by the fire for the rest of the evening. By now, steadfastly immovable until bedtime, he was happy to listen to most things and many serious programmes, slipped in later in the evening, achieved astonishingly large audiences in Scotland.

The plan had worked well against the Light Programme and now seemed to be repeating that success against television. There was an almost petulant tone in the BBC Report and Accounts at the end of the year.

'The people of Scotland appeared to be cautious about accepting the new service. Television drew some listeners from the sound programme... it could not, however, be regarded yet as a large competitor.'

The first television OB unit to have any degree of permanency in Scotland arrived a few months later after the opening of Kirk o' Shotts. The equipment, which had already seen service elsewhere, was on a sharing basis with the BBC's North of England Region in Manchester, an unsatisfactory arrangement that would exist for almost three years. On paper each had the use of the unit for three months at a time, but compromises had to be made to fit immovable feats such as test matches from Yorkshire and the Festival in Edinburgh. It was a sharing process that was workable in theory, but in practice time-consuming and inconvenient and within six months the Director of Television in London would be reporting to the Board of Governors: 'Relations with the Regions are friendly but uneasy. They resent having to share the unit. Feeling on this matter has lately risen considerably and it is true that they can easily quote figures to show that the amount of time the units spend on the road and not on programme sites is very high and with over-long maintenance time.'

The restrictive economic situation of the country had left the BBC with no other option but it was hindering Scotland at a critical moment of national consciousness and the slow progress of television brought considerable adverse comment. It was a time when Scotland should have been awakening to a new and stimulating dimension in broadcasting. Sadly the television service seemed to have slowed to a crawl.

Stung by the criticism and with a healthy pioneering spirit this new breed of professional and dedicated broadcasters rolled up their sleeves and set to work. They cut corners. They used old and unreliable equipment, often begged from elsewhere. They made do with temporary accommodation that was inadequate and foolish from the start. Help from London was largely verbal encouragement – 'you're managing so well' was usually the answer when some local scheme found itself on its beam end, and just to add a touch of zest to the proceedings there was a Head of Television in London who mistrusted Scotland's ability to reach the high standards he had set for the television output.

The foundation of the television service in Scotland was going to be based on ingenuity, chauvinism and ambition. A great deal of help came from some radio colleagues, although radio's rather paternal benevolence would eventually have no place in the new service, and unbelievably an OB unit, which had to be shared with another part of the BBC.

The unit went on show for the first time with a press preview at the end of July 1952. In charge of the technical side was Bill Jackson, supervising a staff of around 30, which included cameramen, technicians, rigger-drivers and sound specialists. The production team was headed by Aubrey Singer and included James Buchan, ex-Glasgow news and fresh from the television training section in London, and Noble Wilson from radio's studio management department. Some 30 years later they would be best known as Managing-Director of BBC Television, Chief Executive of Grampian Television and Controller, BBC International Relations.

The mobile control room or scanner was the core of the television operation. In its cramped and overheated space a rather unique marriage of engineering expertise and production dreams would take place. The producer and his secretary sat on an uncomfortable bench-like seat alongside the sound mixer and the engineer. Behind, standing in a slightly stooped position, not through deference but because of the lack of head room, were those who had come to help, advise or criticise.

The production desk ran almost the complete width of the van, its telephones, dials and faders acting as a constant reminder of the complex chain of technological pitfalls that lay between the programme and the viewer. Between the producer and the two rows of black and white pictures that gave him all his information, because he acted as director and vision-mixer as well, was a subterranean line of 'rack' operators, the engineers responsible for the quality of the picture from each camera.

Usually invisible in the gloom, their voices would frequently report that a camera was no longer usable. With only three cameras available on the unit, a camera breakdown created a considerable amount of tension, particularly as all programmes were live. If two cameras went down things became desperate. One Scottish producer who eventually made a considerable name for himself as a director in London was frequently physically sick after a transmission.

Location Reporting
(l/r) James Buchan, News Assistant, then OB Producer Television, finally Chief Executive of Grampian Television, with Eugene (Gerry) Girot, Mobile Recording Engineer.

The unit had been designed for location work and its cameras were cumbersome and noisy in operation. Changing camera lenses – each turret had a camera of four – used a noisy motor-drive system and there was a distinctively audible carriage movement when the focus was adjusted. Perched high on some scaffolding, covering a Clydeside launch, nobody noticed but when the unit came to be used in the relatively sophisticated conditions of a theatre or concert hall there were a great many complaints.

With the mobile control room were two radio links. These were mobile transmitters used to relay the television signal onward from the programme site to the nearest entry point into the transmitter chain. There was a limit to the distance over which they could operate, usually around 30 miles, and this restricted the deployment of the main unit.

For its first programme from Scotland the newly arrived unit trod familiar ground. Putting its faith in the Scottish tradition of drama successes, it televised an early James Bridie play *The Black Eye* from the stage of the Glasgow Citizens' Theatre on Tuesday 12 August. The producer and adaptor was Jimmy Crampsey (borrowed from radio) and television direction was by Aubrey Singer and Campbell Logan. Amongst the cast were Tom Fleming, James MacTaggart, David Kossoff, Doris McLatchie and her future husband Pharic Maclaren. Pharic, in a few years' time, would become BBC Scotland's principal television drama producer, while James MacTaggart would move to London as a highly regarded television director.

To everyone's relief the play was a success. The London television management were pleased. 'A salty performance that truly captures the Glasgow home and fully justified all our plans', wrote the Head of Television Drama (Michael Barry) to Gordon Gildard. Even *The Listener* saw fit to praise, although it couldn't resist some Sassenach humour and headed its comments with 'A wee keek at the cathode.'

The cameras stayed in the theatre for another programme the following evening. Not drama this time, but a 45-minute discussion: 'A Parliament for Scotland'. Chaired by the Oxford philosopher, H.J. Paton, the speakers were John MacCormick of the Scottish Covenant Association, Walter Elliott, MP, John Wheatley, MP, Dr Robert McIntyre of the Scottish National Party, and Robert Hurd of The Saltire Society. Again the production of the programme was a shared responsibility, this time with George Runcie supervising the content and James Buchan directing the cameras.

The practice of using one site for multi-programmes was to become a hallmark of regional work. Television was already an expensive business and the time and labour needed to de-rig out of one location, travel and move in somewhere else was anything but cost effective. Also, with a shared unit, time was at a premium and there was always a rush to make as many programmes as possible before the MCR moved southwards again.

This high productivity, combined with an unwillingness to turn down any London request, resulted in some striking examples of ingenuity and enterprise. Once, after a rugby match at Murrayfield, the unit stayed on for an interview. The job completed, the London producer came on the line to thank the Scottish director, Bill Stevenson.

'That was okay, thank you. The sound was terrible though. I thought you were in a ladies' lavatory.'

Bill's brief reply, 'We were', brought a stunned silence.

As tales of peculiar location became legion, pride of place surely went to Alan Rees, the television producer who was brought to Scotland when Noble Wilson left to work in London. Rigged into the Locarno Ballroom in Glasgow to cover the ballroom dancing championships, he found himself producing another three programmes: a discussion on the religious significance of pain and suffering; the *Epilogue;* and a general knowledge quiz programme. All from the same site and within a period of three days.

Soon no spacious ground-floor location within 30 miles of Kirk o' Shotts was safe from the prying eyes of television staff. Like predators they stalked their quarry. Halls mostly, and be they drill, burgh, church or masonic, provided they had power and water and a clear radio link path to the transmitter, a use was found for them. On most occasions the unit was well received. Television had quickly assumed the mantle of wonder that had previously enwrapped radio and everyone turned out to see the 'television people'.

As well as making 'built' programmes, the OB unit did find time to operate in its primary role, covering OBs of events. Sport was an obvious candidate, although there were problems with some of the governing bodies. After a year of television in Scotland, the SFA and the Scottish league were still saying 'no' to cameras, as were the Scottish Rugby Union, thought by some to be the most uncompromising of the four home unions.

In the end, it was left to that old preoccupation beloved by radio, watching people at work, to generate a reputation for the new television unit in Scotland. The chance came through a London-based series called *Other People's Jobs,* and for it Scotland was asked to contribute live to the network a 45-minute programme direct from the coalface of the Tillicoultry mine near Alloa.

Other People's Jobs – The Miner had been a gleam in the eye of television for almost four years. Each time a new television transmitter was opened the BBC and the National Coal Board had searched within a wide radius looking for a suitable location. At last, with the opening of Kirk o' Shotts, Tillicoultry mine was identified. The two organisations started detailed planning, working to a transmission date of 25 November 1952 and the first ever pit broadcast was on the way.

The problems were considerable. The unit's vans had to be emptied and a special television control room fitted out over 1,800ft from the surface. Two hundred yards away the cameras and microphones were positioned close to the coalface. During the days of rigging and rehearsal conditions were reasonably dry, but as the evening of the broadcast approached

Open Golf
St Andrews (1955).

water became a distinct problem. Dripping from the very low roof and seeping from cracks at the face it gradually built up around the ankles and legs of the cameramen and commentators. With so much electrical gear in use, there were fears that the programme might have to be abandoned, partly for safety reasons but also because the equipment was in any case becoming unusable.

In spite of this, Aubrey Singer, who was producing, took a sanguine view when chatting to Bruce Allan, one of the cameramen, shortly before the transmission. Straddling a large puddle, his spectacles misting and coal dust covering his face, he beamed, 'This has a 50–50 chance, maybe!'

In fact they made it, although only just and beating the rising water levels by only a few minutes. The three commentators, Alastair Borthwick, Jameson Clark and James Buchan, survived the evening with nothing worse than dirt spattered faces and uncomfortably wet overalls. From every quarter, praise for the programme and the crew poured in. The broadcast had amply demonstrated the appallingly dirty, uncomfortable and dangerous work of the miner, heightened, at one moment, by the look of apprehension that crossed James Buchan's face as a large stone from the roof fell at his back during an interview.

The same James Buchan, five years later, would take the unit to the opposite extremity. This time as producer he contributed a live programme into the Now series siting OB cameras at the very top of the Forth Rail Bridge.

These programmes, and others like them, were the robust side of television. Scotland, particularly within the confines of the Kirk o' Shotts area, had an abundance of 'vigorous' subjects and the three Glasgow-based producers took full advantage, contributing a stream of industrial vignettes into the television service. The chance to use the unit in a more refined atmosphere came very soon after its arrival when, in August, arrangements were made to televise items from the Sixth Edinburgh International Festival.

Television had previously reflected the Edinburgh International Festival (EIF) on film in newsreel items and magazines. It had also, in 1951 and 1952, looked at the Edinburgh Film Festival which ran concurrently with the EIF. It's not surprising, therefore, that the local management now wanted to steer live cameras in the same direction.

Early in the year, shortly after the formal opening of Kirk o' Shotts,

Cecil McGivern wrote from London: 'Now that the 'meagre' opening is over, I am anxious to plan the first occasion when we *really* go to Scotland for a few days.'

He went on to suggest visits either to the Edinburgh International Festival or the Radio Industries Exhibition in Glasgow. In an immediate reply from Scotland both the Controller and Gordon Gildard made it quite clear that the EIF was the proper occasion and shortly afterwards, Scotland submitted a list of suggested items. McGivern took the point and the EIF was pencilled in as a television commitment.

Since its inception in 1947 relations between the Festival authorities and BBC Scotland had always been excellent. The number of broadcasts had steadily increased and all negotiations for radio were conducted directly between the Artistic Director and either the Scottish Controller or Head of Programmes. Television meant a new dimension, not least

Merry-Ma-Tanzie (1956)
Children's television (*l/r*) Noble Wilson, Director, later Controller, BBC International Relations; Kathleen Garscadden, Producer; Bryden Murdoch; Willie Joss; R. Gordon MacCallum; Iain Cuthbertson; Grace McChlery; Joan Fitzpatrick.

because of its London-based chain of command, and because of unfamiliarity and different requirements, negotiations by the new service proved to be anything but simple.

One of the proposals being pursued by television was *Highland Fair*, which the Glasgow Citizens' Theatre was staging at the Assembly Hall in Edinburgh. To keep disruption of paying audiences to a minimum, it was decided not to cover a scheduled performance but instead stage a special excerpt for the cameras on a Sunday evening. When news of this reached the ears of the owners of the Assembly Hall, the Fathers and Brethren of the Church of Scotland, their condemnation was short and to the point and, with the word 'no' ringing loudly in their ears, television abandoned the idea.

There were other difficulties strewn in the way of television coverage. Huge copyright problems that seemed unsurmountable, particularly in the time available, and an almost blanket refusal from both the Musicians' Union and Equity as far as televising concerts, opera or plays was concerned.

Eventually agreement was reached for four programmes specifically tied to that year's Festival. These were the Opening Ceremony on the Castle Esplanade, the Edinburgh Military Tattoo (conveniently from the same location and televised two days later), the Festival Piano Quartet from the Usher Hall and a festival magazine from a 'drive-in' location.

The first two programmes were copybook examples of how to use the unit. Philip Dorte, a pre-war television producer and now Head of Television Films, wrote to the Head of Outside Broadcasts in London after the second broadcast, 'As an elder statesman of television OBS I feel that I must drop you this note to say that I feel that the Edinburgh Tattoo OB last night was one of the best OBS that has ever been staged.' A nice compliment to commentator, Henry Green, and the television director, Aubrey Singer.

But trouble with the Festival was not far away, and it erupted in full measure with the next programme scheduled from Edinburgh: the Festival Piano Quartet from the Usher Hall. From every point of view this was an important broadcast. Not only was it a television 'debut' from the Festival proper but there was also an added responsibility. The live broadcast would be shared with the BBC's Third Programme.

On the night of the concert, as the performance started, so too did the noise of the television OB unit at work. Cameras, emitting a constant ten-kilocycle whine, clunked their way through lens and focus changes. Camera talkback instructions passed between director and cameramen were clearly audible to large numbers of the audience seated in the vicinity of two of the cameras.

At the back of the Grand Tier the doors to the auditorium suddenly swung open revealing the third camera and, with muted grunts and apologies, the unit's riggers proceeded to manhandle the heavy mounting into position alongside the startled audience.

In retrospect it's amazing that the audience controlled themselves as well as they did. Certainly, as the evening finished, more than a few set faces were seen leaving the venue.

Next day the press gave full coverage to the evening's disorder. Several of the audience, including Lord and Lady Harewood, were reported as being extremely upset and the Festival's Artistic Director, Ian Hunter, cast doubts on any future performances being televised. There followed a series of meetings between Melville Dinwiddie and Hunter and a solution was found. For future broadcasts the BBC would install wooden 'kiosks' as hides for the television cameras.

The following year, and for some years to come, these ugly boxes were a feature of all Usher Hall telecasts. They had glass on one side, sadly not optically perfect, and to contain the noise, no ventilation of any kind. The resulting heat that built up inside not only almost asphyxiated the cameramen it also aggravated any latent faults in the cameras.

In its first six months in Scotland television had been about as unobtrusive as a cuckoo in a nest. Radio watched and wondered, fascinated by the thought of using pictures to create programmes, yet sometimes concerned as the even pace of its well-ordered life received some uncomfortable jolts.

The new staff were friendly and wanted everything done yesterday. They cut corners with an easy unconcern and a metaphorical smell of burning rubber seemed always to hang in the air. Their programmes were hugely expensive, almost deliberately so as if they were anxious to pay their way into everyone's good graces. They imposed enormous burdens on Glasgow's administrative services and many radio offices were speechless in more ways than one when told that their script duplicating had been held up because of television.

The social mores of the building began to change. The newcomers, professing not to understand the hierarchical grading that operated within the organisation, proceeded to address all and sundry with an easy informality that dealt a mortal blow to the caste system that had been built up over many years.

Television also brought difficulties over who was working to whom. Who, for example, gave the orders in Scotland? In radio, the channel of command was clear. The post-war commitment to devolution had made the Controller, Scotland responsible for all programmes and programme finance, and under a system known as the Queensberry Rules, he and his Head of Programmes were guaranteed that some Scottish output would also be heard on the national Home Service.

There was no such devolution in television. Indeed such a thought was anathema to those at head office. All programmes from Scotland were considered to be regional OBS chosen and scheduled by London. Even the staff, although based in Glasgow, belonged to London. The Scottish management could advise, recommend, even cajole, but if brought to the brink the final word lay with elsewhere. Even the BCS were powerless to intervene having been carefully excluded from any television responsibility.

Thankfully, serious conflict was rare and only occasionally did the management's wish to reflect Scotland's numerous institutions and customs mean disagreement between the Head of Programmes and the television staff. Most of the time television was left to get on with its small Scottish

Festival Fever (1956) Robert Kemp's television comedy about Edinburgh at Festival time with (*l/r*) Stanley Baxter, Mairhi Russell and Michael Dennison.

commitment, learning what to do best and when not to strive for the impossible and grateful for the help that was willingly given by most of the radio staff.

Sound broadcasting meantime continued to take full advantage of its function as the national broadcasting service. It had none of the restrictions on hours that limited the television output. The introduction of FM broadcasting on VHF (brought into Scotland in 1952 and spreading alongside the television transmitters) was opening the door to better interference-free listening, particularly for music.

Programmes on the Scottish Home Service were tumbling over themselves to get on the air. Perennial favourites filled the early evening schedules almost to bursting point: Scottish dance music, sport, the two House Orchestras, plays and serials, argument and debate took place in *A Matter of Opinion* and Scotland's discernible autonomy in the arts was well catered for in *Arts Review*, *Chapbook* and *Scottish Life and Letters*.

News in Scotland had been substantially improved. A network of more than 100 correspondents now supplied material for the Scottish bulletins. No morning bulletins just yet but ten minutes every weekday at 6.15pm, plus a five-minute bulletin on Saturdays.

Schools department, now located entirely in Edinburgh, was averaging six transmissions a week and over 2,000 schools were taking their courses. In Glasgow, Archie P. Lee had persuaded the BBC to call a spade a spade in its features output. His hard-hitting series, *We*, was examining the Scot and his social problems, using unrehearsed interviews broadcast without comment. Religion, too, was becoming more adventurous, reducing the traditional output of church services and talks. Ronnie Falconer and his staff used every technical facility they could lay their hands on to broadcast programmes about the new *Tell Scotland* movement.

From everywhere there was a feeling of change, a Scottish Renaissance almost, and it was increasingly discernible in Scotland's broadcasting. Opt-out programmes were no longer merely Scottish replacements to the British service. People were singing and talking and writing in ways that were different and new, and it was impossible to ignore this new creativity.

For the arts a great deal of support came from two Edinburgh-based producers, George Bruce and Robin Richardson. Both were generous with their time and talent fostering the new Scottish revival. Sometimes, though, some of the new writing received a less than euphoric welcome.

The Lallans movement, for instance, was described by a senior member of the BBC as 'the damned-up outpourings of passionate young poets.'

Drama, now under the guardianship of Jimmy Crampsey, was also benefiting from new work. There was still no National Theatre in Scotland but the Glasgow Citizens' Theatre and the Gateway Theatre in Edinburgh were now given some theatrical stimulation to Scottish playwrights, all of which had a spin-off benefit for radio. Drama was still the flagship of Scotland's broadcasting. Indeed demand was so great there was now a second producer based in Glasgow, Finlay J. Macdonald from the BBC's Gaelic department.

Gaelic broadcasting was the one department not enjoying what amounted to a pre-television boom. The planners of the radio output were already anticipating competition and in that kind of situation broadcasts in Gaelic were now an obligation. The BBC still maintained that speakers and students of the language were to be adequately catered for but no longer at times of peak listening. As a result the Gaelic programmes were reduced and moved to late evening or afternoon.

Hugh Macphee, the senior Gaelic producer, became noticeably upset. There was less humour in his exchanges with colleagues and even the robust wit of Jimmy Crampsey failed to bring the expected response. At a weekly radio meeting in Glasgow, Macphee, proposing yet another series of Gaelic lessons, this time to be designed as a refresher course, spoke of his search for a suitable title. Could anyone help? In the ensuing pause, Crampsey leant back in his chair.

'Hugh', he said, 'would you consider using *Brush Up Your Erse?*'

The burst of laughter that followed quickly died as everyone sensed Macphee's dismay. For few of Macphee's colleagues knew of the pressures under which he was working. At first he had tried to negotiate for programme space using a touch of humour. Told by Gildard's assistant that it was difficult to guarantee regular places for all Gaelic department items, Hugh Macphee had replied that the disadvantage of having a fixed spot anyway was that it quickly directed attention to cuts or alterations.

Gradually, however, he became more weary. Almost 20 years before, when he had attended the opening of the Burghead Transmitter there had been great purpose in his stride, believing that broadcasting would lead to Gaeldom putting order and life back into its culture and language. Undoubtedly something of that had been achieved, but now in the ratings and survival game there were other responsibilities uppermost in management's mind.

The decline in importance experienced by Gaelic programmes would eventually spread to other departments as audience figures and listener loyalty became even more important. Television had already established a small foothold in Scotland and it would win in the end, of course. But before that happened the Scottish Home Service decided it would flex its radio muscles once more for luck and in what better way than an objective survey of Scotland as a nation – a host of programmes that would examine those three hardy annuals of broadcasting, the history, tradition and culture of Scotland.

The series was *Heritage* and with 40 programmes – features, documentaries, talks and discussions – it was the longest-running and most ambitious radio project of its kind undertaken so far in Scotland. Three men were responsible for the series. Robin Richardson, the Edinburgh features producer, was the project's principal editor. He was assisted by John Wilson, who wrote regularly for radio and was also co-editor of the popular *Sportsreel* programme. The third member of the team was Roderick MacLean, the nearest thing in Glasgow to a current affairs producer.

The series began on Sunday 19 September 1954 and with either one or two programmes transmitted each week, *Heritage* ran until April the following year. Many of the programmes, both in their creation and their execution, were a shop window for the talent and skills available to radio at that time. Neil Gunn wrote about whisky and the Highland Clearances, his first scripts since 1945 for radio in Scotland. Naomi Mitchison described the beginnings of Scotland, the geological processes and the first people. The founding of the Kirk in Scotland was in the care of Robert Kemp and John R. Allan, he of Moultrie Kelsall's *The Farm Year*, traced the story of agriculture. Sinclair Gauldie (the winner of the 1947 Scottish Radio Play Competition) recounted the Industrial Revolution years. Ian Finlay wrote about the craftsmen of Scotland.

The list of players was just as impressive. Filling the studio for programme 20, *The Family Tree*, were close on 30 of Scotland's actors. The cast on that day included Joseph Macleod, narrator of the series, Effie Morrison, Sheila Latimer, Tom Fleming, Brydon Murdoch, James Mac-Taggart, Leonard Maguire, Edith Macarthur and James Sutherland.

As the series ran appreciative comments flowed in. The project had never been thought of as exportable and there had been no attempt to clothe it in tartan. Instead it had relied on the Scot's great passion for reason and knowledge and throughout the winter the editors successfully guided an average of 150,000 listeners through every aspect of their history.

In a fanciful way the BBC's radio service in Scotland had made its case. Now, both metaphorically and in a literal sense, more eyes were on television. How would it run? And would it benefit from its close proximity to radio?

The Scottish management had no doubts about the way its television service should develop. Radio's successful implementation of the Regional Scheme after the war was the blueprint for what must now happen in television. 'Righting the balance of programme items and assisting in a renaissance of the native arts,' was Dinwiddie's description. Others might define it differently but what it amounted to in the end was a need to contrive a significant number of Scottish programmes feeding into the national network plus a growing schedule of Scotland-only opt-outs.

Scotland shared the plight of a shortage of equipment and accommodation. Unlike radio's early days when the whole country had started virtually on the same footing, television's growth throughout the country was proving to be a painfully slow business. The numerous government restrictions on development did nothing to help expansion, particularly as far as premises and new rebuilding was concerned. Progress was also slow with equipment. Television apparatus was of a very specialist nature, much of it developed by the BBC itself, with the latest equipment going straight into London to replace earlier designs – leaving 'hand-me-downs' for the rest.

Making do with what there was and encouraging radio to help whenever practicable, Scotland's television practitioners did what they could. There was certainly a ready market for their ideas. Because of the irregular nature of television's development the service was ever hungry for programmes. There was little or no viable means of recording and film was expensive and in short supply. Provided that you could come up with something that seemed halfway towards being entertaining, and not too expensive, you were pretty sure of getting a slot.

As a result, a fair old mixture of programmes was coming out of

Scotland. Some of the programmes were little more than experiments and thankfully forgotten almost as soon as the last camera shot had faded to black. A couple of departments were conscious that they could ill afford mistakes and that too many eyes were on their very move. For example, light entertainment was usually considered to be a barometer of the state of Scottish broadcasting. Luckily the man who had to shoulder this responsibility, Eddie Fraser, had a background that made him well suited to the new medium.

Eddie had been given his job in radio in 1950 after spending over 20 years as a part-time stage and radio actor. At the end of his appointment he had been playing a small role in the very successful radio comedy show *It's All Yours* which starred Jimmy Logan.

Needing to place someone else in his part – the BBC were very much against producers performing at the microphone – Eddie offered it to Stanley Baxter who he had just seen playing in the Citizens' Theatre pantomime, *The Tintock Cup*.

It was the kind of casting and talent spotting that was to make Eddie famous. Within weeks Stanley had inveigled the show's writers, Andrew McIntyre and Jack Macleod, into creating some new characters for him. One *Bella Vague*, was based on a favourite of Stanley's – a dresser who could never remember a name. Soon her, 'Don't forget, my name's in the book. If you want me thingmy, ring me!' was making Stanley a household name throughout Scotland.

In a later series, *Stanley Baxter Takes the Mike*, Eddie was midwife

Television Burns Club Inaugural Supper (1957) The 'poets end' of the table (*l/r*) Alexander Scott; Douglas Young; Sydney Goodsir Smith; Norman MacCaig; C.M. Grieve (Hugh MacDiarmid) then Iain Cuthbertson and John Russell (standing).

to another of Stanley's creations, this time probably his most enduring, the elderly professor of anthropology who discussed at the microphone some of the stranger habits of speech of the Glasgow inhabitants giving birth to the cult of *Parliamo Glasgow*.

There is no doubt that Scotland's taste in humour was changing, partly through the influence of the various quick-fire comedy shows that now abounded on radio and because of transatlantic imports filling the cinema.

The old style music hall comic, swathed in tartan and whimsical to a degree, was fast disappearing. Even the great Sir Harry Lauder was now only seen in Broadcasting House once a year when he would join with his old friend Ian Whyte and the BBC Scottish Orchestra to record a special programme of his songs for Christmas. Not 'Variety' any longer, just two old friends working together and enjoying themselves hugely.

Eddie Fraser was fully aware that entertainment's new style of sophistication was particularly the province of the middlebrow, the moderate intellectuals who were for the moment the bulk of the television audience in Scotland. These were the same people who were inclined to be over-protective of the image of Scotland, particularly when it was being displayed in front of a southern audience. Knowing this, Eddie must have winced perceptively as the first *Television Music Hall* from Scotland overseen by a London producer went into its finale from the Metropole Theatre in Glasgow.

A middle-class press in Scotland looked down a very long nose the following Monday.

'One may applaud Tessie O'Shea while deploring the kilt and bonnet in which she bounced into the finale,' reported *The Glasgow Herald*. 'There appears in the theatre in general to be a delusion that when a troupe of chorus girls are dressed in frilly little imitations of the kilt and are trained to march and countermarch with thumping leg movements this must be solemnly described as a *"Tribute to Scotland"'* on the screen.'

The next light entertainment show from Scotland was produced by Eddie Fraser. His cabaret from the Banqueting Hall of Glasgow's Central Hotel had a degree of sophistication which helped to restore the nation's self-esteem. Jimmy Logan, his sister Annie Ross and Dave Willis were among the highlights of the evening.

With the proprieties restored Fraser now set about trying out on television some of the artists who had worked with him on radio. What he needed first was a *Scottish Showcase*, a programme, preferably an OB that would allow him to catch London's eye and demonstrate that Scotland was not short of entertainers.

The opportunity came in mid-August 1953 with an OB from HMS *Caledonia* (the Admiralty's establishment at Rosyth). The programme was called *Come on Board* and in it he featured Ian Wallace, Janet Brown, Kenneth McKellar and Dave Willis. He also introduced some tartan into the show but this time it was discreet and well tailored. It was Kenneth McKellar's first appearance in front of the cameras. During the late afternoon as rehearsals were finishing Eddie decided that the spot would be better if Kenneth was wearing a kilt. Kenneth was happy with suggestion although it was something he had never done before. That night, wearing a borrowed kilt and singing *Loch Lomond* and *The Lewis Bridal Song*, Kenneth McKellar launched his considerable television career.

Not long after the Rosyth broadcast Eddie Fraser was associated with London's *Garrison Theatre*, which made frequent visits to Scotland. The first, at the RAF station at Bishopbriggs, featured Stanley Baxter, Jack Milroy, Teddy Johnston and, once again, Janet Brown. Next came HMS *Condor* at Arbroath, this time with Renée Houston, Pearl Carr and the first television appearance by Andy Stewart. After the broadcast Eddie wrote to Andy Stewart to tell him that there had been a host of professional enquiries about him adding, 'I'm glad to think that I was the first to put you on and I'm quite sure that you have a successful future in front of you.' A month later he booked him again for another *Garrison Theatre* this time from Perth.

The last programme of the series transmitted on 7 June 1955 again included Andy Stewart, this time with Duncan Macrae and Margot Henderson and, making another of Eddie's 'firsts' – Chic Murray and Maidie.

Garrison Theatre served Scotland well. It gave Eddie Fraser the chance to bring new faces to the screen without the responsibility of a full-blown series and, because every programme was, from beginning to end, a true OB, there were very few of the technical problems and frustrations prevalent in built programmes. In every way it was an ideal opportunity to ease the experience of radio over into television. It was reassuring too. The more partisan amongst Scottish viewers felt that the pick of Scottish talent was entertaining the whole country and that Scotland was making a reasonable impression on the new service.

There remained one vital test for Scottish entertainment, that touch-stone of its ability to please – the annual ritual of Hogmanay.

In radio it was a tradition that Scotland ministered to the whole country as each year came to a close and television, now that it had a live link with the north, proposed to do the same. Early in 1953, the albatross of Hogmanay programmes winged its way northwards as S.J. de Lotbiniere, Head of Outside Broadcasts Television, wrote to James Buchan in Glasgow:

> Ever since I can remember the BBC has had a problem in greeting the New Year with an appropriate measure of hilarity and sentiment.

It was hardly a reassuring way of commissioning from Scotland in its first live New Year programme.

There had been difficulties for television the previous year so much so that they had described the programme as 'our painful experience'. It had been a television New Year broadcast from St Thomas Hospital, London and the audience had regrettably got more than a little out of control. Everyone was delighted, therefore, when Scotland made clear it was willing to take on the event.

Because of the scars still lingering from the previous year the Scottish programme was planned as a very muted affair. The site chosen was the Govan Town Hall, already a location familiar to the OB unit, and the producer was naturally Eddie Fraser with James Buchan as director. Early on there had been a suggestion that the audience consist of service personnel but this had been vetoed by London on the grounds that, 'A service personnel might consume too much alcohol beforehand and be rather too gay when the time came for transmission.'

Eventually it was agreed that the hall be filled by a combination of carefully selected BBC staff and friends and members of the now Royal Scottish Country Dance Society and to ensure complete sobriety, pre-transmission 'refreshments' consisted of a very innocuous cider cup

The show proved to be well presented, exemplary and, for most of the viewers, dull. Throughout the evening the audience in the hall hardly uttered a whisper and at the stroke of midnight, when the traditional New Year greetings were proffered, all sound from the programme was completely blotted out by the ships on the nearby river blowing their sirens.

The following year the programme came from abroad. 1954 marked the formal start of Eurovision and the festivities were placed in the hands of the European Broadcasting Union. Italy took the final honours for the year and Hogmanay celebrations were presented by the Italian Television Service from the Hotel Continental in Milan. It wasn't until 1957 that Scotland again presented a complete Hogmanay show on television.

For almost five years the OB unit remained the mainstay of television broadcasting in Scotland. The headaches caused by sharing with the North of England considerably eased in 1955 when it was assigned a permanent unit. As a direct result, the number of programmes being made increased and a few of them were shown on an opt-out basis. But money, as ever, was the controlling factor, for Scotland had to pay its own way for its own programmes out of a very limited budget. This encouraged a tendency to always design local productions with an eye to interesting London and hopefully recover the costs of the programme.

They were days of experimentation, trial and error, with often quite monumental odds stacked against the programme because of the inadequacies of the equipment. Camera breakdowns, insufficient lighting, communications and lines continually proved deficient. Yet nothing could deter those involved as they pressed on with their plans.

The programmes bore a strong resemblance to what had already been tried on radio. The policy of a growing harmonisation between the two services, as much as for economic reasons as any other, had the inevitable result of sharing of ideas.

For some time London had been running a prime-time documentary series called *Special Enquiry* in which Robert Reid examined contemporary problems of national concern against a local background. Archie P. Lee, Glasgow's radio features producer, was associated with the programme and it was he who suggested that Scotland be used as the specialist for housing problems.

The first programme scheduled from Glasgow was a live broadcast from a derelict and broken down back-court slum in Partick. For the role of guide and interviewer Archie had chosen Jameson Clark and the opening shot revealed him welcoming the audience with: 'So you've come to Glasgow, to one of the worst slums in the city – squalor, dirt and rats.'

It proved to be a powerful and long-remembered programme. The impact of the pictures was lessened only by the city's cleansing department who had moved in a few hours earlier when word of the television OB reached their ears. The effect of the programme and subsequent visits soon became obvious, particularly in Glasgow, where quite a few priorities of demolition and rehousing were quickly changed.

The programme also resulted in an interesting spin-off for radio. Watching that first programme from Partick had been Andrew Stewart in London where he was now Controller of the Home Service. Almost immediately he had contacted the Scottish management asking them to prepare for his network a radio programme on slums. This Scotland was happy to do and Archie P. Lee and Jameson Clark were picked as the obvious people to make it.

There was another reminder of the power of television when Scotland broadcast *Yesterday's Pet*, an OB from the Glasgow Cat and Dog Home. Once again Jameson Clark fronted the cameras and during the closing minutes of the programme he told viewers that a mongrel bitch found whimpering in a Glasgow back court and christened 'Smokey' by James Buchan, the programme's producer, would be put down unless a new owner could be found. Needless to say, offers came pouring in by phone and telegram from all over Britain. Smokey eventually found a home with a family in Bearsden on the outskirts of Glasgow, the family becoming minor celebrities featured throughout the country's press and appearing on a BBC panel game, *Guess My Story*.

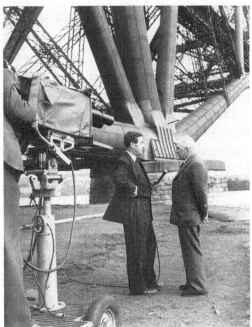

Now UK television series edition
from Scotland (1957)
Alec Beattie, Forth Rail Bridge Inspector,
interviewed by Berkeley Smith.

A few months later Scotland put forward the idea of a regular programme *The Smokey Club*. The idea was accepted and the series ran from April 1955 for almost two years.

It was a runaway success from the very start, so much so that the original presenter, Macdonald Daley, was tempted away by commercial television which had just started in the south and wanted to run a similar series. Barbara Woodhouse offered herself as a replacement and although she was not chosen, she did appear as a contributor in later programmes in the series. Daley's replacement was Dorian Williams with Stanley Dangerfield putting on Daley's editorial hat. In the seventh edition James Buchan decided to present the programme himself and continued to do so until the end of the series.

Of all the programmes coming out of Scotland around this time it was one from Religion that probably made the biggest impact. Ronnie Falconer arranged to televise the American evangelist Billy Graham's Good Friday Service from the Kelvin Hall, Glasgow, in 1955.

It was the first time the American had preached live on television and the programme, directed by Noble Wilson while Ronnie provided the commentary, had considerable impact throughout the United Kingdom. The Scottish OB unit took it all in its stride. It was already well used to Ronnie Falconer's impeccable planning and, because of the number of programmes he seemed to able to cram into an already busy schedule, fully expected one day to find their mobile control room fitted with stained glass windows.

In the few years that had passed since a television OB unit first journeyed over the Border, that 'impeccably dull' official opening from the Edinburgh music studio, Scotland had learned a great deal about improvisation. It had not chosen to specialise in the way some other Regions had done. The West of England, for example, centred on Bristol and made a quite distinctive contribution with programmes on Natural History and kindred subjects.

Scotland's outlook was much wider and constantly changing. Trying to convey the intricacies of being a Nation as well as a Region, probing the planners for suitable subjects that would run in series form, and perhaps attract new money and equipment to support it, but loath to become tied to any one activity for fear of diminishing its ability to take account of Scotland 'as a nation'. It needed major investment in technology and people but instead seemed to be getting a gradual piecemeal growth that by the very nature of its fragmentary style was making Scotland into a Dickensian orphan – forever asking for more.

The television transmission network gradually extended northwards. A temporary transmitter to serve Aberdeenshire was installed at Redmoss

in late 1954 and shortly afterwards was replaced by a permanent installation at Meldrum designed to cover most of the coast stretching from
Elgin southwards to Montrose.

Temporary, and very basic garage and office accommodation was
found for the Scottish OB unit at a site on Glasgow's Parliamentary Road.
It would take until 1959 before a permanent base was occupied, during
which time the unit experienced the near destruction of the roof when a
large tree collapsed on top of it.

There were very rare opt-outs mostly of a very basic kind. Technically they consisted of a quick throw of the switch at Kirk o' Shotts then
over to a location begged or borrowed from the rehearsal time of some
UK-bound production. The first opt-out in Scotland was an OB 'talk'
given by John Bannerman on 9 October 1952. He was speaking about the
National Mod of Scotland and in fact was broadcasting from Rothesay
Pavilion where the 1952 Mod was taking place. The unit was on location to broadcast on the following evening the network OB of the second
part of the Grand Concert given by prize-winning choirs and soloists.
But the programme was not a runaway success. In an exchange of memos
shortly after the broadcast Cecil McGovern, Controller of Programmes,
commented, 'It might be television for Scotland. Surely it isn't for England.
In fact I would say it isn't television at all.'

Clinging to the desire to establish Scotland's nationhood as an early
as possible there were various desultory attempts at Scotland-only programmes, mostly sport, religion and current affairs. An interesting pallia-
tive to the complaint that opt-outs always got in the way of network
programmes came in 1954. The first of a Scottish series called *Compass*,
produced by Noble Wilson and edited by Roma Fairley, went out from
Kirk o' Shotts before evening transmission normally started.

By the autumn of 1955 a small Glasgow music studio, Studio 3 in
Broadcasting House, had been allocated to television. It was the simplest
of do-it-yourself operations and the enthusiasm of those who used it would
frequently turn to black despair as the below standard equipment continually broke down. The studio was suitable for little more than short news
and sports programmes but it was used for much more besides, even though
the results were frequently second-rate and amateurish, encouraging viewers
to discriminate between Scottish opt-outs and network programmes.

When the spirits flagged encouragement came with the promise that somewhere deep down in the caverns of capital expenditure there was provision for a major television development in Scotland. Meantime, as a positive demonstration of intent, some interim improvements began floating to the surface.

CHAPTER EIGHT

New Challenges

THE CONFIDENCE OF the staff was not always shared by the viewers, quite a few of whom were losing patience, either because of the small number of local programmes that were on offer or through embarrassment over the quality of what was being shown. At one time the BBC might have tried to jolly them along, but not now. Competition with commercial television had already started in England and soon the content would include Scotland.

The future television development envisaged by the BBC had already been in the hands of the planners, both civil and the BBC, for some time. The indications were that the ultimate goal, new premises built on the ground adjoining Broadcasting House, Glasgow, was still some distance away. Time was short and with a quick body swerve that surprised even the BBC, Melville Dinwiddie bundled Scotland's principal programmes over the next six years into a temporary studio in Parkhead about three miles way from Queen Margaret Drive.

For £12,000 the BBC in Scotland purchased the Black Cat Cinema in Springfield Road. This money, and what was needed to adapt the building and purchase equipment, was taken from a fund of £50,000 originally allocated to develop television facilities at Queen Street in Edinburgh. Studio 1 was converted to a 'drive-in' studio and a small film unit with telecine facilities was set up.

Once again the Edinburgh staff felt they had been deprived of 'capital' status and for a while were a touch ambivalent over the compensatory £3,000 allocated to improve Queen Street's sound facilities and accommodation. Glasgow, it seemed, had won again and the work went ahead to prepare Springfield Road for television and the new Scottish film unit.

Not everyone was happy with the purchase of Springfield Road. There were quite a few limitations including its distance from Broadcasting House and lack of any expansion possibilities, but these and other problems were brushed aside by those anxious to find a home at last and seeing in Springfield Road the end of their years of peripatetic existence.

Their delight was well founded. From the smiling commissionaire at the front door to the clatter of film editing, the building carried the unmistakable stamp of television. At last the 'cuckoo' had a place of its own and was busy filling it with jobs and titles that had nothing to do with radio history.

Though the premises were small, most of the television services were represented. There were dressing rooms and a make-up area and a fully trained make-up supervisor, Joan Neville. A small television wardrobe department was being put together by Kirstie Colam. Kirstie, tempted away from Howard & Wyndham and the Glasgow Citizens' Theatre, was now everything from costume supervisor to dresser. There were floor managers and production assistants, a film editor and film cameramen, technical supervisors, boom operators and, of course, television cameramen. Even a limited amount of in-house scenic design and supply was now possible.

In the main, most of the skills now being seen for the first time were no more than a token presence and Scotland still needed a great deal of 'bought in' expertise. Sets were planned by freelances. Jack Notman was the principal designer, and the set construction was always done outside, usually by a company such as 'Associated Displays'. This small shopfitting and display firm, with tiny workshops in Glasgow's Dobbie's Loan, was already accustomed to carrying out small economic miracles for the BBC. Its two owners, Bob Booth and his brother, were learning as they went and the BBC owed a great deal to their skill and perseverance in the first decade of television in Scotland.

The film unit, presided over by producer, Harry Govan, functioned only in 35mm, a cumbersome and expensive format inherited by television from the commercial cinema industry. Because of this and the fact that there was only one team, a great deal of hiring of both camera units and editing had to continue, particularly for news and magazine programmes.

A major drawback to Springfield Road was the lack of offices, which meant very extended lines of communication. While crews and other staff were based at the studio or at the OB base at Alexandra Parade, department heads such as Harry Govan had to operate from Queen Margaret Drive, a long and time-wasting journey away.

Holding all this in some kind of equitable balance and at the same time dishing out any money that could be found was the job of the Scotland's Television Organiser, George Runcie. Serving two masters, his Head of

Programmes in Scotland and television in London, George bore the brunt of most of the complaints, an unenviable job that required a considerable degree of patience.

Arranging the first programme from Springfield Road should have been easy. There was no shortage of good entertainment available to choose from and as far as a date was concerned it would have to be before ITV.

Scotland's first commercial station, Scottish Television, was on schedule to open at the end of August 1957. The BBC knew that in order to cover the Edinburgh Festival which had started on 18 August, they would require some of their Springfield Road equipment shuttled through to Edinburgh (the new studio was not completely self-supporting). If the Glasgow studio was to hit the headlines before Scottish Television, and go down in the annals as the first television studio in Scotland, opening night would have to be during the first two weeks of the month.

There were the usual questions about whether the technical work at Springfield Road would be ready but the BBC's engineers had a good record of handing over new installations on time and nobody was unduly worried on that score.

In fact the difficulties that did arise were of a much more emotional kind and were an interesting reminder that in Scotland the old order was slow to change.

The first move to set down on paper what might be done to mark the opening of the studio came interestingly enough from London when Kenneth Adam, now Controller of Programmes Television, wrote to the Scottish Head of Programmes with his first thoughts: 'It seems the right thing to think of it as a pull together of Scottish comedians, singers, etc, which we would take on network, possibly at 10 o'clock for 45 minutes or so as to allow the artists to get out of their theatres. Please let me have a suggested bill and date.'

Normally such an offer from the network would have been too good to miss but to London's surprise a Scottish triumvirate of Melville Dinwiddie, Andrew Stewart (now back in Scotland as the Controller-elect as Dinwiddie would soon be retiring) and Gordon Gildard quickly turned it down. Their refusal stemmed from two things, the first the likely transmission day of a Sunday and the second the embarrassment at the thought of an audience coming to BBC premises located in a broken down part of Glasgow. Sunday broadcasting still had some fairly strict rules about it and Scotland's own broadcasting code was even more exacting. London rushed to make amends. 'I was not at any time proposing the "L.E. programme" to which your most recent memo refers,' wrote Kenneth Adam. Even Scotland's Scottish Variety Orchestra was consigned by him to the sacrificial fire: 'I appreciate your difficulties... therefore no dancing girls, no pop singers, no crude sketches, no svo. Instead a divertissement or magazine or concert or whatever umbrella name is considered suitable for, say, the BBC Scottish Orchestra's strings.'

He was less yielding on the matter of the studio. 'I do not think that the fact that the studio is not in the best part of Glasgow matters, since the viewer will not see that.'

Finally fed up with a conciliatory line he disclosed his irritation: 'If we are going to begin by being rather ashamed of our studio when compared with Thomson's luxuriously redesigned theatre, we shall never lose a sense of inferiority which he will be the first to note as weakness and to attack... I am, I confess, rather surprised that it is London which is pressing on this, rather than Scotland.'

Perhaps it's just as well that others joined in to support Scotland, particularly Cecil McGivern, the Deputy Director of Television Broadcasting. It was he who pointed out that Springfield Road was in no sense a major studio but only a stop-gap designed to fill in while the BBC pursued its development plans for Queen Margaret Drive. Scotland breathed a sigh of relief. Its staff and resources were limited and as yet there had been no chance to train people under typical studio conditions. Kenneth Adam withdrew his suggestion for a gala programme to be shown nationwide. Regretting that it was not

Andrew Stewart
Controller, Scotland (1957–1967).

practicable to make more of a show with the opening, he accepted that instead Scotland would transmit its own opt-out on 16 August 1957.

The August date was a significant one for the planners because it marked the inauguration of the Rosemarkie Transmitter for Inverness and the Black Isle and was a good moment to whet northern appetites. The opening programme, *On View*, lasted 45 minutes and introduced its audience to the BBC's facilities in Scotland. It started with film played in from the new telecine machine at Springfield Road. Alastair MacIntyre, the senior announcer, then introduced shots of previous Scottish outside broadcasts such as the Tillicoultry coal mine and major sporting events. There were brief glimpses of other places and people, including George Young of First Division football champions, Rangers, and a view of the BBC's news and sport staff at work in Studio 3, the much maligned do-it-yourself package in Broadcasting House.

From the studio at Broadcasting House the programme switched to Springfield Road. Here producer James Buchan, now frequently used as a commentator, was waiting to explain the mysteries of what had once been the Black Cat Cinema. Using the OB unit, Buchan unfolded the new facilities as he walked from the small reception area down the corridor and through the double doors into the studio itself. Here the Springfield Road cameras took over, showing brief glimpses from some of the coming productions that would, it was hoped, mean more and better things for viewers in Scotland.

Fifteen days later on Saturday 31 August, Scottish Television broadcast their opening programme. This time there really was a sense of occasion. Called *This is Scotland*, the show was big and glossy, filling the stage of the old Theatre Royal, Scottish Television's headquarters, with glittering stars. A short tram ride away, at Queen Margaret Drive, the BBC seemed to be taking an extremely relaxed view of the event and made no attempt to distract the audience from switching over. The start of commercial television in England two years earlier had been the moment for BBC radio to kill off Grace Archer, a principal character in the Light Programme's popular programme, *The Archers*. Scotland had no such plans and, in any case their biggest radio audience winner, *The McFlannels*, had long since gone from its regular Saturday spot with the death of its author, Helen Pryde. Instead the BBC just watched. As Scots, their fingers were crossed like everybody else's hoping that Scotland would not seem to be making a fool of itself on the national screen. At the BBC they criticised, wondering that anyone could be so foolish as to work anywhere other than with the Corporation.

In an interview with the Scottish press, the BBC's Gordon Gildard was asked about the likely effect of competition on the staff. He had replied that, unlike London, the BBC in Scotland would not lose many people to commercial television.

'Here, every member of the staff knows everyone else. This human element is important. Such an atmosphere cannot, and does not, exist in London where our administrative centres are dotted about all over the city.'

Gildard was equally sanguine about the viewers' reaction to Scottish Television: 'Of course natural curiosity would make him switch channels but he'd be back soon enough to rejoin the familiar, once the fuss was over.'

Despite its outward, relaxed views the Scottish management knew that competition was already affecting the Corporation. The current UK viewing figures for those able to receive both channels showed a less than 30 per cent share for BBC TV, and in the south of the country significant numbers of staff and artists were most certainly changing their allegiance. Obviously the battle for viewers was not going to be determined exclusively in Central Scotland but there was every reason for the Scottish BBC to do what it could to counteract the new challenger.

Despite the strong interest in the arrival of commercial television (the BBC steadfastly refused the word 'Independent' which they felt gave their competitor too great a standing), the Scottish BBC did genuinely believe that as far as local programmes were concerned only a few viewers would switch their allegiance. But just to be sure they'd used *On View* to lay out some samples of what was in store for the future.

Opening the programme with a preview of the new regular news and sport service had been quite deliberate, for this was an area where BBC and Scottish Television were to be in direct competition. Experience in radio had already shown that Scots liked plenty of facts in their broadcasting (a much larger number of the adult population listened to the news in Scotland than elsewhere) and at 6.15pm when each part of the UK broadcast its own radio news bulletin the amount of listening in Scotland was double that of most others.

The new service on television would reflect this with a regular weekday Scottish news summary at 6.05pm and a Saturday sports result programme.

This daily addition to the schedules was part and parcel of a UK development planned for all six BBC Regions and due to start in September. Scotland, however, anxious to be on the air before its commercial competitor, made its own way on to the screen on Friday 30 August, pre-empting Scottish Television and at the same time carrying off the honour of being the first non-London part of the BBC to provide a regular television news service.

The Scottish news summary on television bore a close resemblance to the radio bulletins broadcast on the Scottish Home Service. Both came from the same newsroom, overseen by James Kemp, and relied heavily on specially selected local correspondents and freelance stringers. The stories were almost exclusively confined to events within Scotland and although from time to time an item was considered important enough for inclusion in the national news, these occasions were rare and the main effort went to producing a Scottish news about Scotland for Scotland.

Scotland's treatment of news was serious, perhaps even more ponderous at times, and a visiting London journalist reported back to his editor that it was rather a world on its own, adding, 'there is a feeling here that sometimes their treatment of news is heavy but they are hogs for work and most businesslike.' It was a well-founded assessment and continued to have validity for many years. In truth a weighty treatment was not disliked in Scotland and the measure tones of the staff announcer reading the news added to the general feeling of earnest thought.

One thought could not be disguised however. The bulletins were no more than an addendum to the national news, a factor that upset those Scots who resented having a 'main' bulletin from London. This had been one of the key points in The Saltire Society's evidence to the Beveridge Committee, arguing that all news carried on Scottish transmitters should be written by Scots for Scots. But the case had foundered on two points. A skilful if pernickety reasoning by the BBC that its news policy had always been to select objectively and present impartially and, in any case, if Scotland were to set up a UK-type of bulletin it would be spending a disproportionate amount of its money on buying in from other organisations, such as the Press Association and Reuters.

Running a regular television news was not easy but the 'hogs for work' found that a great deal of their time was taken up with the mechanics of the new service. Television news screamed out for pictures and the challenge was to provide film for the bulletins as frequently as possible. To do this meant hiring from outside the BBC. Springfield Road had brought with it the means of transmitting film but the rest of the process, filming, editing, processing, needed an availability and speed that was only obtainable on a buy-in basis.

Much of the work for the BBC's Scottish news went to Templar Films in Glasgow and this introduced a third location into an operation where time was already short, a certain recipe for frayed nerves and occasional disaster. The film was edited at Templar's then rushed to the telecine machine at Springfield Road. Meantime a commentary had been written and handed to the newsreader in the news studio at Queen Margaret Drive and eventually picture and commentary met on the air, frequently without any chance of rehearsal.

Even without film there was still an air of uncertainty. The television bulletin went on the air at almost the same time as the radio news and people brought to Broadcasting House, Glasgow, were often used in both bulletins. As the two news studios were on different floors and at opposite ends of the building, a great deal of clattering up and down stairs and last-minute dashes took place before the correct person faced the right interviewer.

The principal television reporters were John Lindsay and Maurice Lindsay. John had started working for radio news in the late 1940s and would eventually move 'to the other side' when he became the Independent Broadcasting Authority's Scottish Officer. Maurice Lindsay (the two were not related) was also a long-standing contributor to radio and television and had introduced Scotland's first dramatised musical production on television, an OB of *The Jolly Beggars* performed in Studio One Edinburgh on 25 January 1954. Frequent appearances thereafter had inured him to the vagaries of television, outwardly at least, and he was in constant demand as a broadcaster. But he, too, would eventually cross what the BBC then considered 'The Great Divide', becoming Border Television's first Programme Controller in the early 1960s.

The companion to the daily news was the weekend sports service and again film was important with inevitably football used as the ace card. But attempts to show highlights from one of the day's matches frequently left viewers suffering paroxysms of rage. Bad camera positions and the usual Scottish weather meant that play on the far side of the pitch was practically lost to sight in the grey murk of a Saturday afternoon. There were two film cameras in operation – one equipped with sound for the commentary and the other, silent, used to fill in when the main camera needed to re-load with film (every ten minutes). Fate seemed to decree that the silent camera was always in use when a goal was scored and later from the studio, during transmission, the commentator, George Davidson, would have to simulate an excited commentary as his film report suddenly fell silent at the crucial moment.

The viewers, less than pleased with what they saw, complained: 'You're not nearly as good as London.' They were right, of course, but it was the equipment that should have been blamed. Time after time an exasperated Peter Thomson, the senior sports producer in radio and television, pleaded to be allowed to use OB electronic cameras instead of film. Eventually a plan was devised using recording machines in London as there were still none in Scotland. The improvement in quality (and commentary) was considerable and from then on the Saturday match was covered by two electronic cameras whenever possible.

The new system did have its own kind of mishaps. The first match to benefit from the different arrangement was a Glasgow derby (Celtic v Rangers) at Hampden. After an exciting first half, a telephone call to London was told that the recording was satisfactory. Having given the good news, the London recording engineer then put the protective cap back on the lens of his tele-recording machine and forgot to remove it for the second half. In Scotland later that evening, Archie Henry, introducing the sports programme, explained that the second half of the match would not be shown. The supporters of the winning team, Celtic, just couldn't believe it and were convinced that it was an example of alleged Rangers bias at the BBC. After all Celtic had won 7-1.

It seemed to many that while the general level of technical resources in Scotland continued to improve, benefits specifically for opt-out prog-rammes were still hard to come by. Productions aimed at, or commissi-oned by London had a high priority, sucking in a great deal of the limited skill and resources available, and leaving the 'Scotland-only' group very much the poor relations.

By 1958 the Scottish Region was producing almost four hours of tele-vision a week, about half of which was going to the national network. These UK productions, a mixture of OBs and studio-based drama and light entertainment, were important for Scotland's future, for their success would help consolidate the major expansion being planned for the Queen Margaret Drive site.

Much of the emphasis was on drama, considered by many to be Scotland's best resource in broadcasting. Radio had paved the way, building a fine reputation for plays coming out of Scotland and now there seemed every chance of exploiting that experience, using it as a foundation for a similar success in television.

Drama was a growth area as far as viewers' preference was concerned and, though other parts of the BBC were also competing, they lacked Scotland's ability to subsidise financially from what was an increasingly large opt-out fund. Scotland's 'National' status was also a help, allowing it to schedule some plays for local consumption. It meant a heavy drain on programme funds but it did allow Scotland the opportunity of amassing a useful reservoir of experience and people and, of course, there was always the chance of selling to London a play originally planned for Scotland, with a consequential recoup of costs.

The first play from Springfield Road had been Jimmy Crampsey's production of *The Piper of Ord* by Charles Campbell Gairdner and Rosamunde Pilcher broadcast on 20 August 1957 and it signalled the start of a steady stream of Scottish artists passing through the doors of the studio in Glasgow's East End. For the first time in its existence, the BBC in Scotland were offering actors and actresses a distinct future of full-time employment combining radio and television. Precarious, of course, and subject to vagaries of every kind but it was a start and a considerable cornerstone of development.

Artists were essential but so too were writers and the search for creative work, new writing and new ideas was never ending. Sometimes a decision to use chance talent paid off but there was no guarantee that what worked with one production would succeed with another. Taking risks could bring success but the inadequacy of a studio 'equipped on an extended basis' (the BBC's own description) damped down many ideas.

The axis of responsibility was the producer. Supported by a secretary, the total sum of a 'production office' in radio and television was slow to add to it, the producer had a constant tussle to maintain some kind of equilibrium between a writer's imaginative style and the harsh discipline of the studio. His nervous system bore the brunt of the struggle and it was very evident that though the will was in place experience had to catch up.

An early casualty was Jimmy Crampsey. From the start he had found it difficult to accept the long string of compromises that seemed to entangle most drama productions. Occasional bouts of ill health dogged his work and it was with evident relief that he eventually chose to return to radio, leaving his colleague, Finlay J. Macdonald, to grapple with the demons of Springfield Road.

As Finlay J. Macdonald was still expected to spend some of his time in radio it was obvious that more help was needed. Some assistance was given by using visiting London staff but Scotland also recruited another two Scots, Pharic Maclaren and James MacTaggart. Together they buttressed the nation's drama hopes into the 1960s. The three moderately youthful men, very different in demeanour and style, delivered a patchwork of ideas that saved the Scottish output from becoming too traditional and secure.

As one of the first of the post-war entrants into the BBC, Finlay J. Macdonald had absorbed many of the inspirations and images of the people around at that time and writing for radio. Mixing with these literary scholars of broadcasting he found their work deeply absorbing. Their strong sense of line and shape made extremely effective radio drama and he was determined to carry this into television. Some of his most successful Springfield Road productions were plays previously broadcast on radio. He had liked their patriotism and emotion then and saw no reason why television shouldn't also experience 'some good plays'.

Right Royal by Alexander Scott had started life as a stage play. First produced at the Citizens' Theatre, Glasgow, in 1954, Finlay J. Macdonald had broadcast a radio version on the Scottish Home Service in 1955. Then, in 1958, he brought it to television.

Unusually, *Right Royal* had its own music, specially arranged by Alexander Gibson, Assistant Conductor of the BBC Scottish Orchestra in the early 1950s and a close friend of the producer. The television production used the BBC's Scottish Variety Orchestra. Too large to fit into the studio, for the live performance, it had pre-recorded the music, something that again was fairly unusual in a (Scottish) television production.

The Wallace was produced by Finlay J. Macdonald for television in 1960. Sydney Goodsir Smith's verse drama was a rousing story of Scotland with a splendid background of history and the radio production the year before had marked St Andrew's Night. His television version fulfilled the same function, coming live from Springfield Road studio on Sunday 27 November as a Scottish opt-out from 8.45pm to 10.45pm. In both productions of *The Wallace* Tom Fleming was cast in the leading role and the rich flavour of his Scots tongue tugged hard at emotions already primed with innate patriotism and a sense of occasion.

Pharic Maclaren joined the Scottish staff on 1957, shortly after the opening of Springfield Road. He was a Scot, educated in Glasgow, and had just spent some time working in television in London. Facing what seemed a heavy schedule of work, and with Finlay J. Macdonald having to divide his time between television and radio, he was given some assistance, particularly from James MacTaggart, newly appointed as a production assistant and seen by the management as capable of much more. Of the three, Pharic Maclaren stayed the longest. Finlay J. Macdonald's eloquent and often changing qualities eventually took him into more general programmes, particularly film documentaries and features. But Pharic Maclaren never departed from the elaboration of television drama. Despite a rough time with his health, a series of operations in Glasgow's Western Infirmary followed by polio which left him in a wheelchair for the rest of his life, he was to become the doyen of Scottish television drama. His illness never defeated him and in the first few months of his return to work various BBC colleagues, particularly in the film unit, arranged to manhandle him up and down stairs and around any other irritating obstructions that might hinder him.

Pharic Maclaren's constant cry was for more – more writers, more money for programmes and more facilities to equal what was being done in London. He wanted to overturn what he saw as Scotland's staple diet at that time, Barrie and Bridie, and was particularly supportive of a scheme for a television playwriting competition. Yet at the same time he was never happier than when planning six episodes of Neil Munro's *Para Handy*, which Scotland produced in the autumn of 1959.

The close working relationship between Pharic Maclaren and James MacTaggart became increasingly important during former's illness. When hospitalisation threatened the preparation of the *Para Handy* series, James was the obvious steadying figure and some time later, when the outcome of the play competition was decided and illness again intervened, he again needed no second bidding to grasp the opportunity that was offered.

The competition had evoked a great deal of interest and a shoal of submissions. Of well over 300 entries a dozen were thought to show writers of promise and eventually three prize-winners were declared by the judges, Clemence Dane, Neil Paterson and Donald Wilson. The first prize, £500, went to *Three Ring Circus* by Jack Gerson and two prizes of £350 each were awarded to the Rev J.L. Dow of Greenock and to Alexander Berry, an art teacher from Girvan, for *Job Adam* and *We're No Awa' Tae Bide Awa'*, later changed to *No Thoroughfare* and *Pack Up Your Troubles*. All three plays were produced over a period of two months, a considerable feat for one producer, James MacTaggart.

London, hungry for talent was not slow to notice James MacTaggart's emerging production and writing skills. Soon he was on his way south. It was a loss as far as Scotland was concerned given the style of prodding experimentation that he delighted in.

The third prize-winner, *Pack Up Your Troubles*, was a comedy, described by the *Radio Times* as 'something refreshingly different' for the producer and his cast, but comedy was anything but different, it was just hard to find and Scotland like everywhere else was searching desperately for something to make people laugh. Ideas were found, but inevitably perhaps the bias was towards the tried and familiar, that age-old fusion of drama and nonsense so beloved of the Scottish Music Hall and the pawky characters of *The McFlannels* and *Para Handy* bobbed to the top of the top of the Scottish ratings with predictable buoyancy.

Some of this Scottish comedy exported well. Television audiences on both sides of the Border were entranced with Duncan Ross's adaptation of Neil Munro's stories when the *Vital Spark* set sail on 11 December 1959. It was skippered by Duncan Macrae as *Para Handy – Master Mariner* (the title of the first series) with Roddy McMillan as Dougie, Angus Lennie as Sunny Jim and John Grieve as MacPhail the Engineer.

It seemed as if BBC Scotland had come up with a winner. The series built around a small Clyde coast cargo boat – a puffer – with a wily skipper and some off-beat companions pitting their wits against the conventional world looked as if it could run and run, and for once London, in the person of Kenneth Adam, Controller of Programmes Television, was enthusiastic: 'It is a long time since I got such pleasure out of a preliminary script...

I am sure the series needs to be done well because stories deserve it and we shall therefore not want you to feel yourselves short of money in making it.'

The first series, six programmes, was indeed a huge success, but almost a year later to the day Adam had changed his tune. His last sentence of February 1959 had been taken too literally. Scotland spent £12,000, twice the amount originally allocated to the project.

The basic problem had been the unavoidable need for extensive location filming. A costly business and this compounded by the late arrival of scripts and the illness of Pharic Maclaren put the *Vital Spark* into dry dock for five years.

When it did sail again it was in the Comedy Playhouse series in August 1965. Para Handy was now played by Roddy McMillan but John Grieve still ruled the engine room. This time the script was by Bill Craig and the single story was so successful that another six-part series was commissioned. Named *The Vital Spark*, it ran from January to March 1966. Once again, it was successful and a seven-part series followed in 1967. Bill Craig wrote all the scripts, including the final, and the first in colour, as an extended episode for BBC Scotland's anniversary celebrations on 5 March 1973.

That other manifestation of Scottish comedy, Helen Pryde's gregarious Glaswegians, *The McFlannels*, was not exported to the south, although as a Scottish opt-out it did find considerable favour with the local television audiences. In all, three separate series were produced from Springfield Road, starting on 12 February 1958 with *Willie in Hot Water*.

The television version of *The McFlannels* stuck closely to the original radio stories although there were some alterations in casting. Willie Joss and Grace McChlery remained as Uncle Mattha and Mrs McCotton but the principals of the family were changed. Russell Hunter and Marjorie Thomson played Willie and Sarah McFlannel, with Colette O'Neill and Clarke Tait as their children, Maisie and Peter.

The third series started in March 1959 and by then the BBC were making strenuous efforts to have the plots updated, wishing to retain the characters but with a new writer. This met with head on resistance from Walter Pryde, the author's widowed husband. He held the copyright to the family and was adamant that the BBC must continue to use his wife's original stories. After some discussion he got his way and another six episodes were televised based on the existing radio scripts. There had been 200 of them. But the BBC still wanted a different author – Lavinia Derwent was very much in their minds – and when the moment came to discuss yet another series, this time of 13 episodes, they embarked on what was to be a final encounter with Walter Pryde.

The principal BBC negotiator was Gordon Gildard and in most of the meetings, referred to by Pryde as 'conferences', relations between the two were amicable enough but BBC bureaucratic protocol still demanded that all written communications concerning details on copyright and fees had to be done through the London Copyright department. The inevitable formality that his produced did nothing to further either cause and in the end Walter Pryde refused to yield.

Twenty years before, in 1939, Helen Pryde had written her first letter to the BBC's Copyright section:

Dear Sirs, Thank you for your letter of 17 February. The fee you suggest for *The McFlannels Rub Along* (*Episode 1*) will be quite satisfactory.

In August 1959, Walter's final letter to the same department finished with these words: 'I must say to you, quite frankly, that I am tired of the whole business. How is it to be reconciled? I do not know, if, as seems clear to me, the BBC are determined on a line of action of which I do not approve.'

Removing *The McFlannels* from the Scotland-only schedules was a sad moment for the public but it did bring a passing relief for the planners and administrators. While the show was extremely popular it had been building up some unwelcome headaches within the BBC, not the least of which had been studio availability and space in the schedules.

Before the start of competition in Scotland in mid-1957, the BBC's regular opt-out space had consisted of one 30-minute slot per month. The opening of Springfield Road quadrupled this to 30 minutes per week plus news and sport. It was, said the Scottish management, 'in keeping with staff and technical resources', adding that it would 'stand for a period until we have the measure of the competitor.'

Gradually that measure and the number of programmes crept up as did the programme allowance dished out by London. But as virtually every programme was still transmitted live, the alternative, tele-recording down the line to London was expensive and usually of poor quality, so this required the studio beforehand for setting up and rehearsals, and arranging access to technical facilities was a nightmare. One solution was for programmes to share a time slot, transmitting on a fortnightly basis. It was reasonable logistic answer but the dot-to-dot carry placing did inhibit the growth of a faithful mass audience or, as in the case of *The McFlannels*, caused a great deal of criticism from existing fans.

Stopping *The McFlannels* also saved money, a great deal as it so happens. Though the episodes were short (20 minutes) the costs were high. Local drama, and for all its riotous entertainment *The McFlannels* was financially drama, was an exceedingly expensive business.

Cheap and cheerful was every planner's dream, a programme reasonably low in cost yet high in viewer regard and in Scotland it came swirling out of the mists of Hogmanay in 1957 when for the first time BBC Scotland brought in the New Year with its very own studio party.

The programme producer was Iain MacFadyen, colleague of Eddie Fraser in the Variety department and an ex-balance and control specialist from wartime radio days. Iain's formula was simple and effective – Scots songs and dancing wrapped up in a robust party atmosphere. The public loved it, just as they loved Scottish dance music on the Scottish Home Service and five months later, on 7 May 1958, the first of the series *The White Heather Club* appeared on the screens as a Scottish opt-out.

The New Year programme had been headed by the popular singer Robert Wilson and naturally he had been engaged to act as host for the new series, but the gremlins of television in their unpredictable way chose to rob him of the distinction of hosting the first of the new programmes.

Around the time the new series was to start the Scottish schedules were particularly busy and it was decided that, exceptionally, the new programme would be pre-recorded beforehand down the line to London. This was done and all seemed well. Then, just days before it was due to be transmitted, a serious technical fault was found in the recording. With commendable speed, the Glasgow studio was cleared ready for the day of the broadcast and the complete cast reassembled for a live transmission. All, that is, except for Robert Wilson. He was committed to an appearance in Dublin and couldn't be back in Glasgow in time. Quickly casting around for someone to take his place, Iain MacFadyen picked one of the guests in the show – Andy Stewart. It was a wise choice and Andy's performance was faultless. Iain, much impressed, decided that he would invite Andy

The White Heather Club.

to be the host of the next year's *New Year Party* which this time was to be taken by the complete network.

The success of the 1958 Hogmanay broadcast, billed in the *Radio Times* as a *New Year Party from the White Heather Club*, persuaded London to take *The White Heather Club* on network and later in 1959, Andy Stewart was engaged as the permanent compere. The show became Scotland's top television series running well into the mid-'60s and bringing dozens of names into almost daily use in huge numbers of television households: singers such as James Urquhart and Alistair McHarg, Robin Hall and Jimmie Macgregor (already television celebrities thanks to their appearances on the *Tonight* programme), the Brand Sisters and Moira Anderson, the Scottish Junior Singers and the Aeolian Singers, dancers like Bobby Watson, Dixie Ingram and Isobel James and the White Heather Dancers, the pianist Harry Carmichael, the Joe Gordon Folk Four, Ian Powrie and his Band and, of course, the legendary Jimmy Shand.

It was the very best of Scottish entertainment and it spawned stage shows, special appearances abroad and gramophone recordings, including the two record-breaking songs, *Scottish Soldier* and *The Battle's O'er*, both collaborations between Andy Stewart and Iain MacFadyen.

The successful formula also established a long run of *New Year Parties* on television, held as an annual event from Scotland. They eventually outlived *The White Heather Club* programmes but became increasingly difficult to present. They were confined by their own traditions, struggling for something new and different each year but only managing to reassert the customs and party pieces of many times before.

CHAPTER NINE

A Diversity of Opinion

The public is made up of many audiences, and however much their
likes and dislikes overlap, there are large numbers of distinct and
varied interests which the BBC sets out to serve.

BBC Handbook 1961

AT NO TIME COULD anyone say that broadcasting was in danger of becoming moribund, though its ability to survive as committee after committee
dug at its roots sometimes surprised even the most optimistic of it supporters. Beginning with the Sykes Committee in 1923, six different reviews
and investigations had taken place. Now at the start of the 1960s broadcasting was once again in examination as Committee Number Seven,
under Sir Harry Pilkington, moved into gear.

As usual the BBC extended a warm welcome. Truth to tell they were
anxious to put their case for further advances in broadcasting, listing
amongst these a fourth radio service; a second BBC television channel;
colour transmissions as well as black and white; and an enrichment of
regional broadcasting and contributors.

In Scotland it was an ideal moment to take stock and was certainly
time to review the position of the largest National Region. Change was
already snapping at its heels, particularly in the Scottish Home Service as
the BCS, in cahoots with the Scottish management, set about their formid-
able task of planning the next ten years of broadcasting.

The work to be done had two obvious headings, Radio and Television,
and a third that was less easily defined. Nationalism should have been
the best description but this was a word that worried the BBC, particularly when it had political connotations. Better, therefore, to leave it
unspoken for how else to define that something that was both the pride
and despair of being a Scot, that peculiar mix of patriotism and puzzling
characteristics that made sense to those on the ground but was often
found perplexing and even irritating by people elsewhere.

Radio had been changing for some time and was no longer the main
focus of attention, a fact underlined by audience figures that showed

that the number of Scots listening to all the BBC's sound services when put together was less than that for television. Not only were listening audiences down, the time of listening had also altered. Daytime audiences, once thought to be of minor importance, were now the cherished ones and it was the evening listener who had become classified as a minority.

The style of the programmes was changing with fewer plays but more readings, an increase in music of all kinds and a recognition of the public's growing appetite for discussion and controversy. There were problems of an emotional nature. Broadcasters were as susceptible to a lack of interest as anyone else and with radio fast becoming the poor relation – the 1962 published figures of gross expenditure would show radio being overtaken by television – there was a distant possibility that in some departments 'sound' might become an anteroom for television.

All the signs pointed to a need to underline the continuing importance of radio and this was done by the BCS in their Annual Report for 1961/2.

> The Scottish Home Service should make a selection of the native and of the general and metropolitan, seeking to create a blend of ideas and facts and art, acceptable to Scottish listeners as their own mixture. It should approach Scottish problems through the listeners' own habitual ways of thought and speech, informing them, with the impartiality required of the BBC, about the affairs and controversies which are important to them, broadcasting their forms of Christian worship, expressing their character in drama and stories, presenting their projects and activities, performing their music, reflecting their humour and their entertainment and recreation.

Steadying morale was one thing but satisfying audiences that good could come from the changes happening inside their radio sets was another. Scottish listeners still expected programmes to have a traditional style and anything that was novel or innovative quite often had a hard row to hoe.

One of the earliest Scottish programmes prepared to break the mould was the weekly series *Scope* started in 1957 by James MacTaggart before he moved to television. Its first title had been *Pageant* eventually sunk without trace by the then Assistant Head of Programmes, Aidan Thomson, when he suggested it as it conjured up thoughts of a wet day in Arbroath. At the end of its first season James took a moment to put his thoughts

about the programme on paper: 'I take *Scope* seriously... its success is
the result of a positive attitude to the world around us. This has meant
our not taking some organisations and people as seriously as they take
themselves: a kind of healthy insolence. I believe that it is good leave-
ning by this Corporation of the stodgy, half-baked, cultural smugness of
the self-styled cultural view of Scotland. We have reflected life in Scotland
as we found it, refusing to accept the world of the public relations officers
and mediocre makars would have us see.'

As the programme had managed to upset quite a few of Scotland's
traditionalists during its first year and with its producer now off to television, Gordon Gildard might well have shut it down for good. Instead
he chose to hand it over to a new producer, W. Gordon Smith in Edinburgh.
It was a common-sense move and one that was to benefit the programme
whatever it may have done to the BBC's public relations department.

W. Gordon Smith shared James's editorial stance and revelled in the
youthful assurance of the series. He retained Eddie Boyd as scriptwriter
and presenter Leonard Maguire but altered the programme style considerably by increasing the use made of tape recording. Soon each edition
had anything up to 30 separate pre-edited inserts, a fearsome amount of
tape in those days. This meant leaning heavily on the skills of two BBC
engineers, Bill Milligan and Phil Keane, who between them had developed a way of editing tape rarely used outside Scotland at that time –
copying from one machine to another instead of cutting the tape with a
razor blade and rejoining it with sticky tape.

Under W. Gordon Smith's hand *Scope* ran for five years. It used as
interviewers people such as Denise Coffey, Jameson Clark and Hilary
Paterson, welcomed by some of Gordon's colleagues as a 'sledge hammer
blow at the continuing BBC attitude that you must engage either hack
journalists or solemn pundits to tackle serious subjects of social or
political significance.'

Scope, with its style of sharp and terse understatement attracted a
small but loyal audience, at times critical but mostly always capable of
making their own moral judgements. Occasionally it would raise a whirl-
wind of controversy beyond its immediate devotees. In 1962, an interview
with writer Alexander Trocchi, a self-confessed drug addict, resulted in
a barrage of letters. Writing in reply to an MP, one of whose constituents
had complained about the programme, the Controller, Andrew Stewart,

made an important and revealing statement regarding the problems broad-casting in Scotland faced.

'If this broadcast had gone out on the Third Programme, such comment would have been unlikely but because the Scottish Home Service is a national programme with a wide responsibility under the Charter towards "the culture, interests and tastes" of the Scottish people, its range has to comprise everything from association football to philosophy to literary criticism.'

Scope had embodied ideas of frankness and realism that would even-tually become commonplace in radio, although not always presented with such professionalism as in these programmes, and it represented just one of the many changes discernible in Scottish broadcasting. Many of the traditional outputs established shortly after the war were now moving into a new phase. No longer was it assumed that radio had an audience by right and Scotland's programmes were having to compete both with each other and with other BBC networks.

Scotland's news and current affairs was increased and more attention given to 'metropolitan imbalance' and as an acknowledgement of morning audiences a ten-minute *Today in Scotland*, using studios in Edinburgh, Glasgow and Aberdeen opted out of London's *Today* three times a week.

Programmes with a live audience potential were taken out of the obscurity of the studio and put into the public gaze using modern light-weight OB equipment that made sure that the technical high quality achieved in studio performances was not impaired. In the main these were either entertainment programmes or panel discussions plus, of course, visits by one or other of the BBC's two orchestras to the many festivals that were growing up in Scotland. The Scottish Variety Orchestra's light music and Scottish dances held sway mostly north of the River Tay while the BBC Scottish Orchestra faced more urban audiences.

Inevitably there were changes that gave less pleasure. Some in partic-ular were deeply felt as being the epitome of radio's decline. In 1959, the 9.00pm news on the Home Service, for so long an emotive fixed point in the evening's listening, was dropped and replaced by a 10.00pm bulletin. Less than a year later, in June 1960, BBC Scotland announced the retire-ment of Kathleen Garscadden from her post as *Children's Hour* Organiser – the *Children's Hour* programme was to be axed four years later by the Home Service. In 1961, when the BBC Scottish Orchestra made a welcome return to the Edinburgh International Festival, it was to perform under its new conductor, Norman Del Mar. Ian Whyte, the Orchestra's founder was dead.

The death of Ian Whyte, coming after a long illness, had hit the Orchestra at a time when spirits were already low. For two years recruitment had been frozen with the future of the Orchestra very much in doubt as discussions took place on BBC orchestral policy throughout the Corporation. Ian Whyte was dying of cancer – a fact which for medical reasons had to remain a secret – and as a consequence there existed a perpetual problem of deputies with Scotland's Music department having to fight week in, week out to get conductors to maintain the published output. Then, in 1960, the Corporation chose to regrade the Northern Orchestra, increasing the number of players and making it supersede the BBC Scottish Orchestra as the BBC's second orchestra.

Scotland's management put a brave face on it and continued to fight behind the scenes for symphonic status using the crux of its argument the phrase from the Charter regarding the 'culture, interests and tastes' of the people of Scotland. Who else would broadcast performances of symphonic works by Scottish composers? Eventually the situation was admitted to be inconsistent and over a few years various augmentations were allowed, but in small amounts and usually causing a measure of imbalance. Finally, in 1967, the title was changed to the BBC Scottish Symphony Orchestra, but it was a Pyrrhic victory as its most recent experiences had robbed the Scottish Orchestra of a great deal of its spirit.

The stop-go development imposed on the BBC in the late 1950s had badly restricted investment in new projects with the Regions necessarily having to suffer most when projects were cancelled or delayed. In Scotland there was particular concern over the progress of VHF considered by many to be the most important advance in radio broadcasting. Very High Frequency broadcasting was one of radio's newest weapons in its fight for survival. The tape recorder had brought flexibility and realism to programmes. Cheap portable radio sets and the advent of the transistor meant that listening could happen almost anywhere and now VHF was bringing a promise of better sound quality, interference-free reception and an open invitation to develop stereo broadcasting and community and local services.

The BBC opened its first regular VHF service in 1955 at Wroth in Kent and gradually the system had spread through the country. Each transmitter carried the three domestic services, Home, Light and Third, and in most cases was co-sited with television either as an existing television mast or as new twin-service development. Not surprisingly it figured prominently in Scotland's plans for radio in the 1960s. Interference on both long wave and medium wave had been a constant complaint for some time in the North and West of Scotland and anything that might alleviate this problem was welcome. VHF also meant the chance to bring BBC programmes to small and as yet unserved communities and, equally importantly, it opened the door to area radio.

This particular feature of the new scheme, based on the ability to hive off transmitters either singly or in groups and allow them to broadcast without affecting the main services, was first used in Scotland in 1958 with the start of a service of 'area' broadcasting. Transmitted on the new VHF transmitter at Meldrum and operating out of the Aberdeen studios were two programmes a week, *Town and Country* (described as a pithy magazine) and a weekly newsletter. Both were aimed at listeners in the area lying between Elgin and Montrose. As the VHF network spread other programmes followed also from Aberdeen, Rosemarkie carrying a local service for Elgin and Inverness, and north to Dornoch, Brora and Helmsdale, followed eventually by a service into Caithness and Orkney.

The programmes, scant in number though they were, touched off plenty of interest and gave a useful airing to local topics and interest in the areas served but an undeniable drawback was the cost to the listener of a new VHF set. Only two local programmes a week could hardly be described as a major incentive. In fact, it was obvious that for the moment at least the real function of VHF in Scotland was to extend the coverage of existing services and take radio to the areas that had so far found little chance of listening.

The BBC, as well as wishing to improve reception conditions for listeners, had high hopes that VHF would allow it to extend into a fourth service – local radio. Speaking in Manchester towards the end of 1960 the Director-General, Hugh Carleton Greene, gave a clear policy statement: 'We think that the time has come for the extension of our existing regional and area services into local broadcasting... We believe that the public service system would ensure the local audience a more genuinely local, independent programme than could be offered by any commercial arrangement.'

The Corporation's plans, as with all major broadcasting developments, needed government permission and rather than sit around twiddling its thumbs while Pilkington and others considered the proposition the BBC decided to embark on a series of practical experiments, including two locations in Scotland. The first was a one-day trial in Dundee in August 1961 and, six months later, a three-day version based on Dumfries. During these experiments nothing was broadcast. Instead everything was taped and listened to later when details of staff and equipment could also be considered. It took a surprisingly long time for the BBC to get the go-ahead for local radio – the first station, Radio Leicester, opened in 1967 – and when it happened the National Regions did not appear amongst the first eight stations being planned.

For Scotland and Wales the reason was fairly straightforward. They were Nations and for them radio's first remit must be to underline the national identity. In England the broadcasting centres had no such homogeneity but in Scotland certainly the ties were strong. Radio, as the BCS

National Mod, Stirling (1961)
(l/r) Alex McCaskie; Hugh Macphee; Duke of Montrose; Provost MacFarlane Gray; Fred Macauley; Donald Thomson.

had reported, must continue to develop as a national service serving a large and natural community.

The new network of low-power transmitters gradually extended the reach of both radio and BBC television throughout Scotland and by the mid-'60s coverage of radio had risen to over 96.1 per cent and television to over 97 per cent. Amongst the many projects that contributed to this increase, pride of place went to the Great Glen Chain, a ribbon of links and transmitters that stretched from Rosemarkie to Oban. Completed in 1963 and formally opened by the Secretary of State for Scotland, the Rt Hon Michael Noble, it took BBC programmes across the Highlands to the western seaboard with new stations near Fort William, Ballachulish, Kinlochleven and Oban. It was a magnificent engineering achievement and visible proof that the BBC was in earnest about doing all it could to extend its services to outlying and thinly populated places. This was a responsibility that in Scotland, at least, often proved to be difficult and expensive as was pointed out by the Chairman of the BCS, Sir David Milne, when he said, 'Is this not the land of the bens and glens and the heroes? But it is the bens, and there are so many of them and so much of them, which get in the way of the viewing and listening of the heroes, and the heroes' wives and families.'

Amongst the many words of approval in Oban that day one person introduced a note of caution. Michael Noble in remarking on the feat of radio engineering achieved with the Great Glen Chain said that not since the time of General Wade had the Highlands been laid so open to outside influences and he didn't underrate the dangers to Gaelic culture inherent in what the transmitters would bring.

Mention of outside influences must have struck a chord of sympathy amongst the BCS members who were present. It was something that concerned them deeply, particularly with television, and since back in the late 1950s they had been trying hard to have their authority extended to cover both services. At first the BBC had been most unwilling to support any change despite the fairly cogent argument that audience habits were shifting and if only to keep in step the BCS should move with them. Time passed and despite spending more and more time discussing the effects and problems of television in Scotland, the BCS still lacked any responsibility.

Finally, with the Pilkington Committee looming on the horizon, it seemed the moment to give an almighty push. Assembling a coherent argument and in cahoots with their opposite numbers in Wales they decided to have a trial run by writing to the BBC's Board of Management through the Board of Governors. The initial response, a note by the Director-General to the Governors, was frosty to a degree. Choosing to interpret the suggested change as a thinly veiled attempt to bring pressure to bear for more opt-out time and money, he stressed that it was the policy of the Corporation to regard contributions to the United Kingdom network as the primary function of Scotland and Wales, and that providing separate programmes for their own consumption was an important but secondary object, certainly as long as the BBC had only one national television channel.

Scotland was completely bewildered. It knew that the basic essentials of its nationalism, education and religion, were reasonably well protected through having strong and exclusive committees, but there was a host of other subjects ranging from political broadcasting to moral standards that they could not oversee without parity of responsibility in television.

With Pilkington, the reception was altogether different. Evidence was given both in writing and orally and when the Committee's Report was published it supported the BCS's argument and, what's more, stated that there should be a financial responsibility to allocate adequate resources to the national body. In the first White Paper that followed, the government agreed. The powers would be conveyed in the BBC's new Charter due in 1964, and meantime, the Board of Governors suggested that they immediately treat the BCS as if the powers already existed.

It was good news and doubly welcome coming as it did just before the BBC's 40th anniversary in Scotland. 'Life begins at 40,' said a speaker as he toasted the BBC at one of the many formal occasions that took place. But perhaps, he shouldn't have thrown quite so much caution to the wind. The BBC in Scotland was experiencing a great deal of trouble in coming to terms with the 'Swinging Sixties' in things such as plays, and with a statement from the BCS that said 'a social atmosphere and standards of conduct which may seem to come naturally to the London West End stage are not always equally acceptable when they are introduced into the homes of the people of Scotland.'

It looked as if life was going to be fairly humdrum.

Around this time Scotland was often described as the final bastion of Reithian values. If true, it was not surprising, for its broadcasting had been guided for many years by people known and picked by the first Director-General. Reith, a guest speaker at the BBC's 40th anniversary lunch still remembered and mentioned some of them by name.

'I took him from the ministry of St Machar's Cathedral in Aberdeen (Dinwiddie)... At the age of 18, I almost lost my heart to his sister (Gildard)... Robert Raitt spoke so highly of Andrew Stewart that I engaged him immediately. And indeed I was right to have done so.'

They were called 'Reith's men' by some of their colleagues, a description used in their favour rather than disparagingly and unlike some of their contemporaries in the south, they were happy to consider it a distinction and a compliment.

Scotland, for the moment at least, was still thirled to an order of things that did seem markedly different from what was current elsewhere. An increasing number of UK television programmes were raising a storm of protest from public organisations, the press and individual correspondents, and the BBC in Glasgow, hardened to complaints of mispronunciation and the misappropriation of Scottish achievement, found it difficult to give a reasoned reply to protests over a lack of decency and respect. Sometimes in an effort to keep the locally produced output unsullied, extraordinary rules were enforced which had they been known would have left the audience mystified at the very least.

When a new film version of Buchan's *The Thirty Nine Steps* was about to open in London's West End, the producer of the local Scottish arts programme managed to talk the distributors into letting him have a short clip of the film on his programme, a not inconsiderable scoop in those days. As the film had already been granted a 'U' certificate by the British Board of Film Censors, the last thing to enter his mind that night was the possibility of trouble over sexual impropriety. However, the sight of blonde actress, Taina Elg, peeling off her nylon stockings while handcuffed to Kenneth More was apparently more than the Scottish viewer should have been asked to bear and the following morning the production was carpeted for a gross error of judgement.

There was punishment, too, for tainting the trappings of national identity. In a St Andrew's Eve edition of the current affairs programme *Compass*, the letter x was superimposed on the St Andrew's Cross during the closing titles. As a major item in the programme had been the number of x-rated films currently being shown in Scotland's cinemas, the producer had decided to finish with a visual summary of the question: 'Was Scotland in moral decline?' The next day, far from being congratulated on what had been a very reasonable and fairly balanced item, he was roundly spoken to for blemishing the Scottish Saltire.

The staff quickly learnt to take these excesses of caution in their stride but it was impossible not to have an occasional flicker of anxiety and worry over where this narrowing road of righteousness might lead. Radio, traditionally flexible and imaginative, was not so restricted. It was out of the centre glare of the spotlight of course and over the years had built a reputation of being more stable and responsible. Also, and this probably was the most significant factor of all, its various departments had a long-standing close relationship with London colleagues, something which television lacked.

By the time of the 40th anniversary it was clear that the programme policies of the south were not always to the taste of BBC Scotland. In fact, in television there was a clear divergence of view over quite a few matters, and the BCS, deciding that uniformity with London was not in Scotland's best interests, chose to announce that it had formulated its own Scottish principles. While still wishing to work in co-operation with London colleagues, the BCS 'must gang its ain gait in the interests of its ain folk.'

It was a strangely couthy sentence, oddly out of place in a formal BCS report, an incantation perhaps as if the Scots were throwing a defensive ring around themselves in an attempt to ward off the pressures coming from the south. Certainly there was no thought of loosening the ties with London, the Scots probably having more than anyone else a deep traditional respect for the BBC, but for the moment there was need for time. Time to debate how best to deal with the new emancipation that was moving through broadcasting and how to avoid the seemingly offensive and yet support creative effort and lively professionalism. It was also important to consider how to pursue on the screen Scotland's own native traditions and culture and project them to a wider audience in a way that would bring credit and interest.

Scotland's stance was to prove very difficult to maintain, particularly on the screen. While it could 'gang its ain gait' in locally produced programmes, exerting control over what else was seen by viewers proved to be virtually impossible. Any attempt to influence programme makers elsewhere, not just in terms of moral turpitude but in their selection and coverage of Scottish material, was almost bound to fail, and often caused long-term damage to professional relationships. Even the rather last ditch act of substituting an alternative programme to that being shown to the rest of the country often rebounded and the number of complaints from those denied access to a network production frequently exceeded anything that might have been expected as a result of the original programme.

In London, the Board of Governors seemed unconcerned. 'We have, of course, from time to time, divergencies of opinion,' said their Chairman, Sir Arthur ffforde, adding that the BCS would not be doing its job had it been otherwise. Unfortunately, at executive level, there was not the same magnanimity. Behind the seemingly normal exchanges that continued between Glasgow and London there was growing evidence of a substantial rift between the two managements. As the Director-General, Hugh Carleton Greene, was busying himself accelerating the process of change within the BBC, Andrew Stewart in Scotland felt he had no alternative but to gather a cloak of Reithian values more tightly around himself, determined that nothing would change his honest regard to the long-term and immutable interests of Scotland as he saw it.

Hugh Carleton Greene and Andrew Stewart shared an intense mutual dislike. Their battle over 'tradition' versus 'trendiness' was only one of many confrontations and as their conflict deepened the climate in Scotland worsened appreciably. There were allegations of London interference in the appointment of local staff, with disparate factions forming within the Scottish management group and Andrew Stewart becoming increasingly embittered as he watched the Director-General of the BBC, a post that he must surely have had ambitions to occupy himself, set about breaking down and discarding a great deal of the policy of Scottish broadcasting that had been framed many years before.

Despite these boardroom clashes, however, Scotland, outwardly at least, was in good heart. Radio had now stabilised after the many changes made to its programme structure and was pursuing new audiences through its expanding VHF network. Sound studios were being modernised and new recording suites installed in Edinburgh and Aberdeen. Even Dundee, the neglected bairn of the family, was about to benefit from a scheme of re-equipment. In television, the signs were really encouraging. The spread of the new low-power transmitter chain, particularly in the North and

West of Scotland, was gradually increasing the size of the Scottish audience and programme-making facilities were also extending. In Aberdeen, a small studio and control area butted on to the existing building at Beechgrove, had been opened in July 1962 and in May the following year an even simpler installation was brought into service at Broadcasting House, Edinburgh.

In both cases it meant that live reports could now be fed into the Scottish output, an important factor in the drive to achieve an 'all-Scotland' service, and in Aberdeen's case, where the studio had the added facility of telecine, it was possible to produce local programmes as a bit of flag-waving in the battle with the newly arrived competitor, Grampian Television. Finally, in the most important development of all, Stage One of the new television wing at Broadcasting House, Glasgow, opened in the spring of 1964, putting to an end ten years of frustration and delay that certainly had not been foreseen when the project had first been considered.

There had never been much doubt about where the BBC would locate its first made-to-order television building in Scotland. Tucked away in the eastern end of the Queen Margaret College grounds in Glasgow was a private bowling green and tennis club, and though the Corporation had left it undisturbed when it had bought the College in 1937, it had always kept in mind the possibility of using it one day for a major extension. It was an ideal site for television and early in 1953 the BBC's Civil Engineer gave the go-ahead to start planning its development.

Almost at once the BBC found itself up against stiff resistance. Nearby householders were strongly opposed to any kind of large-scale development in what was a residential area and their case was helped by the existence of an 80-year-old document clearly stating that the ground in question 'shall be used as a pleasure ground... and shall not be feued or sold for building purposes.'

It took almost three years before a public enquiry, held early in 1956, finally delivered judgement in favour of the BBC and unfortunately the long delay was to take its toll. The government's insistence on cutbacks and penny-pinching over the licence fee meant that BBC finances were once again in a perilous state and as it was too late to build anything in time to meet the deadline of commercial television in Scotland (hence the BBC's hurried move into the Black Cat Cinema), it was decided there would be a delay in the bowling green project of at least six years.

The news that completion would now be 1962 at the earliest brought considerable disappointment, not just within the BBC but also to some of the groups that had lent their support. At one point, Glasgow Corporation had applied to the Secretary of State for permission to alter its development plan for the area, changing the zoning of the Queen Margaret College grounds from 'a private open space' to one 'for cultural purposes'. Clearly a silver lining was needed and in an attempt at conciliation the BBC came up with two hopeful suggestions. One was a hint that the enforced delay might mean more money for a better building and secondly, that 'as an insurance against future expansion', Scotland should acquire additional ground by purchasing a semi-derelict nursery garden which lay close to the bowling green, provided that it cost less than £6,000.

Scotland was cock-a-hoop and though it soon became clear that the asking price for the nursery, £8,000, was not open to negotiation, it was confident that the price would eventually fall. A long period of waiting followed and still there was no sign of progress on either of the two Glasgow sites. Then with an inevitability that was now almost wholly predictable, someone pushed Edinburgh back into the limelight.

This time the instigator was Andrew Stewart, suggesting that the development of television facilities take place in Edinburgh, not building from scratch, but based on an existing building, and that by doing so, the BBC might save £250,000 on capital expenditure. The project would have a life of ten years and 'would buy time in which the breathtaking technical developments in television could settle and crystallise so that, before the end of the period, we should have a much better idea as to what our requirements in Edinburgh and Glasgow really amounted to.'

The scheme was intriguing enough to attract a working party from London, but after an on-site investigation and an intensive examination of the adaptation costs involved, the idea was conclusively rejected. Had the decision been otherwise, it would certainly have changed the way television developed in Scotland. It would also very probably have altered the future topography of a small part of Festival Edinburgh, for the building in question was the Synod Hall leased by Edinburgh Corporation to Messrs Poole as a cinema and destined in a few years to become the city's 'hole in the ground'.

One benefit did result from Andrew Stewart's proposal. The Working Party's report, while advising against the Edinburgh alternative, recommended that work start immediately on Glasgow's bowling green site. The Director-General quickly agreed and within a few months Stage 1 was at last on its way. There was still the unfinished business of the vacant nursery site next to the bowling green but few people worried or doubted that it would come the BBC's way eventually. After all, who else would be likely to purchase the ground? Almost two years to the day, after work had started on Stage 1, a very worried Scottish administrator, Peter Dunbar, was able to answer that question as he dashed off a memo to London: 'I hear a rumour that Wimpey have acquired the nursery site for the building of multi-storey flats.' Quickly the rumour was confirmed. The site had indeed gone, bought by Wimpey's at a new asking price of £10,000, provided they could get planning permission to develop it for residential housing.

The BBC had waited too long. Now its only hope was to block the proposed development and then offer to buy the ground back from Wimpey. Setting off for the second time down the weary road of arguments and enquiries, the BBC once more put its faith in Glasgow Corporation and in Dame Jean Roberts, an ex-Lord Provost of the City and a member of the BCS. As before, it was a lengthy process, the consultations and discussions continuing for well over two years. Then in November 1963, with both Corporations close to agreement, the BBC quite unwittingly almost torpedoed the whole operation.

The trouble arose from a special Scottish edition of *Panorama*. Transmitted live from a location on Clydeside, the programme not only painted the worst kind of picture of conditions in Glasgow, it also chose to illustrate some of its points by using film that was quickly proved to be faked. The city was outraged. There was a formal statement of regret from the BBC in London but the Lord Provost's comment, 'this is a lame apology and it has come too late.' showed that Glasgow was in no mood for conciliation and that considerable work would now have to be done to bring relations back to normal.

Thankfully the fact that *Panorama* was London-based helped to reduce the blame laid at Scotland's door. After a few months of cooling down the two Corporations were once again in reasonable harmony, and in April 1964 the hoped-for statement came. Glasgow Corporation would support the BBC and recommended that negotiations open to acquire the nursery site from Wimpey's. The timing of the announcement couldn't have been better. With the final coat of paint almost dry on the Stage 1 building it would have been difficult avoiding speculation about the future.

The following year, the BBC bought the ground from Wimpey's for £18,000. It was a vastly different figure from the initial £8,000 but allowing for inflation it was perhaps not too high a price to pay to guarantee Scotland's future expansion well into the 1980s.

The Stage 1 development, built on the old bowling green and tennis courts, had changed in detail anything up to six different times but in essence it was still a major bit of progress for Scotland. The hub of the new building was the television studio. It was technically bang up-to-date, large enough for most major drama and audience shows and well supported with dressing rooms, workshops and all the other parapher-nalia of television production. At its formal opening on 10 June 1964, Kenneth Adam, the BBC's Director of Television, well aware of Scotland's long wait, spoke of the studio giving the lie to complaints that the BBC built first-class facilities only in London. But his underlining of this bit of BBC largesse had a faintly hollow ring to it, certainly for those in the audience who knew of the tussle that had recently taken place over who would use the studio during the next few years.

Glasgow Studio A, so called to distinguish it from the small refur-bished Studio 3, now known as Studio B, was the first BBC studio out-side London that could make programmes on different line standards (either 405 lines or 625 lines). This bit of technical wizardry had not gone unnoticed by London who were finding themselves desperately short of 625 line facilities for its new television channel, BBC 2. Casting covetous eyes on Scotland's Studio A, they proposed that some drama productions planned for BBC 2 should be shipped into Glasgow when-ever the new studio was ready. For a brief period it looked as if there was to be another disagreement between Scotland and London. Andrew Stewart had counted on the new studio making a major contribution to Scottish output. Substituting programmes from London, the word 'hosting' was quickly coined to describe what some thought was a parasitical action, would be of little benefit to Scottish-based actors and production staff. There was also the emotive factor of Scotland's not seeing any of the transmissions. The new service of BBC 2 had made a start but only in the London area and it would be at least two years before the channel was available to viewers elsewhere.

It could have developed into another of Scotland's famous stand-offs, but needs must when the devil drives and, in any case, gone were the days when a Region owned all its resources. The requirements of the new channel were paramount and within a short time of the Glasgow studio being brought into service the first of the classic serials for BBC 2 was in rehearsal. Thankfully the list of productions included adaptations of such recognised Scottish standards as John Buchan's *Witchwood* and Scott's *The Heart of Midlothian* and this helped assuage the resentment that had bubbled up in some quarters. Also the BBC 2 commitment was not taking up all of the available time in the studio, and there was still an opportunity for some Scottish productions to benefit from the new resources.

Organising a recognisable Scottish drama output took a little time to get under way. At the start of 1965 both Equity and a House of Lords Debate criticised the lack of Scottish drama on television but by the end of the same year there had been a considerable improvement, and drama, that traditional barometer of Scotland's success, had swung upwards once again thanks to some excellent productions such as Robert McLellan's *Young Auchinleck*, Robert Kemp's *Green Pastures* and Evan John's *Prelude to Massacre*.

Hosting also prospered in Scotland. A shortage of facilities in London had been the prime reason for the first move north and there is no doubt that for a while both visitor and host circled each other warily expecting the worst. But the London teams met only co-operation and interest and working conditions that were far superior to what they had left behind. The Scots for their part were also pleasantly surprised. Expecting arrogance and over-statement, instead they found that the continual coming and going of London-based personnel brought an important professional relationship from which they could and were willing to learn. Outward shibboleths from both sides of the border quickly disappeared and hosting remained to become an important strand in BBC Scotland's annual plan of work.

Often it took clever scheduling to fit London commitments and Scottish aspirations together in the same jigsaw of resources, but the increase in professionalism brought about by the visitors was sufficient reward and there is no doubt that Scottish productions benefited from the greatly improved techniques and resources that hosting encouraged.

There was also a move towards making the visiting productions more obviously Scottish and soon it became impossible to distinguish any difference in the pedigrees of *The Borderers*, (a hosted production set in the bad lands of the Scottish Borders in the 17th Century), *Dr Finlay's Casebook* (a London studio production set in the Scottish Trossachs in the 1920s) and *This Man Craig*, (produced by BBC Scotland and centred on a contemporary school in Glasgow).

CHAPTER TEN

'Tiger at the Gate'

IN THE MANY YEARS that had passed since David Cleghorn Thomson had first introduced the Scottish Regional Scheme, control of Scotland had changed hands only twice. That there had been really only three masters spanning a period of over 40 years was exceptional, even for the BBC, and as the time came for Andrew Stewart to retire there was considerable speculation about who could succeed him.

Early in September 1967 the guessing came to an end with the announcement that the next Controller would be Alasdair Milne and that he would arrive almost at once although the actual handover would not take place until July, the following year.

In name at least the new Controller was already well-known in Scotland. After joining the BBC's Television Current Affairs department in London in the mid-'50s, Alasdair Milne had quickly swung into prominence as producer and later in editorial charge of the hugely successful *Tonight* programme. Then, in the early 1960s, he had been given a management post and responsibility for such diverse activities as *Panorama* and the satirical and irreverent *That Was The Week That Was*. These programmes had at times brought him into sharp contact with the Scottish management and he had endured a threat that the Scottish border would be closed to his team of reporters. More recently he had caught Scottish

Alasdair Milne
Controller, Scotland (1968–1973).

attention with an unsuccessful bid for the Central Scotland ITV franchise. He had resigned from the BBC in 1965 and shortly afterwards had brought together a consortium of distinguished Scots hoping to dislodge Scottish Television from its so far unopposed position.

Inevitably, the press made much more of the more turbulent aspects of his background but of his brilliance there was little doubt. Clearly Scotland could count itself lucky to have attracted such a person at what was a crucial time in its television development and the staff waited patiently for the lengthy handover to be completed.

In reality the projected nine months of familiarisation lasted little more than nine weeks. News leaked that Andrew Stewart was intending to accept an offer of a non-executive seat on the board of Scottish Television and with little grace the BBC brought forward his retirement to the end of the year, putting Alasdair Milne in complete charge of the BBC from 1 January 1968. At first staff and broadcasters alike waited for the cataclysmic changes prophesied in the press. One headline that had stuck had been in *The Scotsman* newspaper: 'Milne: A Tiger at the Gate', but in the event the tiger's heart was wrapped in a professional hide. Eager though he was to test his views on how broadcasting in Scotland could be improved, Alasdair Milne was by his own admission fairly cautious.

'I have a lot to learn, he said, 'and there's not much point in upsetting people when you've got to work with them.'

Understandably a great deal of his attention was focussed on television output, which to his mind badly needed some professional help. Until his arrival every member of the Scottish management group had been radio born and bred and, though anxious to do their best for what would ultimately become the most important element of broadcasting, they had lacked first-hand knowledge and experience. The radio service was ticking over reasonably well and had maintained its considerable reputation despite the problems of declining audiences, but television, particularly the local output, had an air of tawdriness about it that was very evident to the new Controller's practised eye.

An immediate remedy would have been massive injections of cash and people but local television programmes had a very low priority with the moguls of Television Centre in London where there was little sympathy for the argument that a National Region resigned to the second-rate would never become a vigorous and active contributor to UK programmes. Help from London might come later but for the moment any remedial work would have to use existing staff and facilities.

Less than three weeks after the turn of the year the BCS were reading the first of half a dozen papers outlining progressive alterations to Scotland's television policy. The proposals covered everything from the style and presentation of programmes – to become freer and more relaxed – to the way in which financial resources would be allocated in the future, enriching one particular vein of programming each year instead of the existing system of scattering money across the board.

For viewers the first sign of change was in the Scottish news. The programme had altered little since the first pioneering edition in 1957 apart from some technical improvements such as better film resources and an improved studio. It was still Glasgow-based and no longer seemed able to give an adequate report on the life of Scotland. As the BBC had studios in Aberdeen and Edinburgh, both sitting empty for a large part of the working week, it was decided that the best way of competing efficiently with Scottish Television and Grampian Television was to do what they couldn't – to bring the whole of Scotland together in one news programme. Under the new title of *Reporting Scotland*, it took to the air on 1 April 1968 with a style of production that was considerably freer and easier than anything that had gone before. Its first presenters were Mary Marquis, who subsequently became an iconic figure in the history of the programme, Douglas Kynoch, Gordon Smith and Donny B. MacLeod, who joined the team shortly afterwards on completion of his contract with Grampian Television. The barriers between news reporting and comment were beginning to break down and by the end of the first month the audience gave its verdict, a clear and distinct nod of approval that pushed the figures up by an estimated 70,000 viewers.

Soon other changes and alterations were filtering through the system. There was the start of a move away from the old regional tradition of the same producers working in both radio and television with single production departments feeding both services. This had been very necessary in the pioneering days of the late 1950s when experienced radio staff had contributed style and ability and a considerable amount of unwritten guidance. But now television had a shape and character of its own. It had already shaken itself loose from the theatre and was now casting aside many of the custom and practices of radio. What was more it was also growing very expensive and was no longer able to consider the sometimes haphazard and beguiling habits of radio. Radio, too, was to become much more cost-conscious in its operation but not until the end of the decade.

Television was now a business on its own. It had to be practical and systematic and as Scotland began to establish some clearly defined television production elements, one of the first being a television documentary unit, started early in 1968, under the charge of Finlay J. Macdonald, there was a corresponding drive to re-examine how best to place programmes for transmission. Scheduling television broadcasts had never been easy and with competition between BBC and commercial television now quite merciless no channel Controller in London was prepared to deliberately plan a throwaway item into his evening's viewing. As a result Scotland's opt-outs, programmes intended only for transmission in Scotland, were frequently to be found at irregular intervals and at inconvenient timings. Even with the support of the network there could still be problems and quite often a play or a documentary, made by Scotland for UK transmission on BBC 1 or BBC 2, could be overlooked in the mainstream of the output and be in danger of passing unnoticed.

The remedy eventually devised fitted well with the change in production units. The old principle inherited from radio was dropped in favour of a much more structured framework of fewer single programmes and more strands. Even documentaries and features, for long the traditional exponents of the single subject, were encouraged to explore more of a thematic approach.

This compression of the output, no longer wayward and a touch self-willed but instead organised into a semblance of a pattern, made it a degree more manageable for the planners and as Alasdair Milne's determination to improve the general standard of professionalism began to take effect the viewers became better disposed to Scotland's programmes than before.

As the mechanics of Scottish broadcasting began to alter there was a corresponding change in programme subjects and treatments. Features and documentaries already bidden to take a thematic approach were also told to devote as much of their output as possible to the future of Scotland rather than the past. The BBC announced two competitions for Gaelic writers, one for plays and the other for short stories. Even more important in the fight to keep the language alive, Alasdair Milne made a ten-minute speech in Gaelic at the close of the 1968 Mod in Dunoon demonstrating that for the first time in 45 years there was a fluent Gaelic speaker at the helm of the management of BBC Scotland.

Change was more difficult in the high-cost areas of drama and light entertainment where it wasn't easy to argue against the quite remarkable popularity of Scotland's customary successes, mostly Scots songs and dancers and the works of Stevenson and Scott. In any case these were programmes where London was usually the paymaster and not Scotland. But Television Centre was beginning to indicate a certain sympathy with the Scotland's need to explore beyond the limits of tradition, and with the climate now very different from the defensive one of five years before there were hopeful signs of a better understanding between the two centres. One factor stood in the way – the fact that the development plan to take Scotland's television resources fully into colour had a very low priority.

The least surprising shift in programme content took place in current affairs. Here Alasdair Milne was on home ground. This fraction of the output, with its name changed from *Checkpoint* to *Current Account* returned to the schedules after a summer break clearly intent on trading ground that had always been out of bounds to BBC Scotland. Asking uncomfortable questions and worrying at disagreeable facts, it edged much closer to the social and political facts of life in Scotland than had been the custom before.

One of its interests was to reflect the growing sense of nationalism in the country, a topic that had already been the subject of a major programme earlier in the year. In April, an 80-minute edition of *Checkpoint* with the title, *Where Do We Go From Here?* had set out to examine the facts and the mood behind the upsurge of nationalist sentiment in Scotland. Using MPs and various experts representing a cross-section of opinion amongst economists, it had been presented before a selected studio of 100 Scots.

It was the first time television in Scotland had attempted to get to grips with whether or not Scotland had considered some of the more perplexing questions raised by what was happening, and if a reason was needed for such a programme – a surprising number of people were against it – an article in the *Radio Times* written by James Kemp, the BBC's Scottish Editor of News and Current Affairs, included a fairly lucid one:

'Certainly there does appear to be a strong current running in favour of the Scots having a greater say in and control of their affairs. The growth in the number of votes for the Scottish National Party since 1964 is clear evidence of that, and it is impossible to dismiss the result of the Hamilton by-election as a freak, as a protest vote, or as a lucky break arising from the admitted attractiveness of Mrs Winifred Ewing as a candidate.'

The programme attracted a huge Scottish audience and also a great deal of criticism especially from Scottish MPs who complained that it had been ill-balanced and misleading. But there were just as many people ready with praise, including the BCS where the general opinion was that it was time politicians realised that there was a mood abroad in the country. Left unsaid was recognition of a new mood circulating in broadcasting thanks largely to the enthusiasm and political nous of the Controller, now busy prodding the BBC into recognising that there was more to nationalism than just cultural achievement, history and tradition.

Four hundred miles away in London there was less enthusiasm than at Broadcasting House, Glasgow. *Checkpoint* had been seen only in Scotland, and London had gained an uneasy impression that during the programme a kind of tidal drift of the odds towards the Scottish National Party set in. Some six weeks after the transmission a playback was organised in the Concert Hall and the Governors' Dining Room for an audience that was to include all the Scottish MPs. Ironically, something went wrong with the distribution of the invitations, arranged by the Whips' Office at 12 Downing Street, and Mrs Winifred Ewing, the Scottish National Party MP for Hamilton, received no notification of the *Checkpoint* playback. It was a strange muddle that served to increase the tensions caused by the programme.

When the BBC launched regular colour transmissions on its BBC 2 network on 1 July 1967, a full colour service being available six months later, alarm bells rang in a lot of offices in BBC Scotland. Altering studios to colour was a complex and expensive business with London inevitably at the head of the queue. Conversion work would take time to move out elsewhere, Scotland being scheduled for 1970/71, and in the meantime Glasgow was in danger of losing many of its network markets. Lack of colour facilities had already put a stop to hosted drama visits for BBC 2, Scotland's own drama output would soon be under threat and, with BBC 1

due to be in colour in 1969, Scotland's extremely exportable light entertainment series faced an uncertain future. The local opt-out programmes
would again suffer odious comparisons this time through being in black
and white and the hard-won ground of viewer acceptance was probably
going to be lost.

Altogether it was a bleak forecast and Scotland pressed hard for something better than 18 months of Scottish programmes in monochrome while
the bulk of those from the networks were in colour. It chose its moment
well. The Chairman of the Board of Governors and the Director-General
attended a meeting of the BCS and they came expecting criticism of the way
they had bypassed the BCS in the appointment of Alasdair Milne. A switch
of complaint paid off and, as it was in any case customary to bring gifts
from the south on the appointment of a new Controller, the two wise men
agreed that the BBC would be sympathetic to Scotland's position.

At the end of 1969, a colour mobile control room and colour video-
tape facilities arrived in Scotland to be used on a drive-in basis for Studio
A in Glasgow. Predictably the first colour programme from the Queen
Margaret Drive studio was *Ring in the New* for that year's Hogmanay.
It starred Moira Anderson, Bill Simpson, Chic Murray, Bernadette and
Alasdair Gillies and had some of the excitement and drive of past OBs
but lacked the up-to-date sophistication that could only be achieved by
using a properly converted studio. Nevertheless the uneasy alliance of
OB colour and monochrome studio served a purpose. For the next 12
months Scotland was able to register itself as colour-capable and at the
same time gain valuable experience adapting to the new medium.

By the end of 1970, the electronic partnership had run its course and
the studio complex was completely shut down for six months to allow
a full colour progression to take place. Alasdair Milne knew only too well
that it was traditional for television management in London to judge a
competence on the quality of a last offering – you were only as good as
your last show. The colour work from the studio during 1970 had been
competent but nothing more and to get Scotland into a position for the
next leap forward he would have to pull something impressive out of the
bag, something that could be made largely on film while the studio was
shut down and which would make full use of natural locations. His
conversation with Pharic Maclaren was characteristically short and to
the point: 'Scotland must break into the network on a regular basis.

What is the best book available to us, distinctive enough to invest a lot of money in? And what about *Sunset Song*?'

Sunset Song, the first novel in Lewis Grassic Gibbon's trilogy, *A Scots Quair* was a bold choice. Some might even have called it a dangerous gamble. Notwithstanding its success as a radio play – after its first broadcast in 1948 listeners had been unanimous in ranking it as a classic – *Sunset Song* did have some inherent qualities that could prove troublesome in television, not least of these being the need to set the play in its home context, using the rich, ringing accents of the Howe of the Mearns.

Having talked the project through with Pharic Maclaren, Alasdair Milne went to London to talk to Robin Scott (Controller of BBC 2) finally selling him the idea as a television serial in six 45-minute episodes for BBC 2. 'Sell' is perhaps a misnomer. It would be better to say a bargain was struck. BBC 2's habit of pleading poverty resulted in Scotland agreeing to pay a percentage of the production costs, a burdensome undertaking that would last for many years to come.

Sunset Song was an immediate success. At the end of the first episode as the closing notes of the specially composed title music by Thomas Wilson died away, BBC Scotland uncrossed its fingers knowing that it had finally lifted itself on to the next step of professional skill. The evidence was clear for all to see. Marvellously directed by a vastly competent Scottish director, Moira Armstrong, Lewis Grassic Gibbon's profoundly moving story sat comfortably on the television screen as if it had never been intended for anything else. The book had been adapted for television by Bill Craig with a sympathetic understanding that was put to good use by an outstanding Scottish cast and with almost half of each episode on film, beautifully shot by cameraman Stuart Wylde, the quality and atmosphere of the countryside was often quite stunning.

A sense of satisfaction and pride quickly spread to everyone in BBC Scotland regardless of whether they had been directly concerned with the production or not. If there was such a thing as a pass mark in television then BBC Scotland had certainly achieved it. From now on, Glasgow's Queen Margaret Drive would be expected to make its own way into the high-cost schedules of television drama without always needing the support of London production departments, still a useful adjunct and, like hosting, destined to continue but in the eyes of some people inclined to verge on colonisation by London.

The success of *Sunset Song* signalled the fulfilment of a long-cherished ambition for BBC Scotland – to be recognised as being capable of operating at the highest levels of television competence. For the first time everyone *felt* they were in the profession and with this came an assurance clearly seen in many of the programmes that followed.

This new-found positiveness received an added boost later the same year. Close on the heels of this success, came what was without doubt the outstanding event of the year, the 1970 Commonwealth Games, hosted by Scotland at the Meadowbank Stadium in Edinburgh. BBC Scotland personnel were largely responsible for both the planning and the administration of the massive broadcasting coverage, drawing on resources from practically every part of the United Kingdom, and once again there was admiration and praise that added even more to the confidence that was now bubbling through the nation.

The following year, with the full colourisation of the Glasgow studio complete (there still remained the problem of monochrome studios in Edinburgh and Aberdeen) and enough development money to expand the supporting staff into five-day working, Scotland increased both the amount and the quality of its output. The range of programmes was wider than ever before. Network television commitments were considerable, particularly drama and documentaries, and in Scotland itself there was an increase in the output from nearly every production unit. Additional videotape facilities now meant it was possible to hold London material for later transmission and this avoided the criticism of deprivation when placing Scotland-only programmes.

This all pointed to a growing harmony between programme ambitions on the one hand and technical improvement and reorganisation on the other. The years of catch-as-catch-can had gone. Twelve specialist departments able to tap into an adequate range of ancillary facilities meant that Scotland could now define its annual supply of programmes against a background of resource allocation and control. *Ad hoc* schemes were gradually replaced by a coherent and assured initiative and, notwithstanding the BBC's continuing financial deficit, Scotland at last felt it was within sight of its single most important change. All Scottish productions were now working to a single standard and the end of local low budget and inelegant programmes justified only by being 'Scotland-only'.

It was a move that was coming not a moment too soon. The quickening political and social changes taking place within Scotland were demanding a broadcasting service of the highest professional standard that would stand comparison with any other, something that the broadcasters had been striving to reach for years and were now likely to achieve thanks to the new image of Scottish identity that was demanding recognition.

When Alasdair Milne made his decision early in 1968 to leave radio virtually untouched, he was not only acknowledging its popularity with listeners. Knowing that London was already busy planning radical changes to broadcasting he saw sense in holding his hand at waiting until the UK position was clear.

Apart from some piecemeal tinkering the BBC's sound services had remained virtually unaltered since the resurgence of broadcasting in the immediate post-war period. Now, urged on by money problems, and a fundamental change in the nature of the radio audience, the BBC took the first steps in a major reorganisation designed to take into account the new needs and tastes of listeners while at the same time introducing proper financial and administrative structures to manage radio's many disparate resources more efficiently. In broadcasting, business management and 'the arts' were unaccustomed bedfellows and there were people in plenty convinced that such an arrangement would sound the death knell of creativity and originality. There were dire warnings that the basis of broadcasting would very quickly become quantity at the expense of quality and that the traditional intellectual categories and minority programmes of the BBC were bound to be emasculated. In truth, however, there was little else for the BBC to do. Money was short and the drastic shift in listening habits had already made it clear that the old days of the wireless as a focal point of family evening entertainment had all but gone. The high-cost programmes that by tradition still filled the evening schedules now looked increasingly alone and self-indulgent and it was high time that broadcasting followed its audience tailoring itself to daytime broadcasting and the increasing demand for light music and information.

For listeners, the first palpable change came in 1967. A bright pop channel joined the old warhorses, Light, Third and Home. All were given new titles alongside a promise that the character of each network – Radios 1, 2, 3 and 4 – would make it easier for listeners to find the kind of programme they wanted. Programme intentions were to remain the same, it was said, but the settings would change.

A campaign of heated debate and intervention was soon up and running and with continual newspaper stories, usually alarmist and often inaccurate, it was guaranteed the widest possible interest. But interest did not necessarily mean complaint. As one senior executive was to point out, the BBC received fewer than 1,000 letters from ordinary listeners, far fewer than, for example, when the decision had been made to take off radio's long-established soap opera, *The Dales*.

In Scotland the new plans had a mixed reception. The move to rationalise radio into four distinctive networks was generally welcomed with only those who had a particular knowledge of broadcasting voicing concern over whether the BBC's coverage north of the Border was capable of making sense of it all. There was also a small question mark hanging over where Scotland stood in relation to developing local radio. The BBC planned to forge ahead with this in England hoping eventually to have the Postmaster General's approval for about 40 stations covering 90 per cent of the population in the south. At the same time the traditional English regional system would be progressively superseded and the old broadcasting 'boundaries', North, Midlands and South and West Regions, would be replaced with eight smaller versions socially more representative and designed with an eye to future television needs, such as feeding the national news and current affairs programmes.

No such restructuring was planned for the three Nations. Each was already serving homogeneous communities and Scotland, always quick to hammer home its role as a national service, certainly had no wish to become a group of local units, but it did have an interest in 'area' broadcasting. Since the early experiments of the 1960s Scotland had been convinced that this was a better option than city-based local stations and had, for some time, been running two modest services on VHF serving the North and North East using spare studio capacity in Aberdeen and hoping for money to develop a station in Inverness.

But the inescapable truth was that broadcasting in the 1970s had to save money rather than spend it. Any area development in Scotland would mean an extra tier of broadcasting on top of the existing service and London was adamant that money was only available for change. Develop along these lines if you wish was the message but you pay for it yourself, diverting some of your existing resources from running the national service.

It was a situation already familiar to Alasdair Milne from the days when he had first set about improving television in Scotland. Then he had been happy to argue a special case and he saw no reason why he shouldn't do the same thing now and with fingers crossed Scotland decided to press for new monies for its beleaguered radio coffers, but even as the whys and wherefores were being committed to paper something new and much more pressing grabbed everyone's attention.

Once again the trouble was money. If the BBC were to achieve their plans for broadcasting in the 1970s extra finance would have to be found somewhere. A high proportion of radio's annual costs went to music, live musicians and the BBC's House Orchestras. Using broadcasting requirements as a yardstick rather than the tradition of patronage the BBC had realised that with a greater use of recorded music it could reduce the large number of house musicians that it employed. A list of orchestras had been prepared which in the Corporation's own words, 'we have no broadcasting need for and which financial responsibility can no longer remain with the BBC'. Heading that list was the BBC's Scottish Symphony Orchestra in Glasgow. With a sense of foreboding the Scottish management prepared itself for a long siege.

The crisis turned out to be shorter than expected. Neither the public nor the unions was prepared to accept a change in the Corporation's long tradition of music patronage and the longer it remained a possibility the greater the resistance. The deadlock was finally broken by the Postmaster General, John Stonehouse. Urging the BBC to change its mind he promised an increase in the 1971 licence fee of just over eight per cent. Although not overly generous it was clearly enough to underwrite the start of 'Broadcasting in the Seventies', the BBC's immediate area of financial concern. With a sense of relief the Corporation accepted that a bargain could be struck and the threat to the orchestras was removed.

For Alasdair Milne and his colleagues the immediate question was how to make the Symphony Orchestras' position in the cultural life of Scotland more secure. Early in the crisis appeals to local authorities for financial help towards the cost of the orchestra had demonstrated a depressing lack of belief in its viability and this would have to be changed. One obvious way of bolstering confidence was to take it out of the studio and into the concert hall, to be seen as well as listened to and appreciated as something more than an expensive broadcasting alternative to gramophone records. To begin with the plan met with considerable resistance. Valuable time had to be spent haggling with the Musicians' Union, who believed that BBC orchestras should remain based in the studio, and in discussions with the Scottish National Orchestra who feared for their hard-won touring income. Gradually, however, opposition fell away. The BBC were able to schedule a growing number of public concerts in Scotland, most notably at Glasgow's City Hall, and soon a strong and valuable sense of partisanship developed amongst the orchestra's followers.

Of all the BBC Regions, Scotland probably suffered the deepest anxiety during the music crisis. Disbanding the Symphony Orchestra would have had deplorable consequences for Scottish musical life and would have reflected badly on the BBC and the BCS, but alongside this another worry had troubled the local management. This was the fear that, because of the prestige attached to the large Symphony Orchestra, a last-minute attempt might be made to sacrifice the long-established BBC Scottish Variety Orchestra (renamed the BBC Scottish Radio Orchestra in 1967) instead. Had this happened Scotland's important output of light entertainment programmes for network television would have been put at risk, jeopardising the next wave of expensive developments planned for the main television studio in Glasgow, and that, as far as the future of BBC Scotland was concerned, would have been a critical postponement.

It had also been a difficult time for the BCS. Its public stance had been to regret the decision concerning the Symphony Orchestra, but to point out that no other economies could be achieved that would be less injurious to broadcasting in Scotland. It was a statement that most members were in final agreement with, although they hadn't liked the way it had

Brian Fahey and The BBC Scottish Radio Orchestra (1973)

Strings – Bill Baxter; Duff Burns; Philip Button; Christine Cartwright; Ronnie Duncan; Mabel Glover; Christine Nelson; David Smith; Alan Suttie; Ian Tyre (Leader); Andrew Wilson plus 2 deputies; Flute – George Horsfall; Saxes – Ronnie Baker; Tony Brooks; Frank Pantrini; Bob Watson plus deputy; Trumpets – Don Bateman; Paul Eshelby; Jim McComb; Dave McLellan; Trombones – Bob McDowall; Roger Rae; Billy Steele plus 1 deputy; Piano – Alan Cameron; Guitar – Iain MacHaffie; Bass Guitar – Alan Walley; Drums – Roy Sneddon; Percussion – John Chambers.

(© Alan Bunting)

been arrived at for no one had entrusted them with any information ahead of the first public announcement of the cuts. Shortly before the publication of 'Broadcasting in the Seventies', Scotland's National Governor, Lady Baird, had been given early warning of what was afoot but told to keep it to herself and as a result BCS members had been caught unprepared. It was a belittlement that many of them deplored, understandably for it had left them without proper time to consider the relevant facts, and it was some time before tempers cooled.

Out of the BCS's displeasure and protest came the suggestion that a special meeting be held each year to discuss obligations, budgets and plans. The management agreed and in future years the Annual Review became an important focus of Scottish development adding considerable strength to the role of the body.

'Broadcasting in the Seventies', even before its start, had caused a deal of commotion in Scotland. There had been some benefits. Scotland was to have a small share of the Postmaster General's eight per cent. The two orchestras had survived and would stay in existence for at least a few years, and thanks to an offer by London of funds equivalent to the cost of one English local radio station, Scotland's plans for community radio could now be boosted by a new station in Inverness.

But the biggest upheaval was still to come. The new radio service destined to start on 4 April 1970 was to offer listeners four 'generic' channels. Except in Scotland where, because of the need to maintain a 'national' service, it would pack everything – and that included comedy, music and current fish prices – into one single channel (the new Radio 4), and still find room for the fixed points of London programming. Not only did it seem a denial of the new-found faith in generic planning, it was a plan that just wasn't going to work. In truth nobody ever thought that it would and soon the tradition of radio opt-out was inhibiting any chance of designing a national service. Without the support of an English local radio system Scotland needed a service that was 'popular'. But the old traditions of a national service, including specialist production staff in serious music, religion, agriculture, drama, etc, would have to change, and until that happened radio listeners would have to desert in droves, mainly to the new Radio 2.

Scotland continued to debate and re-examine the problem for years. Many of its programme areas were militantly defended by advisory committees and other influential support. Problems were also thick on the ground in technical areas, particularly the lack of VHF channels and the inherited hotchpotch of medium wave and long wave. As the early years of the 1970s began to pass the possibility of a one-channel Radio Scotland with a national identity seemed remote.

Television, on the other hand, was in a position to be more positive about its future. Development money once again flowed northwards, this time for investment in light entertainment, documentary films and schools programmes. With prudent budgeting there was also money to start new local programmes – *Bonn Comhraidh,* a monthly current affairs magazine which gave a much needed boost to Gaelic, a television version of radio's *Scope* which set out to cover the arts in Scotland, and *Left, Right and Centre* dealing with parliamentary and local government affairs.

The old Scottish bogey of poor quality coverage of Saturday football was finally exorcised thanks to the ability to deploy a two-camera electronic unit every weekend, and even more credit was amassed with the promise of massive coverage of the Open Golf at St Andrews and the Commonwealth Games in Edinburgh. Within the limitations imposed by a monolithic service the television output was close to fulfilling its main purpose – a limited dip into the Scottish ethos and a more frequent presence on the UK networks, the greatest measure of success.

In time many situations would have to be resolved, but for Alasdair Milne, the 'Tiger at the Gate' of the late 1960s, his work was done. Head Office beckoned and in 1973 he left Scotland to become the BBC's Director of Programmes in London, later Managing Director Television, and finally Director General. BBC Scotland was now the responsibility of Robert Coulter as it entered a period of radical change when no-one wished the significance of broadcasting to be concealed. The arithmetic of how Scotland was financed would become the subject of constant debate, perhaps as unanswerable as how to contrast the glaringly obvious fact that much of what was being done was middle-of-the-road and middle class. As one element was dealt with it would seem that two would take its place and no amount of acclamation would lessen the responsibilities placed on the art of broadcasting.

For a moment though there was a chance to reflect. Radio, and television, had for years seized on anniversaries as legitimate grounds for remembering other people's events. Now in 1973, 50 years of the BBC

Robert Coulter, Controller, Scotland with National Governor, Lady Avonside at the launch of a series of Open Days at Queen Margaret Drive, Glasgow, to celebrate BBC Scotland's 50th anniversary (1973).

in Scotland was ready for a similar commemoration. Special programmes filled the air on radio and television, of course, and the press paid homage to many of the Corporation's achievements. Long queues formed in Queen Margaret Drive as, over a period of a week, more than 32,000 people travelled to the West End of Glasgow to visit an exhibition in the main television studio at Broadcasting House. Its popularity overwhelmed the BBC with embarrassment, surprise turning to amusement when one old lady, overcome with giddiness on the first day, returned each day after hoping correctly that another hoax 'stagger' would again be rewarded by a stout arm from a BBC commissionaire and a warming cup of tea.

Old friends abounded and reminiscences about past events and experiences ranged from how a story about a blue fairy and a red fairy had to be dropped from *Children's Hour* because an election was pending, to reflections on how when *The McFlannels* were on the air, the GPO reported that telephone calls throughout Scotland dropped by 75 per cent.

On the appropriate day, 6 March, a celebratory lunch was held in the Ca' d'Oro Restaurant, a little more than a five-minute walk from 202 Bath Street, Glasgow. There was a warm welcome from the many distinguished people who were there and as the clatter of the coffee service finally died, Professor Sir Robert Grieve rose to speak...

Index

100 Favourite Scottish Love Poems

Edited by Stewart Conn

ISBN 978 1906307 66 0 PBK £7.99

Poems of passion.

*Poems of compassion.
Poems of cherishing.
Poems of yearning.
Poems that celebrate and
illuminate. Poems vibrant
with the tenderness and
heartbreak of love.*

Embracing love reciprocated and love
unrequited, this selection ranges from
irrepressible optimism to longing and
loss; from lovers' abandon to parental
affection. There are poems for every
lover and loved one to savour and share,
and to touch the heart. But leaving
plenty room for humour and a whiff of
sour grapes.

Stewart Conn mines Scotland's rich
seam of love poetry in its different
tongues – from traditional ballads,
Burns and Scott to MacCaig, MacLean,
Morgan and the vitality of Liz Lochhead
and Jackie Kay; from 'Barbara Allan',
'The Blythesome Bridal' and 'Lassie Lie
Near Me' to 'Hot Chick', 'Yeah Yeah
Yeah' and 'Out with my Loves on a
Windy Day'.

*This lovely little book takes in just about
all the major and most of the minor
Scottish poets of the centuries by means
of their most memorable writing.*
THE SCOTSMAN

Arts of Resistance: Poets, Portraits and Landscapes of Modern Scotland

Alan Riach and Alexander Moffat,
with contributions by Linda MacDonald-
Lewis

ISBN 978 1906817 18 3 PBK £16.99

Arts:

1 Any imaginative or
   creative narrative, or
   non-scientific branch of
   knowledge eg literature,
   history, fine art, music

2 ingenious abilities or schemes

Resistance:

1 Standing firm, refusing to submit

2 A covert organisation fighting for
   national liberty in a country under
   enemy occupation

*The role of art in the modern world is to
challenge and provoke, to resist stagnation
and to question complacency. All art,
whether poetry, painting or prose,
represents and interprets the world. Its
purpose is to bring new perspectives to
what life can be.*
ALEXANDER MOFFAT and ALAN RIACH

*... an inspiration, a revelation and
education as to the extraordinary richness
and organic cohesion of 20th-century
Scottish culture, full of intellectual
adventure... a landmark book.*
TIMES LITERARY SUPPLEMENT

Beyond the Sun: Scotland's Favourite Paintings

Poems by Edwin Morgan

ISBN 978 1905222 72 8 HBK £9.99

For years Scotland has nurtured the relationship between literature and art. Indeed, many of Scotland's most prominent writers began their careers at art school.

In September 2005, readers of *The Herald* voted for their ten favourite paintings in Scotland. Topping the list was the stunning Salvador Dali's Christ of St John of the Cross. Edwin Morgan, Scotland's most popular poet, was so fascinated and inspired by these paintings that he immediately penned a poem to honour each one, and sent the handwritten originals to Lesley Duncan, poetry editor at *The Herald*.

These poems perfectly complement the paintings and the result is a moving collection which comes at a time when Scotland is yet again defining its cultural status in the world with the re-opening of Kelvingrove Art Gallery and Museum.

This excellent book will be appreciated by all who enjoy both fine art and great poetry.
AM BRATACH MAGAZINE

Homage to Caledonia

Daniel Gray

ISBN 978 1906817 16 9 PBK £9.99

If I don't go and fight fascism, I'll just have to wait and fight it here.
JOHN 'PATSY' McEWAN, *Dundee*

What drove so many ordinary Scots to volunteer for a foreign war?

Their stories are simply and honestly told, often in their own words: the soldiers who made their own way to Spain over the Pyrenees when the UK government banned anyone from going to support either side; the nurses and ambulance personnel who discovered for themselves the horrors of modern warfare that struck down women and children as well as their men. Yet for every tale of distress and loss, there is a tale of a drunken Scottish volunteer urinating in his general's boots, the dark comedy of learning to shoot with sticks as rifles were so scarce, or lying about their age to get into the training camps.

Daniel Gray has written a deeply human history, moving and thought-provoking, not only of those 549 people, but of two nations – Scotland and Spain – battling with an evil that would soon darken the whole of Europe.
THE HERALD

Poems, Chiefly in the Scottish Dialect: The Luath Kilmarnock Edition

Robert Burns

With contributions from John Cairney and Clarke McGinn, illustrated by Bob Dewar

ISBN 978 1906307 67 7 HBK £15

Poems, Chiefly in the Scottish Dialect, was the first collection of poetry produced by Robert Burns. Published in Kilmarnock in July 1786, it contains some of his best known poems including 'The Cotter's Saturday Night', 'To a Mouse', 'The Twa Dogs' and 'To a Mountain Daisy'. *The Luath Kilmarnock Edition* brings this classic of Scottish literature back into print, after being unavailable for many years.

New material includes an introduction by the 'Man Who Played Burns' – author, actor and Burns expert John Cairney – exploring Burns' life and work, especially the origins of the *Kilmarnock Edition*. Looking to the future of Burns in Scotland and the rest of the world, Clark McGinn, world-renowned Burns Supper speaker, provides an afterword that speaks to Burns' continuing legacy. This edition is illustrated throughout by original line drawings by top political satirist Bob Dewar.

Out of Pocket: How collective amnesia lost the world its wealth, again

Clark McGinn

ISBN 978 1906307 82 0 PBK £12.99

Written by a senior banker with many years' experience, this book takes the long view. It shows how simple the basics of banking are and tells the stories of how we lost money in similar ways over the centuries. Read it and you might just lose less money next time!

If only the world's finance ministers, bank CEOs, non execs, customers, borrowers, little old ladies, all of us, had read this book three years ago, or 30 years ago, we wouldn't be in the mess we're in. But we are. So read this book and weep. And take solace in the fact that financial calamities have happened many many times before, and will happen again.

I started writing this book three years ago to amuse my fellow bankers. Little did we all know what was about to happen. But we should have. Sorry.
CLARK McGINN

This is an intriguing book by an experienced banker... the book expresses its themes with literary flair.
THE IRISH TIMES

The Prisoner of St Kilda: The True Story of the Unfortunate Lady Grange

Margaret Macaulay

ISBN 978 1906817 65 7 PBK £8.99

One shotgun wedding.

Two kings.

Thirteen years incarcerated.

Married to a Scottish law lord, Lady Grange threatened to expose her husband's secret connections to the Jacobites in an attempt to force him to leave his London mistress. But the stakes were higher than she could ever have imagined. Her husband's powerful co-conspirators exacted a ruthless revenge. She was carried off to the Western Isles, doomed to 13 bitter years of captivity. Death was her only release.

The Prisoner of St Kilda looks beyond the legends to tell for the first time the true story of an extraordinary woman.

It's a stunning story and Margaret Macaulay has done it full justice.
THE HERALD

A story of political intrigue, betrayal and personal tragedy.
THE SUNDAY POST

Reportage Scotland: History in the Making

Louise Yeoman

Foreword by Professor David Stevenson

ISBN 978 1842820 51 3 PBK £6.99

Which king was murdered in a sewer? What was Dr Fian's love magic?

Who was the half-roasted abbot?

Which cardinal was salted and put in a barrel?

Why did Lord Kitchener's niece try to blow up Burns's cottage?

The answers can all be found in the eclectic mix covering nearly 2,000 years of Scottish history. Historian Louise Yeoman has uncovered material ranging from a letter to the King of the Picts to Mary Queen of Scots' own account of the murder of David Riccio; from the execution of William Wallace to accounts of anti-poll tax actions and the opening of the new Scottish Parliament. The book takes pieces from the original French, Latin, Gaelic and Scots and makes them accessible to the general reader, often for the first time.

Louise Yeoman makes a much-needed contribution to the canons of Scottish historiography, providing eyewitness, or as near as possible, to events which have shaped the country over two millennia.
THE HERALD

Scottish Photography: A History
Tom Normand
ISBN 978 1906307 07 3 HBK £29.99

 What served in place of the photograph; before the camera's invention? The expected answer is the engraving, the drawing, the painting. The more revealing answer might be memory. What photographs do out there in space was previously done within reflection.
JOHN BERGER

Scotland has made a rich contribution to the art of photography throughout the world. Beginning with the stellar images of Hill and Adamson, and progressing through the vivid landscape and documentary traditions, Scottish photographers have created a resonant and dramatic photographic culture. Today, the radical experimentation of contemporary Scottish photographers continues to push photography to new heights, and towards assuring its own status as an art form.

A stimulating, remarkably comprehensive account of a fascinating subject.
NORTHERN EXPOSURE

Stramash: Tackling Scotland's Towns and Teams
Daniel Gray
ISBN 978 1906817 66 4 PBK £9.99

 Fatigued by bloated big-time football and bored of samey big cities, Daniel Gray went in search of small town Scotland and its teams. Part travelogue, part history, and part mistakenly spilling ketchup on the face of a small child, *Stramash* takes an uplifting look at the country's nether regions.

Using the excuse of a match to visit places from Dumfries to Dingwall, *Stramash* accomplishes the feats of visiting Dumfries without mentioning Robert Burns, being positive about Cumbernauld and linking Elgin City to Lenin. It is ae fond look at Scotland as you've never seen it before.

There have been previous attempts by authors to explore the off-the-beaten paths of the Scottish football landscape, but Daniel Gray's volume is in another league.
THE SCOTSMAN

A brilliant way to rediscover Scotland.
THE HERALD

This Road is Red

Alison Irvine

ISBN 978 1906817 81 7 PBK £7.99

It is 1964. Red Road is rising out of the fields. To the families who move in, it is a dream and a shining future.

It is 2010. The Red Road Flats are scheduled for demolition. Inhabited only by intrepid asylum seekers and a few stubborn locals, the once vibrant scheme is tired and out of time.

Between these dates are the people who filled the flats with laughter, life and drama. Their stories are linked by the buildings; the sway and buffet of the tower blocks in the wind, the creaky lifts, the views and the vertigo. This Road is Red is a riveting and subtle novel of Glasgow.

One of the most important books about Glasgow and urban life I've read in a very long time. It offers an insight into city life that few Scottish novels can emulate.
PROFESSOR WILLY MALEY

Blind Ossian's Fingal

James Macpherson

ISBN 978 1906817 55 8 HBK £15.00

To the accompaniment of the harp, Ossian enchanted his third-century listeners with tales of savage battles, magnanimous victories, graceful defeats, doomed romances and bloody feuds.

The rediscovered Ossianic epics inspired the Romantic movement in Europe, but caused a political storm in Britain and up to recently have been denounced as one of the greatest literary hoaxes of all time.

When James Macpherson published his translations of the poetry of Ossian, a third-century Highland bard, they were an instant success. However, the plaudits soon gave way to controversy. Were the poems part of a great Gaelic oral tradition, or the work of Macpherson's imagination?

They contain the purest and most animating principles and examples of true honour, courage and discipline, and all the heroic virtues that can possibly exist.
NAPOLEON

A Word for Scotland

Jack Campbell

ISBN 978 0946487 48 6 PBK £12.99

 The inside story of a newspaper and a nation. Five tumultuous decades as they happened.

A Word for Scotland was Lord Beaverbrook's hope when he founded the *Scottish Daily Express*. That word for Scotland quickly became, and was for many years, the national paper of Scotland.

Jack joined the infant newspaper at the age of 15 as a copy boy and went on to become the managing editor. He remembers the early days of news gathering on a shoestring, the circulation wars, all the scoops and dramas and tragedies through nearly half a century of the most exciting, innovative and competitive years of the press in Scotland.

This book is a fascinating reminder of Scottish journalism in its heyday. It will be read avidly by those journalists who take pride in their profession – and should be compulsory reading for those that don't.
JACK WEBSTER

Beatrix Potter's Scotland

Lynne McGeachie

ISBN 978 1906817 43 5 PBK £12.99

 *I don't know what to write to you, so I shall tell you a story about four little rabbits whose names were Flopsy, Mopsy, Cottontail and Peter...*

BEATRIX POTTER, 4 September 1893, Dunkeld (from a letter to Noel Moore, the five-year-old son of her governess).

The name of Beatrix Potter, author and illustrator of the world-famous 'Peter Rabbit' books, is automatically associated with the English Lake District. It was, however, a different place that first inspired her imagination: the beautiful countryside of Highland Perthshire.

Spending every childhood summer for 11 years in Dalguise House near Dunkeld, Beatrix Potter fell deeply in love with Scotland. Memories of enchanted summer days and long adventurous rambles were a never-dwindling source of inspiration. And it was when she returned to Scotland as an adult that Peter Rabbit was born.

Lynne McGeachie allows Beatrix Potter's voice to ring out in her own letters and diary entries. They tell the tale of one of the best-loved writers in Britain.

Scottish Family Legends

Various

ISBN 978 1906817 93 0 PBK £7.99

 *Scottish Family Legends* is a treasure trove of true tales written by people from all over Scotland. These stories were collected by Scottish Book Trust as part of a nationwide project to encourage people to get writing, inspired by their remarkable relatives.

Hundreds of people of all ages took part, and this book contains a selection of the best family legends, including specially written stories by Scottish authors Robert Douglas, Mae Stewart, Willie Robertson and Stuart Donald.

The tales recall lives domestic and military, urban and rural, work-a-day and extraordinary – but never boring! Bursting with drama, heartache, celebration, character, warmth, gratitude, love and loss, *Scottish Family Legends* is a celebration of the people, places and events that make up our collective heritage – it is truly a book to be treasured.

For generations Scots have seen storytelling and recording their own stories as a birthright. [This] publication... maintains this proud tradition.
THE SCOTSMAN

A Gray Play Book

Alasdair Gray

ISBN 978 1906307 91 2 PBK £25.00

 A Gray Play Book is an anthology of long and short plays for stage, radio and television, acted between 1956 and 2009. It also includes an unperformed opera libretto, excerpts from the *Lanark* storyboard and the full film script of the novel *Poor Things* by Alasdair Gray.

Gray wrote plays before becoming known as a novelist, and has recently had new works staged. Over 50 years of them are collected here with prefaces, making this a Scots playwright's autobiography.

Over 50 years' worth of Alasdair Gray's dramatic works appear in the hugely enjoyable A Gray Play Book... Fans of Gray's self-termed 'comic fantasies' will also enjoy the candid prefaces that explain how each play was written and produced.
SCOTTISH REVIEW OF BOOKS

Luath Press Limited

committed to publishing well written books worth reading

LUATH PRESS takes its name from Robert Burns, whose little collie Luath (*Gael.,* swift or nimble) tripped up Jean Armour at a wedding and gave him the chance to speak to the woman who was to be his wife and the abiding love of his life. Burns called one of 'The Twa Dogs' Luath after Cuchullin's hunting dog in Ossian's *Fingal.* Luath Press was established in 1981 in the heart of Burns country, and is now based a few steps up the road from Burns' first lodgings on Edinburgh's Royal Mile.
Luath offers you distinctive writing with a hint of unexpected pleasures.

Most bookshops in the UK, the US, Canada, Australia, New Zealand and parts of Europe either carry our books in stock or can order them for you. To order direct from us, please send a £sterling cheque, postal order, international money order or your credit card details (number, address of cardholder and expiry date) to us at the address below. Please add post and packing as follows: UK – £1.00 per delivery address; overseas surface mail – £2.50 per delivery address; overseas airmail – £3.50 for the first book to each delivery address, plus £1.00 for each additional book by airmail to the same address. If your order is a gift, we will happily enclose your card or message at no extra charge.

Luath Press Limited
543/2 Castlehill
The Royal Mile
Edinburgh EH1 2ND
Scotland

Telephone: 0131 225 4326 (24 hours)
email: sales@luath.co.uk
Website: www.luath.co.uk